Conversations with James Ellroy

Literary Conversations Series
Peggy Whitman Prenshaw
General Editor

Conversations
with James Ellroy

Edited by Steven Powell

University Press of Mississippi   Jackson

To my father, Thomas Raymond Powell

www.upress.state.ms.us

The University Press of Mississippi is a member
of the Association of American University Presses.

First printing 2012

∞

Publisher: University Press of Mississippi, Jackson, USA
Authorised GPSR Safety Representative: Easy Access System Europe -
Mustamäe tee 50, 10621 Tallinn, Estonia, gpsr.requests@easproject.com

Library of Congress Cataloging-in-Publication Data

Ellroy, James, 1948–
  Conversations with James Ellroy / edited by Steven Powell.
      p. cm. — (Literary conversations series)
   ISBN 978-1-61703-103-8 (cloth : alk. paper) — ISBN 978-1-61703-104-5 (pbk. : alk. paper) —
ISBN 978-1-61703-105-2 (ebook) 1. Ellroy, James, 1948––Interviews. 2. Authors, Ameri-
can—20th century—Interviews. I. Powell, Steven, 1983– II. Title.
  PS3555.L6274Z46 2012
  813'.54—dc22
  [B]
                                    2011021821
British Library Cataloging-in-Publication Data available

Books by James Ellroy

Brown's Requiem. New York: Avon Books, 1981.

Clandestine. New York: Avon, 1982.

Blood on the Moon. New York: Mysterious Press, 1984.

Because the Night. New York: Mysterious Press, 1984.

Suicide Hill. New York: Mysterious Press, 1986.

Killer on the Road. New York: Avon, 1986; originally published as *Silent Terror*.

The Black Dahlia. New York: Mysterious Press, 1987.

The Big Nowhere. New York: Mysterious Press, 1988.

L.A. Confidential. New York: Mysterious Press, 1990.

White Jazz. New York: Knopf, 1992.

Hollywood Nocturnes. New York: Otto Penzler Books, 1994.

American Tabloid. New York: Knopf, 1995.

My Dark Places. New York: Knopf, 1996.

L.A. Noir. New York: Mysterious Press, 1998.

The Dudley Smith Trio: The Big Nowhere, L.A. Confidential, White Jazz. Arrow: London, 1999.

Crime Wave: Reportage and Fiction from the Underside of L.A. New York: Vintage Books, 1999.

The Cold Six Thousand: A Novel. New York: Knopf, 2001.

Breakneck Pace. Contentville Press, 2001.

The Best American Mystery Stories 2002. Houghton Mifflin, 2002.

Destination Morgue! L.A. Tales. New York: Vintage Books, 2004.

The Best American Crime Writing 2005. Harper Perennial, 2005.

Blood's a Rover. New York: Alfred A. Knopf, 2009.

The Hilliker Curse: My Pursuit of Women. New York: Alfred A. Knopf, 2010.

Editor (with Otto Penzler), *The Best American Noir of the Century*. Boston: Houghton Mifflin Harcourt, 2010.

Contents

Introduction

As a novelist who has devoted much of the latter half of his literary career to both the mythmaking and myth-debunking of American history, James Ellroy has rather fittingly capitalized on his status as one of America's most sought after interviewees to weave myths about his own life and work. As Ellroy would say to Ron Hogan in 1995, "every interview I give is a chance to puncture the myth I've created about my work and refine it."

Ellroy's life story reads like a brutal, hyperbolized realization of the American dream. He was born Lee Earle Ellroy in Los Angeles in 1948; his mother was a registered nurse and his father was a freelance tax accountant and failed entrepreneur. His unusual upbringing was split between his divorced, promiscuous parents. Both his father and mother had the propensity to exaggerate the truth or conceal it from Ellroy. When his mother was murdered in 1958, one of the first things Ellroy did after learning of her death was to fake tears; already Ellroy the storyteller was learning to formulate narrative and performance. Twenty-nine years later, Ellroy transmogrified his lust/hatred relationship with his mother with his fictionalized account of the murder of Elizabeth Short in *The Black Dahlia*. In doing so, he finds a fictional solution to his mother's murder by proxy, but not an emotional solution. It would not be until he reopened his mother's murder case with Detective Bill Stoner that Ellroy could find a compromised peace, an acceptance which Ellroy described in his interview with Charles L. P. Silet: "The only closure is that there is no closure." Ellroy's father's death in 1965 after a series of strokes left the seventeen-year-old high school dropout without a family and precipitated the worst years of Ellroy's moral and physical decline—alcohol and drug abuse, a three-year period of breaking and entering into the upper-middle-class houses of Hancock Park to commit acts of sexual voyeurism, multiple arrests for petty crimes and several stints in the Los Angeles County Jail. That Ellroy could emerge from this life, reinventing himself as the crime novelist James Ellroy with the publication of his first novel, *Brown's Requiem*, in 1981 is a testament to the American dream, albeit his iconoclastic version of it, as Ellroy says in the prologue to

American Tabloid: "America was never innocent. We popped our cherry on the boat over and looked back with no regrets."

Ellroy's life story lends itself easily to distortion, and throughout the interviews in this collection Ellroy consistently tries to correct the misconceptions of journalists. Yet he has also found misrepresentation useful. In interviews with Fleming Meeks and Martin Kihn, Ellroy explains how during the difficult early period of his literary career he marched into the office of respected crime fiction editor Otto Penzler at the Mysterious Bookshop, New York, and declared himself "the next King of American Crime Fiction," even though the manuscript of his third book had been turned down by seventeen publishers. Although Penzler was unaware of this fact at the time, he was initially skeptical of Ellroy's bravado. But this meeting would prove to be the start of a long and creative partnership between the two men. If this moment marked the beginning of Ellroy's "Demon Dog" literary persona, it was also the genesis of his ability to weave myths about his life and work in interviews. Indeed, the opening interview of this collection may form a unique part of that mythmaking process, for Duane Tucker claims he never conducted "An Interview with James Ellroy" for *Armchair Detective* in 1984 and has suggested Ellroy may have used his name to write the interview himself. It should be noted that the former editor of *Armchair Detective*, Otto Penzler, claims that such a scenario is impossible and would never have been allowed. Ellroy himself declined to comment on the authorship of the interview, other than saying he had "no recollection" of it. However, there are a few instances within the text that suggest Ellroy did indeed write the piece himself. There is the use of the unusual term "contrapunctually structured" in the interviewer's introduction, a term Ellroy has used elsewhere to describe the parallel narrative of his novel *Blood on the Moon* (1984). Also, there is the conspicuous use of the term "ikon." This uncommon spelling of "icon" appears twice in the Tucker interview. Parenthetically, in his later novels Ellroy deliberately misspells words by adding or changing letters to a "k," a technique partially stemming from his fondness for alliteration and for American dialects. Tucker may have conducted the interview, and there may be a straightforward explanation for the inclusion of these terms and the unusual interplay between Tucker and Ellroy, which makes this interview read like no other Ellroy has ever given.

Inevitably in a collection of this kind there is some degree of repetition, but Ellroy is very skilled at retelling stories and expressing opinions without them ever becoming stale or overly familiar: new details emerge with every return to an anecdote, ideas evolve and develop nuance, but occasionally the interviews record a remarkable change of opinion or a contradiction. In every volume in the Literary Conversations Series, the interviews are arranged chronologically in the order they were conducted, not the order they were published. Thus, these interviews, spanning 1984–2010, address the full breadth and diversity of Ellroy's literary career, from his debut novel, a private eye story, to the police procedural novels featuring the maverick detective Lloyd Hopkins, to the historical fiction of the L.A. Quartet and Underworld U.S.A. novels and his painfully candid autobiographical works *My Dark Places* and *The Hilliker Curse.* Just as in every crime novel there are parallel narratives of discovery which intersect and modify each other—the mystery storyline with the personal, emotional investigation of the main protagonist into his own identity—these interviews explore the relationship of and the parallel, shifting, and intertwining narratives of Ellroy's life and work. In an attempt to provide context to these conversations, I have added notes wherever appropriate.

I would like to thank Professor David Seed at the University of Liverpool, Walter Biggins at University Press of Mississippi, the archival staff at the University of South Carolina, Lisa Stafford in L.A., my wife Diana, and above all the Demon Dog himself, for being such a fascinating interview subject.

SP

Chronology

1966–1969   Ellroy becomes an alcoholic, drinking copious amounts of scotch and Romilar CF cough syrup. He also becomes a substance abuser of amphetamines and Benzedrix inhalers. He goes through periods of homelessness, often sleeping in the parks of L.A., and begins to break into the houses of wealthy young women who live around Hancock Park.

1968–1975   Ellroy is arrested multiple times for offences such as burglary, petty theft, driving under the influence, and is sentenced to several short terms at the Los Angeles County Jail.

1975–1977   Ellroy becomes seriously ill after suffering two bouts of pneumonia and nearly dies of a lung abscess. He suffers a breakdown and is diagnosed with post-alcoholic brain syndrome. Ellroy joins Alcoholics Anonymous and quits drinking and substance abuse. Ellroy gets a job as a caddy at the Hillcrest Country Club but is sacked for fighting with a fellow caddy. He resumes working as a caddy at the Bel-Air Country Club.

1979   Ellroy begins writing a novel he titles *Concerto for Orchestra*.

1981   Ellroy changes his name to James Ellroy with the publication of his first novel *Concerto for Orchestra*, retitled at the publisher's insistence to *Brown's Requiem*.

1982   Publication of *Clandestine*.

1981–1984   Ellroy moves from L.A. to Westchester County, New York, upon the publication of his first novel. He gets a job caddying at the Wykagyl Country Club. He writes the first two parts of a historical novel, "The Confessions of Bugsy Siegel," which is never completed or published. He also completes a novel titled "L.A. Death Trip." It is rejected by Avon (who published Ellroy's first two novels) and seventeen other publishers. Ellroy's literary agent drops him as a client. Ellroy walks into the Mystery Bookstore in New York and introduces himself to crime fiction editor/publisher Otto Penzler as either the "Demon Dog of American crime fiction" or the "Next King of American crime fiction." Penzler introduces Ellroy to Nat Sobel who becomes his agent at the Mysterious Literary Agency. Penzler and Sobel persuade Ellroy to make extensive rewrites of "L.A. Death Trip."

1984   Publication of *Blood on the Moon* by the Mysterious Press, a heavily rewritten version of "L.A. Death Trip." It is Ellroy's first novel to feature the character of Detective Sergeant Lloyd

Hopkins. "An Interview with James Ellroy" by Duane Tucker is published in the crime fiction journal *Armchair Detective* edited by Otto Penzler. The interview may not have been conducted by Tucker and was possibly written by Ellroy. Publication of *Because the Night*.

1986   Publication of *Suicide Hill*. Publication of *Silent Terror*; the title is chosen at Avon publisher's insistence over Ellroy's preferred title *Killer on the Road*.

1987   Publication of *The Black Dahlia*, a critical and commercial success. It is the first novel in Ellroy's L.A. Quartet series. Ellroy writes an outline for a fourth Lloyd Hopkins novel to be titled "The Cold Six Thousand." The project is quickly abandoned.

1988   Release of James B. Harris's film adaptation of *Blood on the Moon* which is retitled *Cop*. Publication of *The Big Nowhere*. Ellroy marries Mary Doherty.

1990   Publication of *L.A. Confidential*. *Silent Terror* is reissued with Ellroy's chosen title *Killer on the Road*.

1991   Divorce. Ellroy marries the feminist critic and writer Helen Knode.

1992   Publication of *White Jazz*, the final novel of the L.A. Quartet.

1993   Ellroy is hired as a columnist for the magazine *G.Q.*

1995   Publication of *American Tabloid* to great critical acclaim. It wins *Time* magazine's Novel of the Year and is the first novel in Ellroy's Underworld U.S.A. trilogy.

1996   Publication of Ellroy's memoir, *My Dark Places*, which includes an account of the reinvestigation into his mother's murder.

1997   Release of Curtis Hanson's film adaptation of *L.A. Confidential*, a critical and commercial success, which is nominated for nine Academy Awards.

1999   Publication of *Crime Wave: Reportage and Fiction from the Underside of L.A.*

2001   Release of documentary *James Ellroy's Feast of Death* directed by Vikram Jayanti. The film contains a scene in which Ellroy and *L.A. Times* writer Larry Harnisch discuss the Black Dahlia murder with L.A.P.D. homicide detectives. Ellroy endorses Harnisch's theory that Dr. Walter Bayley was the killer of Elizabeth Short. Ellroy donates his original manuscripts and personal papers to the University of South Carolina's Thomas Cooper library. Publication of *The Cold Six Thousand*, the second novel of the Underworld U.S.A trilogy, not to be confused with the outline of the unwritten fourth Lloyd Hopkins novel which bears the same title. Ellroy embarks on an exhaustive publicity tour of Europe and North America to promote the novel. During the tour, Ellroy suffers from panic attacks and becomes paranoid that he has developed melanoma. The remaining dates of the tour are cancelled with Ellroy citing ill health and exhaustion.

2003   Ellroy becomes addicted to painkillers and suffers from three overdoses. He is admitted to rehab and overcomes his addiction.

2004   Publication of *Destination Morgue! L.A. Tales*. Ellroy writes the foreword to the paperback edition of Steve Hodel's *Black Dahlia Avenger*, in which he endorses Hodel's theory that Dr. George Hill Hodel was the killer of Elizabeth Short.

2006   Release of Brian DePalma's film adaptation of *The Black Dahlia*. Divorce. Ellroy returns to live in Los Angeles for the first time in twenty-five years.

2009   Publication of *Blood's a Rover*, the concluding volume of the Underworld U.S.A. trilogy. It is announced that Ellroy will write four novels, a second L.A. Quartet series, which will be a prequel to the original Quartet.

2010   Publication of Ellroy's second memoir, *The Hilliker Curse: My Pursuit of Women*.

Conversations with James Ellroy

An Interview with James Ellroy

Duane Tucker/1984

From *Armchair Detective: A Quarterly Journal Devoted to the Appreciation of Mystery, Detective, and Suspense Fiction* (Spring 1984), vol. 17, no. 2. Reprinted by permission of Duane Tucker.

With only three novels behind him, James Ellroy must already be considered a major hardboiled writer, an appraisal borne out of the plaudits earned by his first two books.

Brown's Requiem (Avon, 1981) was nominated for a Private Eye Writers of America "Shamus" award; *Clandestine* (Avon, 1982) was nominated for a Mystery Writers of America "Edgar" and won a bronze medal from the *West Coast Review of Books*. His third novel, *Blood on the Moon* (Mysterious Press), was just published.

All three novels are Los Angeles-set and feature violent, sexually driven heroes; men who are perilously unsympathetic. Beyond that, they differ markedly in texture and scope. *Brown's Requiem* is the story of Fritz Brown, an ex-cop car repossessor and a "private eye" in name only, accurately described by a minor character as an "urban barracuda." In his early thirties and an alcoholic, he has never investigated anything beyond delinquent car payments and when the book opens is nine months into frightening sobriety, waiting for something to happen. Something does happen—a real "case"—and Brown is thrust into the middle of a pervasive spiral of murder, arson, and welfare fraud. He unravels the mystery, opportunistically seizing upon it as a means to avenge his sleazy life, line his pockets, and earn the love of the woman who hovers at the case's center. In the end, he is rich with blood money but has lost the woman. He has reached for the best within himself, bringing up the most brutal along with it. Winner takes nothing.

Editor's note: There is some discrepancy regarding the authorship of this interview. See introduction.

Clandestine is a long novel set in L.A. in the early 1950s. The hero, Fred Underhill, is a young cop who hustles golf for quick money and lonely women for one-night stands. When one of his overnight paramours is found murdered, Underhill, in a rare moment of remorse, begins with an investigation. Soon his real motives surface: he wants glory and promotion to the Detective's Bureau.

Underhill's ambition gets him (temporarily) what he wants—but the price in innocent lives destroyed is great. Along the road toward the capture of the killer, he falls in love, and the relationship between Underhill and Lorna Weinberg, a crippled Deputy D.A., provides the depth and scope which makes *Clandestine* a major departure from *Brown's Requiem*.

Blood on the Moon, a contrapunctually structured, present-day thriller, told from the viewpoints of a psychotic mass murderer of women and the womanizing police detective obsessed with his capture, is a thematic and stylistic departure from both of Ellroy's previous books, a relentless story of a twenty-year reign of terror. Just published, it reads like Cornell Woolrich out of Joseph Wambaugh out of tabloid journalism and seems certain to arouse controversy for its graphic depiction of L.A. cop/criminal life.

I met with James Ellroy at his furnished basement "pad" in a large house adjoining a golf course in Eastchester, New York. He is a tall, strongly built man of thirty-six who sports loud, preppy clothes and a continual grin. While we spoke, his landlady's Siamese cat stared at us with what Ellroy called "ikon eyes."

Interviewer: Thank you for consenting to this interview.
Ellroy: Thank *you* for giving me the opportunity to flap my jaw on my two favorite subjects—my books and myself!

Interviewer: Ha! Getting down to business, you've covered a great deal of both narrative and stylistic ground in the course of three novels. *Brown's Requiem* was a tight private eye story, *Clandestine* a long, discursive period tableau, *Blood on the Moon* a psychological thriller *cum* police procedural. Most young genre writers stick to one formula. You haven't. Why?
Ellroy: Quite simply, the storylines of my three books *required* different styles, and I simply put on paper what the story dictated. The story always comes first with me, and *it* dictates the thrust of my characterizations. As for the diverse thematic contained in my books, again the story dictated theme and moral substance. Beyond that, of course, I was looking for the strongest possible voice. For now, I think I've found it.

Interviewer: The voice of *Blood on the Moon*? Multi-viewpoint third person. What you might call a "neo-noir" urban horror story.

Ellroy: Well put. Correct on all counts. I've just finished my fourth novel, *Because the Night*. In it, I've refined many of the themes of *Blood on the Moon*—deepened them, refining my style in the process. All good writers have a thematic unity embedded in their subconscious. Mine is deeply intertwined with a knowledge of crime fiction exigencies: plot complexity, pace, and suspense. The third-person crime novel allows the reader to inhabit the minds of both hunter and hunted, and, in the case of my two new books, it allows *me* to develop suspense through characterization, since the killer's identity is revealed early in the story. A sense of impending doom pervades both *Blood on the Moon* and *Because the Night*, which are structured contrapuntually: killer-cop, killer-cop, and so on. The reader knows that the two stories will converge, but at what point in the story? And how?

Interviewer: A moment ago you mentioned "theme" and seemed to imply it "came to you" coincidentally to your developing a viable plot. Do—

Ellroy: No, you're mistaken. My themes emerge from my plots and are intrinsic to them. It's interesting. I've been writing for five years, and only recently have I reached the point where I can say: "These are the things which concern me as a writer and a man."

Interviewer: Ha! Well, what are they?

Ellroy: Ha! Yourself. You've just given an unabashed gloryhound a soapbox. Thanks, Daddy-O.

Interviewer: That's what interviews are all about. Well?

Ellroy: I'm interested in people who tread outside the bounds of conventional morality; displaced romantics ill at ease in the 1980s; people who have rejected a goodly amount of life's amenities in order to dance to the music in their own heads. The price of that music is very, very high, and no one has ever gotten away without paying. Both cops and killers fall into that category, to varying degrees, walking the sharpest of edges between their own music and the conventional music that surrounds them. Think of the potential conflicts. A modern-day policeman, equipped with technology and a pitch-black skepticism, a man who would have been a good medieval warrior, meets a psychopathic killer who maneuvers in the real world yet is fueled by an indecipherable, symbolic language—in other words, pure insanity. I've given you an admittedly extreme example, and a brief synopsis of

Blood on the Moon. Within that framework, though, think of the opportunities to explore psyches and moral codes under incredible duress. Think of how precious physical sacrifice and human love stand out when juxtaposed against the severely contained universe I just described.

Interviewer: One which you yourself describe as extreme, though.
Ellroy: Extreme only because its facts are made explicit. Beyond that, highly prosaic, even vulgar. Eschewing the tabloids completely, pick up a copy of any newspaper. You'll find elliptically worded accounts of psychopathic slaughter in most of them.

Interviewer: A frightening thought. Is there a salient motivating factor in this new "universe" of yours?
Ellroy: Yes, sex. I've gone back and read through my four novels recently and was astonished how close to the surface it has been from the beginning. In this specific "universe" you just mentioned, the dividing point is obvious: in the hellish unreality of the psychopath, sex is a weapon; in the displaced romantic cop's quasi-reality, it is the love of unattainable women, unattainable only because the cop would have to submit to vulnerability to earn their love, which of course he would never do. Again, one example, and an extreme one. Pauline Kael once wrote, "Sex is the great leveler, taste the great divider."[1] As these themes become more dominant in my work, I'm going to have to learn to offset them in subtle variations, and, in general, infuse this so-called "universe" of yours with a greater degree of recognizably human behavior. Literature is tricky, Daddy-O. Just when you think you've got something down pat, you realize you have to shift gears or go stale. Tricky.

Interviewer: Shifting gears, slightly, do you have an overall goal or ultimate goal as a writer?
Ellroy: James M. Cain said that his goal was to "graze tragedy." My goal is to hit tragedy on the snout with a sixteen-pound sledge hammer.

Interviewer: In other words?
Ellroy: In other words, I want to develop a finely delineated tragic vision and sustain it throughout my career as a crime novelist, producing better and better books as I go along.

Interviewer: What about your background? Can you give me a brief bio?
Ellroy: Sure. I was born in L.A. in '48. My father was sort of a Hollywood frin-

gie—an accountant for the studios and small-time entrepreneur. My mother was a registered nurse. I was an only child. My father taught me to read when I was three, and books became my life. All I wanted to do was read.

When I was ten, my mother was murdered. A man picked her up in a bar and strangled her. My reading took on a distinct focus: mysteries and the crime documentaries. I read them by the truckload. My mother's killer was never found. By the way, *Clandestine* is a heavily fictionalized account of her murder—a fact-fiction pastiche.

My voracious reading continued into my teens, my taste maturing as I got older. I started out with the Hardy Boys and Sherlock Holmes, then went on to Nero Wolfe and Mickey Spillane, with hundreds of junk books devoured along the way. When I was fifteen, my father, who was elderly, became seriously ill. I exploited his infirmity and ditched school at every opportunity, stealing detective novels from Hollywood area bookstores, reading them in Griffith Park, and daydreaming about becoming a hotshot novelist myself.

In '65, I was kicked out of high school for fighting and truancy. My father signed for me to join the army. He died when I was in basic training. I hated the army. They took me away from my Nero Wolfe books and made me get up at 5:00 A.M. and do push ups. I capitalized on my father's recent demise and faked a nervous breakdown, securing an unsuitability discharge.

I returned to L.A., to the old neighborhood, and got strung out on booze and dope. Now I had my *two* loves: getting smashed *and* reading crime novels. From '65 to '7, I lived mostly on the streets, flopping out in parks, with about fifty arrests for drunk, trespassing, shoplifting, disturbing the peace, and other Mickey Mouse booze-related misdemeanours.[2] I imagine I did a total of about six months' county jail time. It wasn't particularly traumatic, by the way: I was big and strange enough so that no one said "Boo" to me.

During the early '70s, I read Chandler and Ross Macdonald and flipped out over their tragic power. I must have read every one of Ross Macdonald's books at least ten times. I consider him, along with Joseph Wambaugh, as my greatest teacher.

Wrapping this up, I almost croaked from a series of booze- and dope-related maladies early in '77. Realizing that it was live or die, I opted for life. I've been sober since August of '77. Needless to say, my perspectives have changed. I began the writing of *Brown's Requiem* in January of '79, shortly before my thirty-first birthday. The rest you know about.

Interviewer: I'm sure you can anticipate my next question.

Ellroy: Yes, yes. The cause and effect is patently obvious. If my mother hadn't been murdered, I might have become a writer of Disneyesque kiddies' parables. Who knows? Strange, and perhaps perverse, but I have a very healthy respect for the rather dark events that have formed me. From a standpoint of pure efficacy, they have certainly supplied a marked contribution toward making me the fine writer that I am today.

Interviewer: That sounds very callous.
Ellroy: I disagree. To me, it's a classic case of mankind profiting from tragedy. You like that? It sounds like a definition of literature in a nutshell.

Interviewer: Do you think that literature has a social responsibility?
Ellroy: If you mean do I think that literature's ultimate purpose is to create needed social change, no. W. H. Auden[3] said, "For poetry makes nothing happen. It survives, a way of happening, a mouth." Since we're dealing specifically with crime fiction, I would say that in *general* the crime writer's only responsibility is to entertain.

Interviewer: What about your individual responsibility as a writer?
Ellroy: Entertaining the reader stands as a bottom line. Beyond that, I want to create a verisimilitude that will give my readers the feeling of being uprooted from their daily lives and thrust into the heart of an obsession. My responsibility is to combine the natural, raw power of the crime novel form with my own narrative gifts to build an obsession so compelling that the reader will willingly move with its flow—regardless of where it takes him.

Interviewer: Where is *that*?
Ellroy: It varies. In *Brown's Requiem*, it was to the heart of a lonely man, a decent man too corrupted and paradoxically innocent to be called tragic. In *Clandestine*, it was to L.A. in the early 1950s. In *Blood on the Moon* and *Because the Night*, it was to the ultimate terror: human beings beyond love or reason and *their* obsessions.

Interviewer: Do you see any general trends emerging in hardboiled fiction?
Ellroy: Unfortunately, I don't read enough in the field to be able to spot trends. I just don't have the time to read. Sad. My instincts, however, tell me that the cop will replace the private eye as the hardboiled ikon.

Interviewer: Why?

Ellroy: Let's divide crime fiction readers into two categories: those who read to escape reality and those who read to confront it and gain a handle on the pulsebeat of the dark side of life. Put hardboiled readers in the second category, and, while you're at it, consider the fact that crime in America is rapidly escalating, assuming as many bizarre forms as there are lunatic perpetrators to give them form. The reader out to sate his dark curiosity and inform himself on the violence that surrounds him will want a hero, or anti-hero, who meets the requirements of a realistic vision. In one of the 87th precinct books, McBain's hero Steve Carella ruminates that the last time he ran across a private eye investigating a murder was never.[4]

Interviewer: Do you consider yourself a nihilist?

Ellroy: No, although I have absolutely no desire to upgrade the fabric of life in America today or actuate any kind of social change. I think that cultivating a literary vision entails developing an affection for things the way they are. Write it down the way it is, reach into your own soul for whatever it takes to provide illumination, and give it to the reader. Maybe your vision will inspire compassion, maybe it won't. The important thing is to look at things the way they are and not flinch, then look at yourself the way *you* are and not flinch. Only the reader should flinch—but only momentarily. You have to compel him to need to know the way *you* need to know.

Interviewer: You sound obsessive on that subject.

Ellroy: I *am* obsessive on that subject.

Interviewer: Moving on, what are your future writing plans?

Ellroy: I'm going to write three more present-day L.A. police novels, none of which will feature psychopathic killers. After that, I plan on greatly broadening my scope. How's this for diversity: a long police procedural set in Sioux City, South Dakota, in 1946; a long novel of political intrigue and mass murder in Berlin around the time of Hitler's Beer Hall Putsch; the first complete novelization of L.A.'s 1947 "Black Dahlia" murder case; and the reworking, rethinking, and rewriting of my one unpublished manuscript—"The Confessions of Bugsy Siegel," an epic novel about the Jewish gangsters *circa* 1924–45.

Interviewer: The manuscript is completed?

Ellroy: Halfway. Four hundred pages. It's a mess. Even my noble agent hates it.

Interviewer: How old will you be by the time all those projects are realized?
Ellroy: About fifty.

Interviewer: Will you have mellowed?
Ellroy: No. Being mellow is okay, if you aspire to becoming a piece of cheese. The trouble with being a piece of cheese is that someone is likely to spread you on a cracker and eat you.

Interviewer: Ha! Let's conclude with some non-sequitur-type questions and answers. Do you have non-writing hobbies and pastimes?
Ellroy: I love classical music and boxing and enjoy going to the movies.

Interviewer: What is the one thing that you do not possess that you would most want to possess?
Ellroy: Need you ask? The love of the unattainable, but hopefully attainable, woman. Maybe she'll read this interview and stalk my heart. Who knows?

Interviewer: Why is that cat staring at us so insistently?
Ellroy: That's Chico, my mascot. He's memorizing your features. If you write anything bad about me, he's going to be my avenger. Very sharp teeth.

Interviewer: I'll watch out for him. Any last words? On whatever subject you like?
Ellroy: Yes. A pledge to crime fiction readers everywhere. I pledge to never relent in my determination not to flinch and my determination never to grow stale; never to give you anything less than my best.

Notes

1. Pauline Kael (1919–2001) Influential American film critic.

2. The number of times Ellroy was arrested is difficult to ascertain as the number he gives often differs from interview to interview. It should be noted, however, that Ellroy's police record, which is available to view at the Thomas Cooper Library, records fourteen arrests between 1968 and 1973: eleven by the LAPD, two by the Santa Monica PD, and one by the Santa Barbara PD.

3. Wystan Hugh Auden (1907–1973) Anglo-American poet. An excerpt from his poem "Dance of Death" is used as the epigraph to Ellroy's novel *Because the Night*.

4. Ed McBain was the main pseudonym of Evan Hunter (1926–2005). McBain created and wrote over fifty novels in the 87th Precinct series. McBain's novels of the 87th precinct series created a level of realism in the police procedural subgenre as opposed to the more stylized private eye novels of Chandler and his imitators, as McBain said in an interview conducted by Evan Hunter in 2002: "In fact, most private eyes—in fiction and in real life—aren't hired to investigate murders."

Don Swaim's Interview of James Ellroy

Don Swaim/1987

From the Donald L. Swaim Collection, Mahn Center for Archives and Special Collections, Ohio University Libraries. Available from Wired for Books, WOUB Center for Public Media, http://www.wiredforbooks.org/. Reprinted by permission.

Interviewer: Well, I did read *The Black Dahlia,* and it looks to me that you spent quite a bit of effort to learn the jargon and the way people talked and the slang and everything.

Ellroy: Of the 1940s, yeah. I was born in '48, the year after the murder occurred, and grew up in Los Angeles and have always been obsessed with the Los Angeles of the past, the years before I was born. So it was inbred in me, the interest, the customs, and I read a lot of the novels of that period. So essentially, when it came down to write the book, all I had to do was the formal research into the case.

Interviewer: Yeah, I think you really captured the sounds and the forms of the 1940s. The hardboiled . . .

Ellroy: Yeah, noir, yeah.

Interviewer: One thing I was surprised about is the foul language, somehow; I know we were all sheltered when we grew up, and I'm somewhat older than you are, but I remember the 40s pretty well and nobody seemed to talk like that. Of course I was a kid in kind of a fine Mid-western family.

Ellroy: Here we're dealing with policemen and criminals and lowlifes almost exclusively, so you have to figure that their florid colloquialisms are up a couple of notches from the general populace.

Interviewer: In fact, I remember, my father is now eighty, and I took him to see a movie some time ago called *Platoon*[1] and everybody is foulmouthed

11

in it. And here's an eighty-year-old—he was shocked, and he said, "People don't talk like that." And I said, "Well, Dad this is the 1980s."
Ellroy: Times have changed. Yeah.

Interviewer: But now I'm getting the feeling that maybe people talked like that in the 1940s.
Ellroy: In the 1940s yeah. Well, cops and men on the edge, and criminals certainly.

Interviewer: Why did you develop such a fascination for the Black Dahlia murder case? In fact, in some of the dialogue in the book the hero complains, "Why a hundred cops on this case?"
Ellroy: I'll give you the historical perspective on the case first, then I'll digress a little bit and tell you how I personally became interested in it. It's 1947, Los Angeles; there are five daily newspapers; there are circulation wars. Brutal sex murders were not as prevalent then as they are today. The body of a young woman, nude, chopped in half at the waist, bearing marks of prolonged torture, is found in a vacant lot in South Central L.A. She was twenty-two years old, her name was Elizabeth Short. She was quite lovely. She came west from Medford, Massachusetts, to be a movie star like forty-six trillion other impressionable young girls of that era and ended up bisected, on a vacant lot. And a police reporter assigned to investigate Elizabeth Short's recent past learned that she dressed totally in black to attract the attention of casting directors, and he called her the Black Dahlia. The newspapers, particularly the Hearst newspapers, seized upon it as nothing else before or since and blew it way, way, way, way out of proportion. And the police were under a great deal of pressure to solve it. So imagine if you will in 1987, forty years later, one single sex killing taking up front-page headlines for six weeks. No. A couple of days in the daily news maybe. Six weeks—never.

Interviewer: I'm amused at the clippings that were sent with the publicity material: the front-page headlines of the newspapers of the day. And they're not that much different. There's a train wreck. Bill Tilden[2] was involved in a sex case—I didn't even know that. I knew him as a great tennis star. I had no idea. And then a number of murders and things like that. In a way I guess the news wasn't so much different. We look upon that period as kind of a benign era, but I'm not that sure that it was.
Ellroy: Well, compared to now I suspect, and the numbers point it out, but

parenthetically the florid prose of that time exceeded the *Post*[3] at its most dubious. And yet there was a lesbian angle on the Black Dahlia murder case, and they couldn't use the word "lesbian." They said, quote: "The affection of women came as easily to Elizabeth Short as the affection of men."

Interviewer: I'm not sure in reading *The Black Dahlia* where the facts ended and your imagination took over. Could you tell me?

Ellroy: Interesting, the book is scrupulously researched insofar as the main central characters Elizabeth Short and her family, the names of some of the suspects, the milieu, the addresses, the fact that she was missing for five days before her body was found. We're dealing now with America's most famous unsolved homicide. It has never been solved. Of course I solve it in the book. I would never cheat the reader that way because the book wouldn't be published if I did.

Interviewer: You solve it several times in the book.

Ellroy: There are some false endings in the book. A great deal is known about the girl. A great deal is known about the case. What people don't know is who killed Elizabeth Short. So I digressed fictionally, gave you a supporting cast of fictionalized characters and dealt essentially with the innuendo of the times, the rumors that circulated, what people were whispering about. The lesbian angle, for instance, is gone into in detail in my book. The circulation wars, the newspapers, the political infighting, the behind the scenes intrigue with the Los Angeles Police Department, all these are gone into based on what I know about the times; based on the general tone of the times; based on some real life characters that I'd read up on. So it's a crazy quilt of fact and very much fiction and some personal demons in there as well.

Interviewer: You were probably also motivated by a particularly shocking event in your own childhood.

Ellroy: Yeah, yeah I was getting to that. When I was ten, my mother was murdered. A man picked her up in a bar and strangled her. She was a good-looking redhead, a registered nurse, divorced from my father for some four years. I lived with her in El Monte, which was a white trash suburb, just east of downtown L.A., and I came home from a weekend with my father—it was Sunday, June 22, 1958, I was ten—and learned that my mother had been killed. A man had picked her up in a bar. She was seen drinking with a man and a woman in a bar: the man strangled her, she wasn't sexually abused, and wrapped her up in an overcoat and dumped her in the bushes nearby Arroyo High School. I went to live with my father then, and the killer was never found. And the following year I read a hauntingly written ten-page account, a summary of the Black Dahlia murder case, that was included in Jack Webb's nonfiction paean to the Los Angeles Police Department, a book called *The Badge*. And I was obsessed like nothing else before or since. It was all the horror of my mother's death and a whole lot more. It was brutally, graphically sexually explicit. She was young, she was beautiful. It was a time, in the forties, that I had already become interested in, and it happened about four miles from where I was living with my father at the time.

Interviewer: Well that was a devastating event but somehow you appeared to have recovered from it. What were the motivating factors that led you to become a writer?

Ellroy: Well, I had never wanted to do anything else, essentially. I was literate at an early age although not precocious in other ways: I couldn't tie my shoes until I was eight or nine. It took me a long time to learn how to tell time. My father taught me to read at three and a half, and so although not precocious—I can't do arithmetic to this day very well—I could speak like an adult at six or seven with a reasonable adult vocabulary. And that produced with it a sense of isolation, and I would read anything that wasn't nailed down. That was my one gift at that time: kids' books, newspapers, magazines—soup labels. And that summer of '58 when I went to live with my father, my reading took on a distinct focus, which was crime novels. First I started out with the Hardy Boys and Ken Holt and that kind of thing and graduated to Nero Wolfe and Mickey Spillane, who was quite graphic, and devoured, devoured the books. My father, who was quite solicitous to me that first summer we lived together, would buy me several Hardy Boys books a week, and it wasn't enough. I'd go through one a day. So I'd go to a local bookstore and steal the damn things, and that sort of started me out on this little life of petty crime that I had that lasted until my late twenties.

Interviewer: You had a life of petty crime?

Ellroy: Oh yeah, yeah. I drank and used drugs. I've been sober for ten years now, which is essentially what turned my life around. I probably got sixty-five, seventy arrests: drunk, disturbing the peace, shoplifting, shoplifting, shoplifting, drunk driving, breaking and entering, resisting arrest. So I imagine I did eight, nine, ten months county jail time all totaled, five-, ten-, fifteen-, twenty-day stretches.

Interviewer: You were a wild kid. You grew up in a broken home and the tragedy of your mother's death. It was a difficult adjustment.

Ellroy: Difficult adjustment. All I wanted to do essentially was take drugs, drink, and read crime books and live in these fantasies of mine of becoming a great crime novelist some day.

Interviewer: Because you grew into maturity in the sixties when that was the prevalent attitude.

Ellroy: It was prevalent. The drugs were available. What I couldn't procure on the street, I would steal in drugstores. I would steal cough syrup and drink it. I would steal nasal inhalers, swallow the cotton, and go on amphetamine trips. I'd steal cheap wine. I'd steal steaks and sell them to a guy I knew, a pimp, who lived down the street from me. I would break into places and prowl around and look at the way other people lived, that kind of thing. I did that for years.

Interviewer: In Los Angeles.

Ellroy: In Los Angeles, yeah.

Interviewer: How did you turnaround?

Ellroy: Essentially got real bad with booze, REAL BAD, like DTs. I was over at a friend's place, and I saw a bus right there in the room with me. I'd been drinking for days and not sleeping; I was dehydrated, hadn't been eating, and there's a bus. I said, "Oh no man, this can't be it; this is the heebie-jeebies." So I don't know how to get away from this bus, I'll go into the bathroom. So I went in the bathroom; I was going to sit down on the toilet, and I opened up the toilet lid to sit down and this big monster jumped out and got me. I said, "'I think you'd better get sober." I didn't have the revelation then, but had it in the ensuing days. And that was that. I got sober.

Interviewer: Just got sober. All by yourself?

Ellroy: Yeah. I had the help of some friends. My friend Randy, a guy named Randy Rice[4] who I'd been friends with for years and years. We used to spend HOURS hashing over the Black Dahlia case and talking about crime fiction. He'd gotten sober first; I just sorta followed his lead.

Interviewer: By the time you got sober you were in your early twenties?

Ellroy: No, I was twenty-nine. I was pushing in on thirty. So I lived from about the age of seventeen till the age of twenty-nine sleeping in boxes, going to jail, cheap pads, prowling around.

Interviewer: You supported yourself through petty thievery didn't you? You didn't have a job.

Ellroy: I would essentially shoplift things or hire out as a day laborer at the slave markets on skid row. Get some work that way. Work for temporary agencies, get some money. For a while there I had $150 a month from my mother's double indemnity insurance policy administrated by my aunt in Wisconsin. I had a $150, and it went a lot further then. You'd get a pad then for $75 a month. So that helped out a little bit, but essentially I just played it catch as catch can. If I needed a shirt, I'd go to a thrifty drugstore and steal a shirt. If I needed clean socks, I'd go steal some clean socks. If I was hungry, I'd go to a restaurant during the noon rush, have several martinis for guts, order a big meal and beat the check. Dine and dash.

Interviewer: You were twenty-nine, thirty when you got away from the booze, but what did you do then?

Ellroy: I had been caddying for a couple of years at country clubs in the Los Angeles area. The Hillcrest Country Club and Bel-Air Country Club which is a subculture that I used, that I explored, in my first novel *Brown's Requiem*. Now 95 percent of most country club caddies, particularly on the West coast where it's a year-round proposition, are alcoholics, drug addicts, and compulsive gamblers. It's great tax free cash that stood me in good stead through the writing of my first four books until the money got okay. And I would just go to the golf course in the morning and make my, oh God, twenty, thirty, forty bucks, whatever, and come home. So that was sort of a transitional time in my life between age twenty-seven and twenty-nine when I got sober.

Interviewer: So you launched a career as a caddy while you were writing?

Ellroy: No, I had started caddying first and launched my career as a novelist while I was caddying. In fact I wrote part of *Brown's Requiem* and *Clandestine*, my first two books, in the Bel-Air Country caddyshack with card games going on around me.

Interviewer: When were they published?

Ellroy: *Brown's Requiem* was published by Avon as a paperback original in 1981. *Clandestine* as a paperback original in 1982; it was nominated for the Edgar award and won a medal from the West Coast Review of Books. And I've been with the immortal Mysterious Press, the Rolls Royce of mystery publishing ever since.

Interviewer: One of your books has just been filmed. I think I just I saw an ad for it. It's running this week, I believe.

Ellroy: No. The book that was filmed is *Blood on the Moon*. The first of my trilogy about a policeman named Lloyd Hopkins, and James Woods plays Hopkins in the movie. I don't know what it will be released as. There's controversy over the title, *Blood on the Moon*, which is an old RKO Western. Maybe it will be released next month in October.

Interviewer: I probably got confused as there is a movie that James Woods is currently in . . .

Ellroy: Yeah, that's called *Bestseller*. And it may be released in January, that's up in the air right now, but it's finished. It's been filmed—and the check cleared—which is always nice.

Interviewer: What brought you east? Here's a lifelong Californian practically . . . All of a sudden you pop up on the East Coast.

Ellroy: I was thirty-three years old. I had never been East. I had never been anywhere but in Los Angeles and in trouble, essentially, and I wanted to wake up in the city that doesn't sleep and boogie-woogie down Broadway to the Gershwin beat and meet East Coast women and this kinda thing.

Interviewer: In Westchester county!

Ellroy: Because I couldn't afford to live in New York City! And so I found a good basement pad down in Eastchester,[5] and I've been there for six years.

Interviewer: And do you supplement your writing with any other income?

Ellroy: No, the money got good about three years ago, and it's got steadily better, and so I haven't had to caddy. I was caddying out at the Wykagyl Country Club out in New Rochelle in circa '81, '82, '83, '84, summer of '84.

Interviewer: How's your relationship with Otto Penzler and Mysterious Press?

Ellroy: My relationship with Otto Penzler is enormously strong. I am fiercely loyal to the man; he is one of my dearest friends. He is my mentor, and he has taught me a great deal.

Interviewer: Are you still reading fiction other than your own? Mysteries?

Ellroy: I don't have a helluva lot of time to do it, and I get absorbed in my books, and I work mornings, go to the gym in the afternoon, and work most evenings as well. And it's pretty all-consuming for me. I don't wanna be influenced by other writers. I don't wanna live in words. So if I have spare time, I would just as soon see friends or brood: stare up at my ceiling with the lights off and some music on the radio.

Interviewer: Do you plan to stay in the genre?

Ellroy: Yeah, yeah I have a contract with Otto Penzler at Mysterious Press for three more novels, and I'm mid-way through the first book now. And *Black Dahlia* begins, is the first novel in a quartet, which will explore Los Angeles from the years 1947, the year of the Black Dahlia murder case, through to 1959. The volume I'm writing now, which is about the Red Scare, is set in 1950. Subsequent volumes will be 1956 and 1959. And what I wanna do is re-create the Los Angeles of my past, which I am totally obsessed with. So there'll be a few recurring characters—there'll be a lot of true-life characters as well putting in appearances.

Interviewer: Bucky make a return?

Ellroy: Bucky Bleichert, the hero of *The Black Dahlia*—no. Not planned at this time. Fred Underhill, the hero of my book *Clandestine* will return in the final book of the quartet. Ellis Loew, the unscrupulous District Attorney of *The Black Dahlia*, is even more unscrupulous as a Red Hunter in *The Big Nowhere*, the 1950 book that I'm writing now. And I have a marvelous demonic Irish cop named Dudley Smith in *Clandestine* who is a focal point of *The Big Nowhere* also. Nice to bring Dudley back!

Interviewer: Well we look upon the 1940s as the good old days, but boy the way the cops knocked people around I'm not so sure that's good. Especially someone like yourself, as you as a petty criminal and a kid, I imagine particularly in the forties, you would have been easy prey. The cops select their victims.

Ellroy: Yeah. I have nothing but the highest regard for the Los Angeles Police Department. And back in the sixties and seventies when I was getting arrested, I never saw them beat up anybody. The L.A. Sheriff's Department, they patrol the unincorporated area, that's their job, their bailiwick as well as the jails. I saw them do some pretty brutal numbers—not the LAPD.

Interviewer: Well, theoretically those days are gone. We have citizen's watchdog committees, this sort of thing. And also I was surprised—I was reading the City of Dallas was looking for police officers, and they require their officers to have two years of college. In New York, of course, you don't have to have college just a high school degree and pass the civil service exam, although they get rigorous training here. So the New York police are generally considered among the best of the police forces.

Ellroy: Most of the LAPD high brass have master's degrees.

Interviewer: Of course in *The Black Dahlia* the police officers get so emotionally involved in the crime.

Ellroy: Yeah, you're dealing with two extremely volatile men cast into the heart of sexual obsession, and the book is seen through their eyes—primarily Bucky Bleichert's. And the cops who surround them, there's some good men and some bad men too.

Interviewer: In real life, though, I don't think the police get that involved. Maybe sometimes. Just like some of the medical shows you see on television where the doctor gets involved with his patient, goes out to the house—and that doesn't happen, the doctor wants to go home and play golf with you as the caddy!

Ellroy: And stiff the caddy too, undoubtedly. Doctors were stiffs. I have to say it, out there. But doctors out there in Radioland, buy my book anyway!

Notes

1. First in a trilogy of films about the United States involvement in the Vietnam War by the American director Oliver Stone. Ellroy's opinion of Stone's film *JFK* is a subject of his interviews with Brad Wieners and Ron Hogan.

2. William Tatum Tilden II (1893–1953) Star American tennis player. His career was effectively destroyed when he was arrested for soliciting an underage male prostitute in 1946. Reputedly the basis for the character of Ned Litam in Vladmir Nabokov's *Lolita*.

3. Ellroy may be referring to one of the Hearst newspapers here, but there was no Los Angeles newspaper called the *Post* at the time of the Black Dahlia murder.

4. Ellroy's first novel *Brown's Requiem* is dedicated to Rice, and there is a character named Randy Rice in *Clandestine*.

5. Eastchester is a city in Westchester County, NY.

James Ellroy

Fleming Meeks/1990

From *Publishers Weekly* (June 15, 1990), vol. 237, no. 24. Reprinted by permission of *Publishers Weekly* and Fleming Meeks.

Dressed in seersucker shorts, tennis shoes, and a crisply starched white shirt, James Ellroy greets *PW* at the train station on a Saturday afternoon looking like he just stepped away from a backyard barbecue. At forty-two, the solidly built 6'2", 195-pound crime novelist, who last month moved with his wife Mary into a rambling fourteen-room colonial house in New Canaan, Connecticut, looks more like an ad exec and an ex-Ivy League footballer than a high school drop-out and former petty thief, golf caddy, and one-time chronic alcoholic.

But Ellroy's readers—his ninth novel, *L.A. Confidential,* is just out from Mysterious Press—know better. Ever since his first book, *Brown's Requiem* (Avon), appeared as a paperback original in 1981, fans of the hardboiled crime genre have been privy to Ellroy's vivid renderings of street life in Los Angeles.

Ellroy's unflinching view of this violent landscape perhaps is born of his experiences. His mother was murdered when he was ten years old, and his father, an itinerant accountant, died when he was seventeen. His knowledge of the seamy side of life was reinforced by the twelve years, from 1965 to 1977, that he spent on the streets of his native L.A., drinking, using drugs and sleeping in parks, deserted buildings, and flophouse hotels.

Thrown out of high school for disruptive behavior in 1965—he says the last straw came when he insinuated himself into a meeting of the school's folk song club and sang an obscene song of his own creation—and following the death of his father, he took up burglarizing houses by night to steal liquor, food, and fresh clothes. In all, through 1975, he was arrested and convicted twelve times on misdemeanors and served some eight months in jail—a record for which he seems strangely proud. Compared to the criminal careers of the characters in his novels, however, he calls it "a bunch of minor Mickey Mouse crime activity."

He says that, during his hellraising period, he spent daytime hours in libraries, "to get out of the sun," and there he'd "sit back in the stacks with a bottle of sneaky pete and just read and drink." In such fashion, he says, he worked his way, chronologically, through twentieth-century American fiction, topping off his literary education with hundreds of paperback crime novels he shoplifted from local drug stores and bookshops.

With no family to fall back on—he was an only child whose parents divorced when he was six—he drifted around his old L.A. neighborhood, a mile-and-a-half south of Hollywood, sneaking into friends' basements to sleep or bunking down in a goodwill box in front of the Mayfair supermarket at Fifth Street and Western Avenue—one of the most treacherous neighborhoods on the West Coast. Through it all, did he have the dreams to sustain him?

"Yeah," Ellroy says, with a guttural groan that frequently punctuates his conversation. "I did a lot of fantasizing about being a great writer." And then, with a chortle that breaks into an almost maniacal laugh, he launches into a series of hilariously obscene stories—so provocative that their subjects can't even be hinted at here—which make it clear that writing has never been his single obsession.

Ellroy didn't start writing until 1979, two years after he sobered up, but he says the dream of being a writer never faded. "Booze and drugs," he says, "are powerful inducers of fantasy." However, it wasn't, perhaps, until 1973, when he read Joseph Wambaugh's *The Onion Field*, that he began seeing how his own experiences could be molded into novels. "Wambaugh gave me real street corners that I had walked on—a real sense of here and now."

In 1977, after recovering from a severe lung abscess and a bout with post-alcoholic brain syndrome, Ellroy, with the help of Alcoholics Anonymous, put away the bottle for good. And with an introduction from an old drinking buddy, he landed work as a caddy at the Bel-Air and Hillcrest Country Clubs in Los Angeles, where he carried golf bags for, among others, George C. Scott, Telly Savalas, and Dinah Shore.

Two years later, while living in a dingy twenty-five-dollar-a-week room at the Westwood Hotel, Ellroy, then thirty-one, began outlining his first book, *Brown's Requiem*, about an ex-cop turned private eye who becomes entwined in a murderous extortion scheme with a skein of L.A. lowlifes. After a few months, he put it down. But, he says, "It just gnawed at me and gnawed at me," until ultimately he was forced to start writing.

How did he finally summon up the nerve to test himself against the fantasies he'd been carrying for all those years? "I was on the golf course. And I actually sent up a prayer to my seldom sought, blandly Protestant God. 'God,' I said, 'would you please let me start this fucking book tonight?' And I've been at it ever since."

Working standing up, using the top of his dresser for a desk, Ellroy wrote his first novel in longhand, on white, college-ruled notebook paper. From start to finish, it took him ten and a half months. After scraping up about $850 to hire a typist and to have the manuscript photocopied, he sent it out to four agents who, he learned from the *Writer's Market 1980*, were willing to read unsolicited manuscripts. All four responded positively within a week. Ellroy went with an agent who promised to auction the book and get him off the golf course. But the sale to Avon brought just $3,500.

In 1981, Ellroy moved across country to a basement apartment in Eastchester, New York, close by the Wykagyl Country Club, where he soon resumed work as a caddy. On his first trip into Manhattan, for lunch in midtown with editor Nellie Sabin, who bought his second book, *Clandestine* (1982) for Avon, he happened onto the Mysterious Bookshop on West 56th Street. Overhearing a conversation in the store about its owner, mystery-meister Otto Penzler, Ellroy marched upstairs to Penzler's office and introduced himself, "I'm James Ellroy," he announced, "the next King of American crime fiction." Penzler, he recalls, replied coolly, "Mr. Ellroy, would you excuse me if I reserve judgment on that?"[1] It proved, nonetheless, to be a fruitful meeting for both men. Penzler subsequently introduced Ellroy to agent Nat Sobel, who agreed to represent him. Sobel's clients include Andrew Greely, Richard Russo, and Hubert Selby Jr., and Penzler's Mysterious Press has published all but one of his seven subsequent books. Just the same, Ellroy, whose monthly mortgage payments now top the advances for his early books, wasn't able to give up caddying to write full time until late 1984.

Sobel works closely with Ellroy in helping to shape and structure his books. Ellroy's current novel is a perfect example of their collaboration. Set in Los Angeles in the mid-1950s, *L.A. Confidential* is the third of a cycle of four novels that form a sort of history of the city's underside from 1947 to 1959. The first in the series, *The Black Dahlia* (1987), was about an actual unsolved murder case that in many ways paralleled the murder of his mother. The second, *The Big Nowhere* (1988), focused in on the Red Scare of the early fifties. The current book, which tops off at 496 pages, picks up where the last left off. It features three protagonists in a darkly drawn police procedural, laced with corruption, pathos, and highly graphic violence—the plot revolves around a bloody mass slaughter in a restaurant meat locker.

To keep track of the action, Ellroy first wrote an intricate, chapter-by-chapter outline, in which he mapped out and cross-referenced the action, point by point. The outline also contained meticulous descriptions of characters and their motivations. He handed over the 211-page outline to Sobel, who scrutinized it, marking twenty pages, to ensure that the plot, characters and themes of the book all came together.

Author and agent then spent two days poring over the outline and Sobel's notes. "Nat and I looked at every story point for logical flaws and looked for ways to punch things up. We were making sure that it was all cohesive, that there were no loose ends, that plot devices and themes were not repeated and credibility was never strained."

"Then," says Ellroy, "I wrote the book." The result though structurally tight, was unwieldy. The manuscript came in at a hefty 809 pages. "Nat and I did another logical, structural overhaul. He said, 'Everything fits, it's dandy, but the book's too long. Cut every word you can.'

"I realized there was not one scene I wanted to cut. But I also realized that Nat was right," he continues. So Ellroy went over the manuscript, line by line, deleting extraneous words and phrases and, in the process, developed a truncated, telegraphic style which speeds the pace of the book. Working for twenty days straight, he cut away 207 pages.

It was only then that he turned the manuscript over to the Mysterious Press and began to fine-tune the book for publisher Otto Penzler. Asked what he thought about Warner Books' acquisition of his publishing house, Ellroy, whose contract with Mysterious Press ends after his next book, says bluntly: "I think that Otto Penzler's editorial skills and eye for crime fiction is so strong, that if he continues to stay with Mysterious Press, it will flourish. But if he leaves, it will die."

What compels Ellroy to be so prolific? He says it's not the money, though with foreign rights and movie options he earned well into six figures last year. "I'd still be writing if it was still $5,000 a book. And I would still try," he says, "with every fiber of my being to be grateful for that." "Grateful," he says, with evident sincerity, "for not being holed up, drinking myself to death in some L.A. rathole. Grateful for the ability to write books and see them published. And grateful for the talent and the will to see it through."

And what compels him to write books that are so graphically violent and psychologically intense? Certainly there are demons from his childhood that he is looking to make sense of. Most notably, his mother's strangulation by a man she met in a bar in 1958, a crime that was never solved. "I want to know," he explains, "what's the psychology of the victim? What's the psychology of the victimizer?"

"One of the recurring themes in my books," he goes on, "is to show the genealogies of violence. To attempt, as much as possible, to take the bad guys back to their childhood and follow their development up to the point where they start killing and maiming people. Hence, to explain those horrible, senseless and otherwise inexplicable acts."

And on his other recurring themes: "Sex, death, horror, love—dying more often than it flourishes—these are the stuff of life and I don't want to flinch from them. I want to take them in their rawest, most complex forms, especially vis-à-vis the myriad of people involved in chains of violent events, and somehow make them cohesive in my mind for the reader."

Ellroy is by no means short on plot ideas or confidence. After finishing up *White Jazz*, the last volume in the L.A. Quartet—for which he has just completed a 164-page outline—he plans to write a sprawling police thriller, unconnected to the previous four books, set in Los Angeles in 1942. And then? He plans a series of as many as ten novels in which he wants to "completely re-create America in the twentieth century through crime fiction. Completely," he repeats, followed by a guttural "yeah." Pausing a moment, he adds, "And I have no doubt I'll succeed."

Note

1. In an interview with Jofi Ferrari-Adler entitled "Agents & Editors: Q&A with Agent Nat Sobel" Ellroy's long-time agent Nat Sobel claims that Ellroy actually introduced himself to Penzler as "the Demon Dog of American crime fiction." A minor difference but important when considering the genesis of Ellroy's Demon Dog persona.

Doctor Noir

Martin Kihn/1992

From *New York Magazine* (August 24, 1992), vol. 25, no. 33. Reprinted by permission of Martin Kihn.

The day his brain stopped, James Ellroy was on a roof. It was his friend Randy Rice's roof, atop an apartment building at Pico and Robertson in West Los Angeles. This was in 1975—four years before he began writing the incendiary crime novels that have made him rich and may soon make him famous. He was just out of a thirty-day alcohol rehab at Long Beach General Hospital, shoplifting Oscar Mayer bologna for raw fuel. And he was trying to formulate a simple thought: *I want to go across the street and buy a pack of cigarettes.*

But he kept missing the synapses. He couldn't think of the next thought, and after an hour or so, he did a dark, primal, *noir* thing—he screamed. And screamed. Rice heard him and called an ambulance, and Ellroy soon found himself in restraints downtown at the county hospital. He was hearing voices *(Ellroy, you killed your father!)* and seeing fearsome, shapeless monsters.

Injected into oblivion, he woke up in a locked ward, his teeth loose, his knuckles bruised, his wrists rubbed raw from the leather restraints. The doctors told him he had a lung abscess and something called post-alcoholic brain syndrome. He'd known he was an alcoholic and a drug addict, but he'd thought he could control it. He was wrong.

Three days later, Ellroy, twenty-seven, checked himself out against the doctors' advice and had a partial seizure on the hospital steps. He lifted a fifth of gin from a liquor store and guzzled it but still wasn't drunk. Lifted another fifth, took a couple of shots, and passed out cold. Randy Rice told him later that he twitched and writhed for twelve hours straight.

"I realized," says Ellroy, now forty-four, peering over a tall iced espresso, "if you keep this up, you're going to die."

There was always a part of Ellroy that wanted to live—to write great books, sleep with beautiful women, leave the squalid past behind him, and grow up. First stop was the Mira Loma Hospital in the California high desert. But he got kicked out for disrupting group therapy with his endless tales of sexual experiences he'd never had. Back in Los Angeles, terrified of drinking, he landed a job caddying at the Hillcrest Country Club. That's when he began his second life.

As Ellroy tells it, his first one—encompassing most of his twenties—was a lurid litany of sneak thievery, guzzling Romilar CF and sweet Thunderbird wine, choking down the cotton wads from the bottom of Benzedrex nasal inhalers, breaking and entering, pornography, reading, and fantasy. All this unsupervised mayhem followed the grisly murder of his mother when he was ten and the monumental indifference of a loving but feckless father, who died when Ellroy, an only child, was seventeen.

His second life was well under way by 1981, when his first novel, *Brown's Requiem*, was published. He moved east to caddy, stayed sober, and wrote five more increasingly assured books. Then, in 1987, his breakout, *The Black Dahlia*, appeared. Based on a real-life Hollywood murder that in many ways paralleled the slaughter of his own mother, the book transcended the confines of the genre and marked Ellroy's debut on the *New York Times* paperback-best-seller list. With *The Big Nowhere* (1988) and *L.A. Confidential* (1990), he perfected a telegraphic prose style that joined brutal and complex plot lines to produce a fictional planet of harrowing power.

Two years ago, Knopf paid more than $1 million for Ellroy's next three novels—this despite his books' having no martini-tippling starlets or madcap Manhattan weekends. They're savage, masculine hallucinations, *noir* minus the smirk. And they've utterly transformed their author—from a homeless L.A. rakeshell into a studious gent with a Connecticut manse, a brand-new dark-blonde wife, and a berth with the country's most respected literary publisher.

"What I like about the work is its ferocity," says Bret Easton Ellis, the L.A.-born writer whose novels share a similar preoccupation with violence. "[*White Jazz*] is so stripped-down, it's almost surreal. It's just wizardly how he got all that information, the sense of detail, the feeling for L.A. during the forties and fifties. I came away from some of the books just appalled by how bloody and horrific a lot of it is, but very impressed."

Ellroy's pared-down, unnerving language reaches its apotheosis in *White Jazz*, to be published this month. (*Publishers Weekly* has already praised it for its pitch and plotting, saying it "makes most other crime novels seem naive.") Its demonic anti-hero, Dave Klein, is pure Ellroy: a psycho cop obsessed by a beautiful woman, in this case a movie actress/murderer. Howard Hughes and real-life mobster Mickey Cohen appear as kingpins of a system so corrupt it's radioactive. When a turf war erupts between the Feds and Klein's own department, Klein becomes a scapegoat for his superiors' sins. And, with a fiendish jab, Ellroy concludes the so-called L.A. Quartet that began with *Dahlia*.

Jazz is more an incantatory prose poem than a novel, so distilled it's almost subverbal. Chapter 60, in full:

> *I bought a new clunker—two hundred dollars cash. I took a detour airport-bound: 1684 South Tremaine.*
>
> *8:00 a.m.—quiet, peaceful.*
>
> *Voices inside—bellicose male.*
>
> *I walked back, tried the rear door—unlocked. Laundry room, kitchen door—yank it.*
>
> *J.C. and Tommy at the table, guzzling beer.*
>
> *Say what?*
>
> *What the—*
>
> *J.C. first—silencer THWAP—brains out his ears. Tommy, beer bottle raised—THWAP—glass in his eyes.*
>
> *He screamed: "DADDY!"*
>
> *EYEBALL MAN! EYEBALL MAN!—I shot them both faceless blind.*

"I want to burn crime fiction to the f---ing ground," trumpets Ellroy, who's still wild-eyed enough to make many people who meet him uncomfortable. "I want to destroy every last bit of niceness and cheap empathy in the American crime novel. All other crime novels are tepid compared to mine. *I want to be known as the greatest crime novelist who ever lived!*"

Writers resemble their work. At six-two and 190 pounds, Ellroy is more garish than life, guzzling coffee the way he once did wine, sporting one of the dozens of outré Reyn Spooner Hawaiian shirts he wears in the summer. He's constantly in motion, jiggling his legs while he sits, springing up to go to the bathroom three or four times an hour. With his moustache, thinning hair, and little round spectacles, he resembles a bearish Adolf Hitler.

And there is the way he talks: quick, clear, irrationally intense. He's often smiling; he's been married to his second wife, writer Helen Knode, for a month, and he actually seems happy. But despite a winning impishness, he is, at heart, a very serious man. Like the veterans of A.A. meetings who've confessed so often they no longer know which stories are true, he delivers his monologues in carefully wrapped packages.

"You can recognize the anger and intensity when you're just having coffee with him," says the author Joseph Wambaugh, a friend of Ellroy's who also writes about troubled L.A. cops. "I always suspect that beneath it there's a performer there. I suspect James wouldn't be saddened if he could find out he couldn't write anymore but could be a major movie star. You sort of know you're being put on when you're with James Ellroy—maybe even when you read him, in a sense. But it's so charming that you don't mind."

After the publication of *The Black Dahlia*, Ellroy was called upon to relate over again the circumstances surrounding his mother's 1958 strangulation. In Ohio, a local television anchorwoman accused him of telling the story dispassionately. His response: "You tell something 6,000 times, it's going to lose some of its punch." He never minded the attention, though, not even when *People* magazine printed a posed picture of him about to impale a cat with a pitchfork in his landlady's backyard. "Better that than nothing," he sighs. "I like talking about myself. I've got a big ego. I discerned a while back that these are difficult books. I need publicity."

Long ago, Ellroy realized that his life was his greatest publicity asset. He was born early in 1948 to an alcoholic registered nurse and a free-lance accountant. Dad had an erratic business doing inventories for pharmacies and, like Mom, a penchant for fleshpots. In the late forties, he'd briefly been Rita Hayworth's business manager, and when Ellroy was about fourteen his dad told him that he'd slept with her.

His parents' divorce, when he was six, was pure Grand Guignol. His mother got custody, as mothers always did then, although Ellroy preferred his father. "I found her in bed with men," he recalls. "I had a lot of uncles." For no apparent reason, early in 1958 she moved with her son to El Monte, a lower-middle-class burg in the San Gabriel Valley.

On Sunday, June 22, he cabbed home from the bus depot after spending the weekend with his dad in L.A. Police cars idled in front of his house. Plainclothes cops, like Jack Webb on *Dragnet*. And he knew, just knew, that his mother was dead. The cops told him she'd been seen leaving a local bar the night before with a dark-haired man of about forty and a blonde woman with a ponytail. That morning, she'd been found by some Babe Ruth League baseball players in the bushes outside Arroyo High School—naked, strangled, not raped, with a silk stocking wrapped around one leg and fragments of beard lodged under her fingernails.

"I think she went with the man and the woman," says Ellroy dispassionately. "She wouldn't f--- the guy, the woman took off. Or the man wanted a three-way, some sleazy deal like that. And she lost her temper—she could be very articulate when she got angry. And he hit her, and one thing led to another." He pauses. "I felt relieved. I remember forcing myself to cry crocodile tears on the bus going back to L.A." His mother's killer was never found.

Ellroy's life with his father was chaotic. They had a beagle, Minna, that was never housebroken, so the house always smelled. His Dad, with his large lack of ambition, was always laughing when nothing was funny and asking him rhetorical questions: "You getting laid?" "Think you'll ever amount to much?" Ellroy once found him in bed with a teacher from his school. Already six feet tall at ten, he started stealing Hardy Boys books from Chevalier's bookstore; although his father gave him a couple every weekend, he scarfed one a day.

Lee Ellroy had his first stroke in 1963 and was discharged from the hospital the day President Kennedy was assassinated. After that, James Ellroy became obsessed with the television series *The Fugitive*—its rootless hero, each week bird-dogging another groovy chick, hanging her up just before the curtain with the words "Baby, I've gotta walk, 'cause I'm a man on the run." Meanwhile, dad was smoking three packs of unfiltered Lucky Strikes a day.

A few days a week, Ellroy went to school to sell the Hang Ten swimming trunks he'd shoplifted. He gypped his father, who was living on Social Security and veteran's benefits, out of change. One day, after being berated for hours by the manager of Mattson's on Hollywood Boulevard for stealing, Ellroy arrived home late to find his Dad being hauled away in an ambulance. He'd had a heart attack. Ellroy began preparing for a life without him.

He got drunk for the first time that summer of 1964. He lifted a bottle of Taylor New York State champagne from a store in his neighborhood, drank it, walked up to this girl he knew from school, unzipped his pants, and started chasing her. He'd been after her for years, but now he had courage. His old man, back from the hospital, found him throwing up at home and said, "You're gonna be an alcoholic, just like your mother."

The rare times he went to school, he was insane. Fairfax High School was mostly Jewish, so he wrote a song criticizing American Nazi Party leader George Lincoln Rockwell to impress a girl. Teachers called him disruptive and suspended him. Now, he thought, he'd have the time to become a great novelist.

So he joined the Army—just as Vietnam was heating up. His father took a turn for the worse and began to die in a Veteran's Administration hospital in

L.A. While taking the Army oath, Ellroy realized he was making a big mistake. He started faking a nervous breakdown by stuttering, then tearing his clothes off and running naked through the Fort Polk, Louisiana, reception station. A psychiatrist bought his act. He was discharged just in time to be with his father when he died.

Dad's last words: "Son, try to pick up every waitress who serves you." And Ellroy thought, "You're free. Now you can get laid, drink, write books."

He got work passing out handbills for a Serbian-Croatian psychic named Sister Ramona. Days of Thunderbird, marijuana, and Benzedrix nasal inhalers. In the back room of a friend's house, Ellroy spent hours losing himself in the music of the German Romantic composers. He began calling nearby homes, and in those days before answering machines, no answer meant the house was unoccupied. So he'd find an open first-floor window, or punch one in, and steal liquor, underwear, books, money, and credit cards, raid machine cabinets, make himself ham sandwiches.

It was a voyeur's cheap thrill. What was it like to have brothers and sisters? Leather couches? Air-conditioning? The thrill ended in late 1968, after someone reported having seen Ellroy sneaking into a deserted house, and a team of L.A. cops barged in with shotguns and arrested him. He got three years' formal probation, and the following year, something told him not to break into houses anymore. It was the time of the Manson killings, and L.A. was getting paranoid.

He served time in the county jail, off and on, over the next seven years. There were convictions for being drunk, driving while intoxicated, and petty theft—some thirty in all, he claims. "County jail is two stupid white guys, two stupid black guys, and two stupid Mexican guys," Ellroy says, "talking about all the foxes they've f---ed, all the crimes they've committed, all their athletic prowess. And it's all bulls---. I always had some germ of circumspection that said, 'White boy, don't open your mouth.' I think I should've been in grad school somewhere."

It was a mangled, dicey period. Ellroy got fired from the Porno Villa bookstore for tapping the till. He had a job repossessing cars but lost it. The money from his mother's life-insurance policy ran out, and he became homeless. He'd "dine and dash" at local restaurants. Sleep up against a back wall in a park or in a pay toilet in an old Spanish building in central L.A. Taking shelter in libraries, he read.

He sank deeper and deeper into madness—until 1975 and the brain freeze on the roof that, in its own ironic way, started his ascent back into sanity.

Around his thirtieth birthday, Ellroy started making notes for a novel he'd felt churning in his subconscious for years. An obstreperous caddy who called his golfers "bwana" and "sahib," he'd been fired from Hillcrest for punching out a guy who owed him money. But he'd been in A.A. and sober since 1977. Looping blissfully now at the Bel-Air Country Club and working briefly as a process server, he tossed the book around in his brain—afraid every night when he went home to his rat trap room at the Westwood Hotel that he wouldn't succeed, that a guy like him could never write anything that was any good.

Finally, on January 26, 1979, he went out onto the green, stared up at the sky, and prayed: "Please, God, let me start this book tonight." That night, standing, writing on his dresser, he did. Ten months later, he sent it to four agents listed in *Writers Market 1980*, all of whom responded positively within a week. The man he went with sold it to Avon as a paperback original for $3,500. *Brown's Requiem* contains the embryo of the later Ellroy: the fallen-cop anti-hero who's an orphan, the *noir* heroine, the machinery of corruption. But its prose outshines its plot.

With his first check as an author, Ellroy got a hooker, paid his back rent, bought a cashmere sweater and a $500 1964 Chevrolet Nova, and took his girlfriend away for the weekend. By Monday, he was broke. But he was getting things done. Seven months later, he sold his second novel, also for $3,500, and—before his first was in the stores—moved across the country, alone, to Eastchester, New York. It was 1981.

"I'd been in L.A. too long," he explains. "I have jolts of fear in Los Angeles that I don't get anywhere else. It's as if L.A. knows me better than any other place, and thus, I'm vulnerable."

Ellroy's second novel, *Clandestine* (1982), a thinly veiled, chronologically altered portrait of his mother's murder and himself as a young boy, was nominated for an Edgar Award, America's premier crime-writing prize. Caddying mornings at the Wykagyl Country Club in New Rochelle, Ellroy put aside a third novel, "L.A. Death Trip," and wrote half of a fourth, an homage to Saul Bellow's *Adventures of Augie March* called "The Confessions of Bugsy Siegel," about the real-life gangster. The bloated "Death Trip" (at the end of which L.A. burns to the ground) was rejected by seventeen publishers. Undaunted, Ellroy marched into New York's Mysterious Bookshop and confronted its owner, mystery Poo-Bah Otto Penzler.

"He said, 'My name's James Ellroy, and I'm the next great one,'" recalls Penzler, who subsequently read Ellroy's books. "I thought, 'This is an extraordinary original talent who doesn't really know how to write a book.' A very powerful stylist, but they weren't particularly well constructed plots.

But he was such a bright guy and had so much raw talent, I never thought for a moment he wasn't going to be a monster."

Penzler agreed to read Ellroy's two unpublished manuscripts and introduced him to Nat Sobel, who has been his agent ever since. During a meeting at Penzler's store, Sobel and Penzler told Ellroy that Siegel was out to lunch but "Death Trip" could be reworked. It was eventually published by Penzler's imprint, Mysterious Press, as *Blood on the Moon* (1984). At thirty-six, Ellroy was able to put caddying behind him, and he's been a very generous tipper ever since.

With *Because the Night* (1984) and *Suicide Hill* (1986), *Blood* forms a trilogy about an evil-genius L.A. cop named Lloyd Hopkins. A pasteboard Nietzschean *uber*man at first, Hopkins becomes by the end of the series the archetypal Ellroy cop, indistinguishable from his prey and tortured by guilt. "Hopkins is essentially a criminal," one of the character's colleagues says. "What sets him apart from a run-of-the-mill street thug is a one-seventy I.Q. and a badge." Martin Plunkett, the serial killer who narrates *Killer on the Road* (1986), is simply Hopkins without the badge.

It wasn't until the L.A. Quartet that Ellroy soared as a writer. He returned to the approximate era of *Clandestine*—L.A. in the late forties. Built on tightly reasoned plot outlines, his stories became increasingly complex, to the point where *The Big Nowhere* (1988) holds some sixty important characters and three simultaneous plot lines. But he'd found his métier; his cops *are* his criminals. The system isn't corrupt; corruption *is* the system.

"What I can generally remember is an older and inchoately perceived Los Angeles of the fifties," says Ellroy, who hates doing research, relying instead on his prodigious, imaginative memory for historical details. "I remember feeling that things were going on outside the frame of what I was seeing. The language I got partly from my father, who swore a lot. It was an older L.A., a man's L.A., where everybody smoked cigarettes and ate steak and went to fights."

Ellroy's attraction to the period began when he first heard about the Black Dahlia murder case. Two weeks after New Year's Day 1947, an aspiring actress named Elizabeth Short was found in a vacant lot, hacked in half and eviscerated. Her murderer was never found. Mentioned briefly in most of Ellroy's previous books, the case is solved fictionally (and preposterously) in *Dahlia*, a personal rite of passage and the author's first truly popular novel. It was "the shocker other writers would kill to have written," said author Harlan Ellison.

"When you live in your imagination, you re-create things," Ellroy says. "I got off my mother's death that way."

Dahlia's follow-up, *The Big Nowhere*, limns twin phobias of L.A. in 1950: Communism within the movie industry and homosexuality. One cop is assigned to infiltrate Hollywood and find Communists, while another goes against departmental policy by investigating a string of gay murders. It's Ellroy's essay on McCarthyism.

The author's next novel, *L.A. Confidential*, is his biggest book thus far (496 pages), and it makes even greater demands on the reader. Constructed around one of Ellroy's hallmark slaughterhouse scenes—this one the "Nite Owl Massacre" of six in the walk-in refrigerator of a twenty-four-hour diner—it is written in prose that avoids adverbs and adjectives. Lookalikes are implicated in crimes, making it very difficult to keep track of suspects.

Some dialogue from *L.A. Confidential*: "'Franchise boys got theirs three triggers blip blip blip. F---ing slowdown ain't no hoedown, Mickey thinks he'll get the fish but the Irish Cheshire got the fishy and Mickey gets the bones no gravy he is dead meat for the meow monster.'"

"He's progressed in the last four books to the point where he's so far beyond the genre he's almost unreachable," says Katherine Dunn, a friend and fellow Knopf author (*Geek Love*). "At this point, he really, truly is a maniac. For a mature writer to maintain that level of passionate anger is a very rare commodity. What we're seeing is a writer drive himself to genius."

Ellroy's Eastchester office is the apartment he moved into after leaving L.A., and it's a shrine to crime fiction—his own. Bookshelves are filled with foreign editions of his novels: French, German, Swedish. It's a dark, smallish studio without a television, and its backyard is a puissant golf course Ellroy looped a couple of times in the old days. On the walls are elaborately framed newspaper and magazine articles. About him. There are boxing magazines and old green curtains. Everything is neat; too neat, perhaps, like a dam against disorder.

Likewise, there's little askew in the two-story rental house in New Canaan, Connecticut, he shares with Helen Knode. It's an austere white Colonial overlooking the Stamford Reservoir, and it doesn't seem to have quite enough furniture. Ellroy and his first wife, a marketing executive, were divorced last September, after two and a half years of marriage. In addition to a house, she got Ellroy's beloved dog, Barko, the four-year-old bull terrier he fondles forlornly on the jacket of *White Jazz*. (He has visitation rights.)

In the basement is a Tunturi step machine Ellroy pounds after a morning's hard work and a health shake. The living room sports a bust of Beethoven and portraits of Schubert and Brahms. One second-floor room is empty. Most of the books on the shelves are his own. Ellroy doesn't read much anymore; outside art is intrusive.

"I live a quiet life," he says, settling into a chair in the small room where his wife is writing her first novel. "I need no outside stimulus. What I do is brood. I sit in one place quietly, or lie down on the bed upstairs, and think. About crime, about politics, about how to market books—my books. About the association of men and women. What else is there? There's art and sex. The whole thing of men and women just blows me away. Love. Death. Sex. What's her body look like after she takes her clothes off? Commitment." It's a mental life so nonstop that years ago, the only way he could get to sleep was by reenacting Hemingway's suicide scene—buy a shotgun, sit in a chair, trip the trigger with his thumbs—in his head. All the way to sweet oblivion.

"A lot of people take James on one level," says Nat Sobel. "The fact that he uses the nickname Dog. That he likes to bark or howl as a form of salutation. The fact that he likes to say totally outrageous things, knowing that he's sending everybody in the room right through the ceiling. But when you get behind that, you see how hard he works. He approaches the art of writing fiction with a jeweler's loupe."

Ellroy works five or more hours a day, scrawling block-capital letters maniacally on lined pads. And his outlines, from *Dahlia*'s 142 pages to *Confidential*'s 211, allow for byzantine plots. Since *Confidential*, he has resorted to inserting fake newspaper and magazine clippings into his text, to bring confused readers up to speed. He hoists an outline he just finished for his next book, *American Tabloid*, about the Kennedys and Marilyn and the Mob. It's 345 pages.

After the writing comes the lengthy edit. The first draft of *Jazz*, for instance, was even more clipped and opaque than the version about to be published. Working first with Sobel, then Knopf editor Sonny Mehta, Ellroy painstakingly added words to the manuscript. "The first draft was extremely challenging," says Mehta. "What James was doing was extremely ambitious. But I think you have to engage people and draw them into the story. And I thought essentially we had to make it a little easier for them."

Even with the revisions, Ellroy's style still demands a certain diligence. On every page, the violence his characters do to one another is matched blow for blow by the violence Ellroy does to the English language. "I thought the last three books have become more and more hard to read," says Otto Penzler, whose Mysterious Press (now owned by Time Warner) published eight of Ellroy's novels before losing him to Knopf. "I think he has gone as far as he can go with making the style as terse as he has, as clipped. And I would still like to see *somebody* there with whom I as a reader can empathize."

Ellroy never apologizes. He explains. "I don't want to entertain readers. I want to shock them. I wanted a hellishly violent story told in a hellishly violent language by a very bad man."

Sonny Mehta found Ellroy eager to please. After all, Knopf had been the home of Raymond Chandler, James M. Cain, Dashiell Hammett, and Ross Macdonald. It had long been Ellroy's ambition to join that pantheon.

In fact, so steeped is Ellroy in the crime-literature tradition that he's weirdly indifferent to Hollywood. Seven of his books have been optioned, but the only film version to appear so far is *Cop*, a tepid 1988 adaptation of *Blood on the Moon*, starring James Woods as Lloyd Hopkins. "I think my books don't translate well to the screen," Ellroy says with clear pride. "I think they're too dense, too complex."

He paints a portrait of high domestic serenity and all-consuming work that is only occasionally disturbed by a letter or review accusing him of being homophobic, misogynistic or mean. Most of his homosexual characters are self-loathing characters, and a lot of his straight women do seem to be ex-hookers. Ellroy is unapologetic; the views are those of his characters locked in a moralistic past, and not his own. "I think that social revisionism and political correctness make for very, very bad crime novels," he says.

Amid the calm, before the tsunami of press and reviews that will surround *Jazz*, Ellroy is regrouping himself for the next step in an ambitious career. He intends to re-create the entire history of twentieth-century America—which he calls "the story of bad white men"—through crime fiction. *Tabloid* is the first step, a "secret history" of the sixties, focusing on John and Robert Kennedy. Eventually he'll have ten, twelve, maybe more books, all of them packed with fervor and historical fact. He even broke down and hired a $25-an-hour researcher to help him with the legwork for *Tabloid*, which starts in 1957 and ends with Robert Kennedy's assassination. It's all part of his bid to become as he puts it, "the Tolstoy of the crime novel."

"*All I have is the will to remember*," says *Jazz's* Dave Klein. "*Time revoked/ fever dreams—I wake up reaching, afraid I'll forget. Pictures keep the woman young.*"

"This whole noir thing—I feel it so strongly," says James Ellroy, snaking a hand around his new wife's waist. "There's a woman, you flush your life down the toilet. But I don't want to live that life. I just want to write it."

Interview with a Hepcat

Brad Wieners/1995

From *San Francisco Review of Books* (May–June 1995), vol. 20, no. 2. Reprinted by permission of Brad Wieners.

The day broke the same as midnight, storm of the century wild. No sunrise. There'd be no sunset. Branches everywhere. Lines down. Traffic snarled. San Francisco in the grip of a March tempest.

Storm of the century or no, the plan remained: meet Ellroy at the Huntingdon, 2 P.M. He arrives at 1:58 during the eye of the storm. He pegs me as the interviewer, "Disheveled, the Ellroy type." We grab a table in the dining room.

In person, Ellroy is more soft-spoken than his narrators, but no less crass. His vulgarity however, is not so much rude—it's not directed at any-one—and the result is, ironically, a more open exchange. He says "yeah" as a period or a comma, a downbeat between phrases that sounds on tape like someone testifying "amen" to what he just uttered.

After a chat about his choice for Connecticut for a home, and his planned move to Kansas City, I asked him my first official question: why the Kennedy's—and, why now?

"This was the story that grabbed me. I read *Libra* by Don DeLillo. I urge everyone to read it. [yeah] And, I said "holy shit this book"—I was never interested in the Kennedy assassination before. And I read it and I got ob-sessed. [yeah] And I thought, 'This book is great, but I could never write my own book on it.' But then I began to see it was a much bigger story. [yeah]

"Also I felt that through the L.A. Quartet books I was really moving to-wards the idea that politics is crime. The L.A. political establishment really moves to center stage in the last three books and I was tired of writing about L.A. and I really wanted to take a big risk [yeah], my biggest risk yet, and write the biggest, baddest, ugliest, most explosive, most revisionist book I could think of, and this story put me over.

"I wanted to burn down an era. [yeah] I wanted to crawl in the gutter of history. I mean, I'll ask you what I've been asking a lot of interviewers—women, men, a gay black guy I talked to last week, 'Wouldn't it be a blast to go back there and pull this shit, to do these shakedowns with Pete Bondurant, to train Cuban exiles?' People who are alive to this are because of the exhilaration of this power."

According to Ellroy, J.F.K.'s demise boils down to "Bobby [Kennedy]'s Oedipal story" playing itself out. "I don't necessarily agree with all of what he said, but I think Malcolm X was basically right on this one, 'the chickens came home to roost.' Kennedy fucked with some people and they fucked him back."

Of course, Ellroy is far from the first to comment on Kennedy's rise and fall or to speculate on what went down at Dealey Plaza. Given his particularly cynical view of J.F.K., I pointed out that he probably wouldn't be congratulated on historical revision.

"Did you see the Oliver Stone movie? I saw it. I liked it for the first hour-and-a-half, until Donald Sutherland came on and started explaining everything.

"The difference between me and Oliver Stone—I think he goes for the whole lost innocence thing. For one thing, he [Stone] has the whole Vietnam thing going on where he wants to believe Kennedy would have prevented the war. But for every piece of evidence that says he would, there are two that say he was getting us in deeper. The biggest difference, between him and folks like Stone," says Ellroy, "is that I think [Stone] believes that his version is the truth. My book is a novel. Fiction."

Describing *Tabloid* as his "biggest risk yet," gave me the "in" I needed for my amateur psychology. His books teem with men with something to prove. What about their author, did he have something to prove?

"That's absolutely right. It's a great classically simple observation. It's very true, I've always dealt with a lot of fear in my life. And I've learned some humility. I mean, as arrogant as I can sound, and as wild as I can behave, I'm basically a very hard-working, reasonable guy. You know how these books are. They're difficult to read. Imagine how they are to write.

"I saw that there was a raging hunger to prove myself. And I think it's what you might call a sane kind of ambition because I do not want to be president and walk over people on my way to the top. I respect people who treat each other kindly and take their risks in their art.

"And it's there very much in my characters, the fears. I've spent my life-time reading crime fiction. In general, fear is the missing component. Every-one's a hard ass, trying to portray themselves as tough guys. I look at that twit Quentin Tarantino,[2] you know, talking about being in brawls, and I take one look at him, this little pip-squeak, and I feel embarrassed for him. I've never been a tough guy really—even when I was going to jail I was outsized, which helped, and crazy looking, but I really survived by the good graces of the people I was in with . . . I don't think I could survive the L.A. county jail system today."

It doesn't take a psych degree to pinpoint the origin of many of Ellroy's fears, and with it the source of his cavalier façade, which he says folks mis-take for a tough-guy pose. When he was ten, his mother was strangled to death. The crime-writer Ellroy shrugs it off and even admits to exploiting her story during the book tour for *The Black Dahlia* (*The Black Dahlia* is dedicated to his mom, "Mother, Twenty-nine years later, this valediction in blood.") Yeah, says the crime-writer Ellroy, that's how it happened, that's how it goes, the babe got whacked.

But if *The Black Dahlia* was Ellroy wrestling with his demons once re-moved, Ellroy is now wrestling directly with her and what her loss meant to his life. And, based on the way that he answers questions about her, it seems that he's judging himself pretty harshly for resenting her, resenting that she "abandoned" him and left him scared.

Last year, with a Los Angeles homicide detective Bill Stoner, Ellroy re-opened the investigation into his mother's murder, reading her files, and interviewing those who knew her. He says he and Stoner have become close friends, perhaps the closest male friend he has. And, as you might suspect, the investigation has already occasioned one piece (by him) for *G.Q.*, and another by a reporter friend for *L.A. Weekly*. Ellroy plans a book on the in-vestigation's outcome, working title: *My Dark Places*.

"I'm starting to think that noir is a cliché," Ellroy reflects, "that I've tak-en it farther than anybody—at least physically—and also in the size of my books. I think it's over. And I think the dividing line is *My Dark Places*."

Whether it is or not, it seems clear that Ellroy will give us a history of the '60s like one we'd never have thought possible without him. And, as he rewrites his own history and ours, it appears we'll get to witness a writer mature out-of-genre, to watch him, as he would say, grow up.

Interview concluded, I grabbed an early afternoon beer in a Bush Street dive bar and interviewed myself. Ellroy? Yeah, he's still a "pig" as they say—digs boxing on TV, speaks in genital expletives and, sarcastically or not, says ethnic slurs a bit too casually, but he is also eager (no shit) to write a fully realized role or two for women and to concentrate on a "greater diversity of experience."

Says Ellroy, "Noir is a shit-can I'm getting off of. Publishers, they want crime writers to write serials, same easily recognized characters. Same plots. I just couldn't do that. I fought hard to be where I am with Knopf, to move on."

1. Malcolm X first made this comment in response to a question about Kennedy's assassination after a speech he gave in New York City, December 4, 1963, titled "God's Judgment of White America."

2. American film director and screenwriter, who, at the time this interview was conducted, was at height of his career with his films *Reservoir Dogs* (1992) and *Pulp Fiction* (1994).

Mad Dog and Glory:
A Conversation with James Ellroy

Charles L. P. Silet/1995

From *Armchair Detective: A Quarterly Journal Devoted to the Appreciation of Mystery, Detective, and Suspense Fiction* (Summer 1995), vol. 28, no. 3. Reprinted by permission of Charles L. P. Silet.

The self-described "Mad Dog" of contemporary crime fiction, Ellroy has led a life as bizarre as one of his ill-fated characters. His mother was murdered when he was ten years old, and in his late teens he dropped out of school and went on the streets, becoming addicted to drugs and alcohol, living in abandoned houses, and gorging himself on crime novels.

By 1977 he sobered up and began writing: first, a classic detective novel, *Brown's Requiem* (1981), a genre that he quickly abandoned; next a sex murder book, *Clandestine* (1982) which was a thinly disguised version of his mother's case; and, finally, a short-lived series of police procedurals featuring detective Lloyd Hopkins—the "Hopkins in Jeopardy"[1] books—*Blood on the Moon* (1984), *Because the Night* (1984), and *Suicide Hill* (1985). After a first-person serial murderer novel, *Killer on the Road* (1986), Ellroy struck it big with the first of his L.A. Quartet, *The Black Dahlia* (1987), a novel about the famous unsolved mutilation death of Elizabeth Short.

The success of this book fueled the writing of the rest of the L.A. books: *The Big Nowhere* (1988), *L.A. Confidential* (1990), and *White Jazz* (1992). In the Quartet, Ellroy explored the underside of postwar Los Angeles with its red baiting, police corruption, racist bigotry, and sexual perversion. He developed an increasingly sparse, realistic style which culminated in a telegraphic prose experiment in *White Jazz*, with its riff rhythms and improvisational narrative. In 1994 Ellroy published *Hollywood Nocturnes*, a collection of short fiction that included the novella "Dick Contino's Blues," based on a nonfictional, investigative piece he wrote for *G.Q.*

Ellroy is now embarked on a series of three large novels, broadly socio-political in scope, that cover American history from 1958 to 1973. *American Tabloid* deals with the years 1958 to 1963; the next volume will cover 1963 to 1968 and is expected to be published in 1997; and the third will deal with the years 1968 to 1973 and will appear in the year 2000. Each volume is planned to be bigger and broader than the last.

Currently, Ellroy is writing his first nonfiction book, *My Dark Places*, the story of his mother's murder and the investigation which failed to discover her killer. He is working with a retired L.A. detective and is reinvestigating the case using modern police procedures. They hope to uncover the murderer, and if he is alive, bring him to justice. Ellroy's lifelong obsession with his mother's death refuses to go away.

The following interview was conducted just after Ellroy's multi-city book tour to promote *American Tabloid*. In it he discusses his past as a petty criminal, drug addict, and crime fiction junkie. His outspoken views on private-eye novels, serial-killer fiction, and series with likable characters will not endear him to traditional mystery fans, but they will surely stimulate serious thought about the art of crime writing.

Interviewer: You have been rather widely interviewed about your checkered past—the murder of your mother when you were ten, your time on the streets, your alcoholism and drug addiction—is there anything new about that period that you'd like to discuss?

Ellroy: As a criminal I was pathetic. As a drug addict and alcoholic, I was always on the cautious side. I was never a tough guy. I broke into houses and sniffed women's undergarments, sure, but I was never a bad-ass burglar. We're talking about the late 1960s primarily, and it was quite simply a different world. People didn't have sophisticated alarm systems; people didn't have telephone answering machines. So if you were called up and got no answer, chances were nobody was home. And finding a loose screen or some window access or a dog door was rather easy. I was always frightened, but the thrill of voyeuristic entry always eclipsed my fear, and I never took anything large. I took cash, I sniffed some undergarments while I was there, I stole drugs. In the summer of 1969, right after the Tate/La Bianca killings,[2] I started to see more and more alarm tape on windows, people were getting dogs, there were stickers for the Bel Air Patrol and Hollywood Patrol, private companies that patrolled the swankier areas, and I simply decided that sooner or later the law of averages was going to catch up with me, I thought, "Let's not do this again," and I didn't.

Interviewer: The ante had gone up.
Ellroy: The ante had gone up, and I didn't want to be caught. I always had that certain level of cautiousness and circumspection going for me.

Interviewer: You've talked about always wanting to be a writer, but there must have been some specific point when you decided that you needed to get serious about it.
Ellroy: I quit drinking and using drugs in 1977, when I was twenty-nine and a caddie at the Bel-Air Country Club in Los Angeles. At the time I was reading some recent crime fiction and rereading some of my old favorites, and I had this sneaking suspicion that I could do better than the people I was reading. I had always wanted to be one thing—a novelist—but it wasn't until a desire to simply write novels overtook me that I was actually able to start. It was a tremendous surprise to me that the story that started developing in my mind was a crime story. Big surprise! I should have been the first one to know, since crime fiction had been the big love of my life. I hadn't thought I had the kind of brain that could come up with complex plots—which, of course crime fiction requires. The first story that came to me was the story of *Brown's Requiem*, a little autobiographical perhaps, but primarily based around some old L.A. crimes. That's the story that came to me, that's the book that I wrote and damned if I didn't sell it.

Interviewer: Were there any false starts, or did you just begin with the idea for that book and stick with it?
Ellroy: I started outlining *Brown's Requiem* in 1978, but I stopped because I was afraid I might write the book and not sell it; I was afraid that I might fail in general. At the time I had quit caddying for a spell, to work for an attorney service. Basically I was a processor server, but I couldn't make any money at it, because it was contingency work and I wasn't very good at finding people. So I went back to the golf course, where I could make my guaranteed $200–$250 a week. And it wasn't until January 1979 that I said, "Fuck it" and wrote the book.

Interviewer: So you really did just sit down and write it?
Ellroy: Yes, from a threadbare outline.

Interviewer: You've talked about how you graduated from the Hardy Boys and Sherlock Holmes to Mickey Spillane and Nero Wolfe and finally to Joseph Wambaugh and Ross Macdonald. And you've said that both Macdonald and Wambaugh were your teachers.

Ellroy: I'd say that Dashiell Hammett taught me much more than Ross Macdonald: and Raymond Chandler, in the end, taught me very little. I think Chandler is essentially very overrated and not as important as he's given credit for being.

Interviewer: What did you learn from Hammett?

Ellroy: I think I picked up the Hammett world view. Hammett wrote the man that he was afraid he was, whereas Chandler wrote the man he wanted to be. I think that my books have evolved more and more into what I like to call "the private nightmare of public policy." Increasingly, I have focused on the bad men of history, on the leg-breakers, and that in essence is what the Continental Op[3] was all about. If there is a book that stands out in my past more than any other it's *Red Harvest*, where the Continental Op is called upon to restore order to a lawless mining town. He plays off all the factions against each other. He is in the pay of the big money of the mining company. He succeeds at restoring order at a great cost. In the end marshal law is imposed, the little guy gets fucked, and the mining company takes over stronger than ever. It's a dark view.

Interviewer: Did your reading affect you stylistically? Were you aware of how they were saying what they were saying?

Ellroy: No, not at all. I read inchoately, I read emotionally, I read for a story, I read for milieu. I read because reading crime novels gave me both a tidy sense of resolution and a sense that the ramifications of violent events would go on forever. Of course, I think that this love of crime fiction derives from my mother's murder. It's a very simple cause and effect to chart. On one level or another I write crime novels because I'm deeply curious, and the only way that I can sate my curiosity on all matters pertaining to crime and psychosexual behavior is by writing the books that nobody could write.

Interviewer: Did your reading also provide a sense of closure for the fears caused by your mother's death?

Ellroy: No. The only closure is that there is no closure.

Interviewer: What triggered you to write *Brown's Requiem*?

Ellroy: I tried to write the story that was talking to me at the moment. I tried to apply some of my own past: my alcoholism and the fact that I was recently sober, my love of classical music, the fact that I was caddying at the time. All that hokey autobiographical stuff that mainstream writers dwell on ad infinitum I got rid of in my first two books.

Interviewer: I was going to say *Clandestine* also has a lot of autobiographical material in it.

Ellroy: Yeah, it's a heavily fictionalized, chronologically altered account of my mother's murder.

Interviewer: In writing those two books did you discover anything about what you wanted to do next?

Ellroy: I wrote *Brown's Requiem*, and I had a tremendous revelation when I finished it. I realized that all modern private-eye novels are bullshit, and that I would never write another one.

Interviewer: The next three books that you wrote were a short-lived series, the Hopkins novels. Where did the character of Hopkins come from in *Blood on the Moon*?

Ellroy: I wanted to write the ugliest and most explicit cop/psycho-killer book of all time. In the first draft the cop, Hopkins, and the killer, Teddy Verplanck, kill each other and L.A. burns to the ground.

Interviewer: In the original version?

Ellroy: In the original. It was Nat Sobel, my agent, and Otto Penzler, who was thinking about publishing me for Mysterious Press, who got me to do an extensive rewrite on *Blood on the Moon*. I look back now and think, "Holy shit, is this moribund." And while we're on this topic of what's dead and what's not, serial killer novels are just as dead as private eye novels.

Interviewer: Yet *Killer on the Road* is a serial killer book.

Ellroy: Yeah, but at least it's strictly from the serial killer's viewpoint and not a *roman policier* on any level.

Interviewer: You started your career writing novels with different central characters, but with *Blood on the Moon* you began a series. Why did you continue with Hopkins in *Because the Night*?

Ellroy: I liked him, and I wanted to do a limited series with him, chart his psychology over a set period of time, and then abandon him on some sort of ambiguous note. There's a liberalism that I despise in crime fiction, and I wanted to create a realistic Los Angeles cop of the time, with a full component of prejudices, and place him in various violent contexts. A quote that keeps coming back to me is Raymond Chandler said that "Dashiell Hammett gave murder back to the people who really committed it."[4] My L.A. Quartet and *American Tabloid* are designed to give crime fiction and violent intrigue back to the men who would really have perpetrated it—and they are *men* and they are *white men*. I see hardboiled crime fiction as a heavily ritualized transit horseshit and largely spun off of Raymond Chandler. Chandler is a very easy writer, which is why so many people have been able to adapt his formula with such success, but I hate that formula, and I hate its sensibility. I wanted to give crime fiction back to the leg breakers of history, to soldiers of fortune, to bad white men, to racist shit-birds and the corrupt cops. I think the chief risk I've taken is to ignore the old warning of crime fiction editors worldwide. Namely, that you've got to create sympathetic characters that your readers can identify with.

Interviewer: Do your readers identify with any of your characters. There are few who are conventionally sympathetic.

Ellroy: I identify with all of them. I want my readers to have an ambiguous response to my characters. I want my readers to identify with my characters on the level of their hidden sexual agendas. I want my readers to say, "Man, what a blast it would be to go back to 1952 and beat up faggots." Then I want them to realize, "Oh, am I really thinking that?" In *American Tabloid*, I wanted people to think, "Yeah, what a fuckin' blast; let's whack out John F. Kennedy."

Interviewer: Is that being on the edge in ways that most readers simply never experience?

Ellroy: Yes, I think crime fiction at its best is touching the fire and getting your hand burned.

Interviewer: You said a minute ago that you had basically planned the Hopkins series as a limited series. So you started out thinking that you would do three books and stop?

Ellroy: Three, four, or five. When I wrote *The Black Dahlia*, Otto Penzler wanted me to write a fourth Hopkins book. I wanted to build on *The Black Dahlia*, create a quartet of interlocking novels, and chart L.A. from 1947 to 1959.

Interviewer: Why the fascination with the past?
Ellroy: I'm from Los Angeles. If I were born in Dog Dick, Delaware, or Moose Fart, Montana, I would write dark crime novels about those places. Luckily for me, my parents hatched me in a place that had a rich criminal history.

Interviewer: Why not write about contemporary crime? What is it about the past that fascinates you?
Ellroy: I like it because everything that's happening today was happening then, only statistically there was a whole lot less of it. I like to call it "the contained apocalypse." As a kid, I sensed there was a secret world coexisting with the outwardly more placid world. I began to consciously rediscover that world as I started writing the L.A. Quartet. Those books dealt with hep-cat musicians, desperate homosexual informants, corrupt D.A.'s, perverts, panty sniffers, pederasts, punks, people like that. And it's a closed world. There's a symbiotic frenzy going on among these people at all times. It's very rare that this inward world spills out into the outwardly more placid world. But it does occasionally in *White Jazz*, and the results are hellish.

Interviewer: Why was that world of particular use to you? What was it that fascinated you about it?
Ellroy: On June 22, 1958, I went back to the place I was living with my mother. The fuzz were all over the place, and a man said, "Son, your mother has been killed." My mother had been shitty to me in the weeks preceding her death. My greatest dream during that time was to go live with my father. All of a sudden my mother is dead, all of a sudden my wish had been granted. I experienced a very ambiguous bereavement. I was frightened of my mother; I was frightened of the hold that she had over me. I felt that I should have loved her more. But some part of me seized upon my mother's death as an opportunity. At the time of her death I was heading toward puberty and was sexually obsessed with her. The next thing I know she's dead, and it's a terrible sex crime, and I'm living with my old man and gobbling up all the crime books I can get my meat hooks on—because I wanted to know why and that curiosity has never left me.

Interviewer: Don't you think your style shifts with *The Black Dahlia*, displaying your growing assurance as a writer?

Ellroy: I'd been wanting to write that book for a long time. I first learned of the Black Dahlia murder case about eight months after my mother's death. My father got two books for my eleventh birthday in March 1959. One was *The Complete Sherlock Holmes*; the other was *The Badge* by Jack Webb, which contained a haunting ten-page summary of the Black Dahlia murder case. The two cases merged in my mind, and in many ways Elizabeth Short, the Dahlia, was the stand-in for my mother. I felt the horror of her death. It was a completely uncompromising horror. I used to have nightmares; I used to be afraid to go to sleep because I knew I would dream about Elizabeth Short. I used to have daytime flashes where I'd see her being tortured. And in 1977, just as I was getting sober and was about to change my life, I read John Gregory Dunne's wonderful, if fanciful novel, *True Confessions*, which is his heavily fictionalized account of the Black Dahlia murder case. *The Black Dahlia* probably would have been my first novel, but I thought the success of Dunne's novel precluded anyone else ever writing about the Black Dahlia. I didn't realize at the time that, *au contraire*, if you have a big, hit book like that, it spawns a great many imitators. And so I wrote my first six books, learned how to write in the process, and embraced the writing of *The Black Dahlia* with a certain degree of consciousness. And I made every effort to differentiate *The Black Dahlia* from *True Confessions*. It was my first hit book, and I realized that I had to make every book from that point on more meaningful than *The Black Dahlia*, this book that I'd waited so many years to write. So I conceived in *The Big Nowhere* a much larger story—a story with a broader societal base. In every way, I think, it's a better book. It's not as accessible as *The Black Dahlia*. The characters are harder to like, and there's no happy ending payoff. From *The Big Nowhere* on I formed a new covenant with myself—a covenant of consciousness. The covenant goes something like this: every book has to be conceived as bigger, better, stronger, and more stylistically evolved than the book that preceded it, or I am fucking up big time and should be considered a second-class citizen.

Interviewer: Certainly *L.A. Confidential* and *The Big Nowhere* are much bigger books, especially in terms of plot, but *White Jazz* is quite different. Among other things, it's a stylistic experiment. Some of the critics had a little trouble with it.

Ellroy: The style evolved this way. My preceding novel, *L.A. Confidential* came in too long in manuscript. I cut sentences, trimmed the book down, and saw that I had developed a unique telegraphic style. I started writing *White Jazz*, in a normally discursive, first-person style, but the book felt flabby to me, so I started cutting words. I realized that I had developed a paranoid tone, a stream of consciousness style that made the book read like a fever dream. That style was uniquely suited to Dave Klein, the narrator—a terrible man whose life is burning down. And so I wrote the book in that style, and a lot of people found it difficult. I think it's a groovy, seamless work of art, and I'm thrilled to death with it. That style was suitable for that one book—and I'll never go back to it again.

Interviewer: You talk about not wanting to entertain your readers but to confront them. What is this confrontation? What is your relationship with the readers?

Ellroy: I want to thrill; I want to horrify; I want to titillate. I want to shock. I'm getting more obsessive as I get older, and I'm getting more controlled and more contained in my obsessiveness. I want to jolt my readers out of their everyday lives and share my obsessions with them. I want them to obsessively read my books.

Interviewer: How would you respond if somebody said, "You're just exploiting people's sickness?"

Ellroy: I'd say, "Fuck you!"

Interviewer: Critics often describe your writing as neo-noir. What are you doing that's different from traditional noir?

Ellroy: I think I've shaped noir far into social history. Nobody's written noir books as big as mine, with their scope and with their heavily detailed societal backgrounds.

Interviewer: You've said that the cop has replaced the private eye as the center of the hardboiled novel. Why do you think that's true?

Ellroy: Because, to paraphrase Evan Hunter, "The last time a private eye investigated a murder was never!" Because Joseph Wambaugh ascended and became the most important writer of realistic intrigue since Dashiell Hammett.

Interviewer: What is it you learned from Wambaugh, specifically?

Ellroy: He has a unique vision. I think he's a right-wing absurdist and how many right-wing absurdists have you run into in your career as a critic? I used to get hassled by the L.A. cops as a young misanthrope about town. I never hated them, even when they were hassling me a bit more roughly than they should have been. I admired them, and I sensed their inner drama—and Wambaugh made that inner drama real for me.

Interviewer: You talk about having an affection for things as they are and not really trying to push for social change or betterment in your books. Can you expand on that idea at all?

Ellroy: I'm a white, Anglo-Saxon Protestant heterosexual born in America, and I've never shared the counterculture ethos revered by so many people of my generation. I get ragged occasionally for being fascist, racist, anti-Semitic, and homophobic—because my characters are. I think some people hate my characters because their fascism, racism, homophobia, and anti-Semitism are in no way defining characteristics—they're just casual attributes. These characters, who are meant to be empathized with, say "nigger," "fag," and "kike," and people don't know how to respond to that. I love these characters of mine. It's as if I lived their lives long ago. Thus I try not to condescend to them, and I show their heroism coexisting with their dubious attributes out of another time.

Interviewer: You've obviously proved that the crime novel is a perfect vehicle for social commentary.

Ellroy: I hope so.

Interviewer: Is it better than the conventional novel?

Ellroy: It beats me—I don't read much.

Interviewer: Let's talk about *American Tabloid*. Tell me about the Kennedy assassination, and the FBI, and America in the 1960s.

Ellroy: I had read Don DeLillo's novel *Libra*, and it blew my mind, fucked my soul, and scorched my sexuality. I felt that, holy shit, now I'm tremendously interested in the Kennedy assassination, but now I can never write about it—because the book is just that seminal. Then I began to see that I could write a novel where the assassination would be but one crime in a long series of crimes. I wouldn't even have to use Lee Harvey Oswald, who DeLillo portrayed so brilliantly. I began to see that all the harbingers of the assassination started to percolate in the late 1950s, and that I could write an epic-length novel about government/criminal collusion with a huge cast of characters. I knew the historical elements I wanted to co-opt: the CIA and their war against Castro's Cuba; the Bay of Pigs invasion; the Kennedy assassination; Jimmy Hoffa and the Teamsters; Bobby Kennedy's war on organized crime; J. Edgar Hoover; Howard Hughes. I realized that these people were all in bed with each other, and more than anyone else, it was Joe Kennedy who got his son killed—because it was Bobby Kennedy's Oedipal drama that resulted in Jack's murder. Bobby had a strong moral sense, and he understood that the gangsters he was chasing were his father once removed. As I started writing the book, I realized that this isn't just one novel. This is a trilogy about America between the years 1958 and 1973. I'm going to write an epic trilogy that nobody else would have the stones or the patience to write.

Interviewer: You have the titles of the next two books?
Ellroy: No, just the dates. Volume II will cover 1963 to 1968: Volume III will cover 1968 to 1973. Just think of American history between those years, and you'll have an idea of the plot.

Interviewer: Let's talk a little bit about your next book, and your first work of nonfiction, *My Dark Places*, which is coming out in the fall of 1996.
Ellroy: In January of '94, my friend Frank Girardot, a reporter for the *San Gabriel Valley Tribune* in California, called up and said, "I'm doing a piece about the L.A. County Sheriff's Unsolved Unit, and I'm going to spotlight five unsolved San Gabriel Valley homicides." Frank told me he was going to see my mother's murder file, so that he could review the case in his piece. I said, "Oh, holy shit, I want to see the file, too." I called up my editor at *G.Q.*, Paul Scanlon, and said, "I want to go to L.A. and write a 5000-word piece for *G.Q.* about the experience of seeing my mother's homicide file thirty-six years after the fact." Paul said, "Go, daddy-O." Girardot had told me that he was dealing with two cops about to retire from the sheriff's homicide bureau: Bill McComas and Bill Stoner. I called up Stoner and talked to him. He said, "Yeah, you can see the file," and made arrangements for me to come out and look at it. In April of 1994, I went out and saw my mother's homicide file. I saw her nude on the morgue slab. I saw her dead on the road where she had been left after she was raped[5] and strangled, and as I read through the file, it completely blew all my preconceptions about the case apart. It was just as shocking as you'd think it would be. I realized this isn't over. Bill Stoner impressed me too. I had never met a cop quite as intelligent, quite as humane, quite as perceptive as this man. He seemed to be a very evolved human being.

I went back home to Connecticut and wrote the piece for *G.Q.* It was a wrenching experience, and it left me wanting more. I realized what I had to do. I called up Nat Sobel, my agent, and told him that I wanted to turn the *G.Q.* article into a full-length book. I mentioned it to Sonny Mehta, the boss and my editor at Alfred A. Knopf, and he said that he heard about the *G.Q.* piece and was hoping I would want to expand it. He read the article and said, "Yes, let's do the book."

I see the book thusly. It would be my autobiography, my mother's biography, Bill Stoner's biography, and it would have two basic dramatic thrusts. One, I would go back and re-create the original 1958–59 investigation from official records and surviving witness testimony. Two, if he were willing to help me for a cut of the proceeds, I would enlist Bill Stoner and we would reinvestigate my mother's murder in the present.

So that's the book that I'm doing now. Stoner and I have been at it since late October. He's retired from the sheriff's department now, and we've become close friends. More than anything else, it's exhilarating, and there are times when I feel my mother's presence very strongly. I'm staying in an apartment in Newport Beach because Stoner lives in a neighboring community, and we travel a lot together. I've put up corkboards with pictures of my mother and mugshots of various perverts who were brought in for questioning and later exonerated, maps of the area where her body was found, and lists of the witnesses that we need to find. I can feel her, and I can smell her after thirty-seven years. I can smell the perfume she used to wear, and her breath, suffused with Early Times' bourbon and L & M cigarettes. She's coming into focus in ways that I can't quite assess yet, and Stoner is undergoing the same thing. I'm starting to feel the killer, too, and I'm starting to feel the lower-middle-class, middle-aged alcoholic desperation that resulted in her death.

Interviewer: When you finish this book are you going to return to your larger, ongoing historical project?
Ellroy: Yes, I'm going to go back to the second volume of what I'm calling the Underworld U.S.A. Trilogy, which should be published about two years after *My Dark Places*.

Interviewer: What do you do better than anybody else in your writing?
Ellroy: I think I sustain concentration better than anybody I know. I've brought a rich curiosity and a rich emotional need to the craft, and I have a

strong will to surmount and get better. The older I get, the more self-referential I become, and I don't compare myself at all to other writers. And the older I get, the hungrier I get—which makes me believe I'm going to write a lot of great fucking books.

1. This is one of the few sources that refers to the "Hopkins in Jeopardy" title. It appears the series title would have been used more prominently if Ellroy had written a quintet of Hopkins novels as originally planned. The James Ellroy archive at the University of South Carolina contains an outline Ellroy wrote in 1987 for a planned fourth Hopkins novel titled 'The Cold Six Thousand', a title he would later use for the second volume of the Underworld U.S.A. trilogy.

2. A series of murders committed by members of the Manson Family. Sharon Tate was an American actress and the second wife of film director Roman Polanski. She was murdered by four members of the Manson Family on August 9, 1969. Pasquilino 'Leno' and Rosemary LaBianca were murdered the following night by Charles Manson and four of his followers.

3. Dashiell Hammett's unnamed private detective the Continental Op appeared in thirty-six short stories, mostly published in *Black Mask* magazine between 1923 and 1930. Several interlinked stories were published as the novels *Red Harvest* and *The Dain Curse* in 1929.

4. "Hammett gave murder back to the kind of people who commit it for reasons, not just to provide a corpse; and with the means at hand, not hand-wrought dueling pistols, curare and tropical fish." From "The Simple Art of Murder" first published in *The Atlantic Monthly*, December, 1944.

5. This reference to his mother being raped is inconsistent with Ellroy's other interviews and with his article "My Mother's Killer" for *G.Q.* and the memoir *My Dark Places*.

The Beatrice Interview: 1995

Ron Hogan/1995

From *Beatrice.com* (1995). Reprinted by permission of Ron Hogan.

Dig it: Howard Hughes holed up in a hotel suite, strung out on heroin and receiving daily blood transfusions. James Riddle Hoffa at war with the Kennedys. Jack Kennedy ready to jump on anything in a skirt. Sam Giancana and Carlos Marcello scheming to get back the casinos in Havana. Jack Ruby in over his head with some bad, bad men. J. Edgar Hoover sitting in the shadows, watching over everything, listening in through the wiretaps.

This is the world of James Ellroy's new novel, *American Tabloid*, a world where just about everybody's working two or more different angles. There's Pete Bondurant: disgraced L.A. County sheriff, errand boy for Hughes, and private investigator specializing in getting dirt for divorce cases. He ends up taking on side jobs for Hoffa that lead to contract work with the CIA, organizing the Cuban exiles in Miami. There's Ward Littell, alcoholic FBI agent: sick of harassing pathetic, ineffective Communists, he itches to take on the Mob, but his rash decisions have violent repercussions. And Kemper Boyd: G-man who hustles his way into the Kennedy brothers' inner circle, and liaison between the Mob and the Company.

Since the publication of *The Black Dahlia* in 1987, James Ellroy's star has been rapidly climbing. Each subsequent novel in the L.A. Quartet (*The Big Nowhere*, *L.A. Confidential*, and *White Jazz*) sold more and garnered higher praise than the last, and Ellroy's prose developed an increasingly baroque, telegraphic style—his books are what Rudy Rucker is talking about when he asks, "How fast are you? How dense?" Ellroy's novels are so fast and dense that you can whip right through this book, and hours after you've put it down, the ugly parts will still be rebounding inside your head. They combine the dark, shadowy world of *film noir* with ultraviolent atrocity in a nonstop torrent through which his protagonists—and sometimes his readers—try to find some last vestige of morality to which they can cling.

When I spoke to Ellroy in Los Angeles, I could see that he's genuinely excited about the success that his last two novels have achieved, on both the financial and literary levels, and it shows in his exuberance as he speaks. "You know what the biggest thrill of my career is?" he tells me. "Being published by Alfred A. Knopf." In person, Ellroy drops the psychohipster spiel and talks seriously about his craft and his life.

Interviewer: You've said recently that "*noir* is dead" for you now.
Ellroy: It's gone.

Interviewer: What's going on, and what do you see developing in your style as you get out of the *noir* of L.A. and into the big national story of *American Tabloid* and beyond?
Ellroy: *American Tabloid* is history as *noir* on an epic scale. One of the chief ironies of the book is that Boyd, Ward, and Pete get fucked out of the assassination; they don't get to kill him. These guys all start out enamored of Jack to one degree or another, and all end up hating him. Their motives for killing him are really very personal, but they are in the grip of events bigger than themselves and don't even get to kill him. Kemper Boyd dies; he gets off easy. The two surviving protagonists have tried to force history and history has ended up getting them where it hurts the most. The men are getting older. Littell is fifty. Bondurant is forty-three: he's desperately in love with a woman; he's heavily compromised. Kennedy is about to die; he knows who's doing it. He was part of a number of botched plots, but it's going to happen, and there's hell to pay. He and Littell have been exiled to Las Vegas, and they've got a five-year span coming up in the next book in which to confront themselves; I want that confrontation to be gradual and subtle and dramatic and to push them in some very, very odd directions. I want to show a greater diversity of character and motive, and I want to see these bad, bad, *bad, bad* men come to grips with their humanity.

Noir is dead for me because historically, I think it's a simple view. I've taken it as far as it can go. I think I've expanded on it a great deal, taken it further than any other American novelist. What I want to do is take the *noir* elements that I developed in my first eleven books and . . . not soften them, but take them out to different places. I think the dividing line between noir and what follows is the nonfiction book I'm working on now.

Interviewer: That's *My Dark Places*, which is a combination of your auto-biography, your mother's biography, and the story of the two investigations into your mother's murder: the original investigation in 1958, and the re-opened investigation you've recently undertaken.

Ellroy: I'm going to re-create the original investigation as best I can from the documents and witness testimony. I'm not going to extrapolate; I have to adhere to fact. Then, Bill Stoner and I conduct our own investigation. We have no hard suspects. We have a number of call-ins from psychics who wanted to come in and conduct séances for seventy-five bucks. We'll see where it goes. It's going to be an uphill battle . . . I don't know. I honestly don't know. In some sense, and I'm not being disingenuous, you know as much about it as I do, about how it will turn out.

Interviewer: Watching *White Jazz* (the British TV documentary on Ellroy and his work), I got the feeling that in a certain sense, it doesn't matter where it goes, because you're already on a journey in which, no matter whether you find out who killed your mother or not, you've already started coming to grips with your mother, and cleansing yourself of her death.

Ellroy: I go back and forth on it. There's times when I'm intensely deter-mined to make it happen. I'm clenched down; I'm locked in on it, which is my general approach to life. There are times when I realize, "You're simply doing all you can, this is way out of your hands. So let go of it." It's like this: Stoner and I are becoming very close friends; we've been close friends al-most from the gate. I've become friends with Bill's family; my wife Helen has become friends with Bill and his wife Anne, and I think that they're going to be close friends of ours for as long as we live. Toward the end of the summer, I'll need to go away and write the book. Bill will be here if anything comes up. He can call me. We'll be talking every day or so. If we're nowhere, if it's a washout by the time the book goes into production, that's that. Then I think Bill and I will just get together periodically and chase leads.

Interviewer: In terms of the personal journey that you're going through in this investigation, in the documentary you mention that your friendship with Bill Stoner has really helped you to get out of yourself, so to speak.

Ellroy: I have a very intense marriage, and the intense thing with Stoner, and most of my friends are colleagues. Other than that, I like to be alone so I can write. But focus can hurt you. I don't want to be some stress casualty in early middle age. So Stoner is amazing in that I don't have to perform with him. I'm profoundly interested in just about everything he has to say. I can quit being myself, which is a tremendous freedom for such a whacked out personality. If I'm not performing, I feel rather deferential to people. If I'm going to a party or meeting with a group of people, I would much rather not talk about myself. I can do that in front of a podium and have a blast at it, make people laugh. If this were not an interview, and you and I were just sitting around having a cup of coffee, I'd much rather hear about your life. I like to perform, but when I'm not performing, I'm not performing. I've led a colorful life, but I'm always trying to demythologize that life. I was terrified as a kid. I broke into houses, how many times did I do it? Thirty, fifty? I don't know. How much time did I spend in jail? Six months, eight months, four months? Mickey Mouse stuff. I don't think I could have survived in the shape I was in then in the jails today, but that was in an era when a lot of middle-class and lower- middle-class white kids were being arrested because of the availability of hard drugs, so there were a lot of guys like me in jail, which really greased the skids for me. I was always frightened. I was never a tough guy. Every wild thing that I did was tinged with alcoholic and drug-addicted self-loathing and a large degree of fear. Today I put on such a good show, the story is outrageous, and people don't want to hear that I'm basically a reasonable human being. As long as it continues to get me print, I'll continue to perform in an exuberant manner.

Interviewer: What you've been doing in the L.A. Quartet and in *American Tabloid* is connecting your characters to history, but in a way that connects history to people.

Ellroy: As a kid, I sensed history going on all around me, but the basic thrust of it didn't move me. For instance, the events in *American Tabloid*: I was for Richard Nixon in 1960 when I was twelve, because my father was. I was not upset by Kennedy's assassination. I was just a little shitbird nihilistic fifteen-year-old kid, and I thought it was cool that somebody gunned down the Prez. I don't recall the Bay of Pigs. The Cuban missile crisis didn't scare me because I thought it would be cool if the bomb went off. I sensed these things going on all around me, especially as I got older, and as all the social torment of the late '60s occurred, I felt completely divorced from it. But I sensed the bigger stories going on.

When I was a kid, Eisenhower had been president forever, and all of a sudden, everything in the world was all about Jack Kennedy. The primary election—I was twelve, interested in politics; my father was from Massachusetts, had an accent like Kennedy—everything was about him. He handled it with a certain ironic detachment that was appealing. He was amused, he was bemused, and people mistook it for love. Bad miscalculation. Everything was about him for some years, especially after he was elected. I couldn't believe it, because he looked so young and he had his run and he died. It's like being with a woman and she leaves you before the sex gets stale. You're always going to think of her, you're always going to want more, you didn't get enough. That's how America was with Jack. That's why we put this preposterous "loss of innocence" tag on his death.

Raymond Chandler once wrote that Dashiell Hammett gave murder back to the people who really committed it. This was his comment, I believe, on the "tea-cozy" genre, and I think that's interesting. And I think that I would like to do that again. You're under a great deal of pressure, if you write crime fiction, which is what I used to write, to create serious characters, so-called sympathetic characters, with which the readers can empathize, so that you can build a readership. Of course, it can kill you because you have to write the same book over and over again. And I think that Chandler, who I have less affection for by the day, spawned a whole number of easy imitators. His style is easy to adapt to the personal prejudices of the individual writers, which is why you now have the gay private eye, the black private eye, the woman private eye, and every other kind of private eye. But I don't think that's the realistic archetype of twentieth-century violent intrigue: to me, it's these legbreakers, these guys like Pete Bondurant, corrupt cops like Dave Klein, and I take a great deal of satisfaction out of putting these guys back in history.

Interviewer: When I read critics of your work, they often react: "Oh my god, he's writing these horrible homophobic, racist, misogynist, psychopathic books." And I'm thinking: "No, he's not writing from *his* perspective. He's getting into the heads of these ugly characters." You're not endorsing their world by any means.

Ellroy: I think I know what's behind this, especially some of the views expressed by Mike Davis.[1] These are fully rounded characters, and the racism and homophobia are casual attributes, not defining characteristics. These are not lynchers or gaybashers, toadies of the corrupt system. When you have characters that the reader empathizes with, who are carrying the story, saying "nigger" and "faggot" and "spic," it puts people off. Which is fine. I would like to provoke ambiguous responses in my readers. That's what I want. There's part of me that would really like to be one of Dudley Smith's goons and go back and beat up some jazz musicians, and there's part of me that's just appalled.

Interviewer: One of the first major advances I noticed in your style after going back and reading the earlier stuff is that around the time of *The Black Dahlia* you stopped having your protagonists be outside the racism and homophobia, like in *Clandestine*, where the protagonist clearly distances himself from the attitudes. You've allowed yourself to position your characters within that mindset.

Ellroy: I figured out a while back that I'm an unregenerate white Anglo-Saxon Protestant heterosexual. So are my men. Their racism and homophobia are appalling, but it's germane to their characters, and people will either get that or not get it. That's that. You can't really respond to the press and say, "I'm not a racist or a homophobe." Nobody's going to believe you.

Interviewer: Getting back to your comments about Chandler—do you think there are other writers who avoided—not necessarily the mistakes— but the direction that he made it easy to take? Or writers that have particularly influenced you?

Ellroy: I've been tremendously moved by a bunch of odd books. Ross Macdonald is very important to me. I loved the Lew Archer books. I don't know if I could stand them now. I glanced through one the other day, and it seemed to be appallingly overwritten, full of metaphor and so on, not really my bowl of rice. Did he influence me? Yeah, and there's some elements of his lost child motif, and the webs of violence going back generations, in my earlier books. He influenced me, but I can't see how it's made its way into my books for years. My first novel, *Brown's Requiem*, was very heavily indebted to Raymond Chandler. He was an influence, but one that I've had an apostasy regarding.

Hammett, especially *Red Harvest*: big, big book to me. Big book, political book—a book about a toady for the corrupt system restoring order to a town and then turning it over to the National Guard, martial law. The mining company wins, the rival factions are wiped out, and he goes on to another job. I think it's a great vision. James M. Cain at his best. *Serenade, Postman Always Rings Twice, Mildred Pierce, Double Indemnity.* Joseph Wambaugh: **BIG.** The major influence, the biggest. Big, big, big influence; most important crime writer since Hammett.

Odd books. *No Beast So Fierce* by Edward Bunker: the best armed robbery novel ever written. Other than one of my books, if you want to hole up with a great book this weekend and you haven't read it yet, get *Compulsion* by Meyer Levin, his novel of the Leopold-Loeb murder. A brilliant portrait of the Chicago of the '20s, five hundred pages, a great psychological epic. *True Confessions* by John Gregory Dunne. *Red Dragon* by Thomas Harris: even though I think there's some things wrong with the structure, easily the best serial killer book ever written. *Libra*, by Don DeLillo.

Interviewer: That actually brings up an interesting point, in that immediately after finishing *American Tabloid*, I realized that you had produced a very compelling portrait of the Kennedy assassination, what Malcolm X called "the chickens coming home to roost," with NO OSWALD.

Ellroy: There's some things that you don't fuck with. One of them is Don DeLillo's portrayals of Lee Harvey Oswald and David Ferrie. No way. His portrayal of Oswald, as the ultimate American loser, broke my heart. It's the first time I've ever seen such a stupid man developed into such a complex character.

Interviewer: Have you seen *JFK* and if so, what did you think?

Ellroy: I was just enthralled for an hour and twenty minutes. Bravura moviemaking, wonderfully layered and dense and jazzy, and then Donald Sutherland arrives to posit this preposterous theory, and it goes downhill from there. I think organized crime, exile factions, and renegade CIA killed Jack the Haircut. I think your most objective researchers do as well. When Oliver Stone diverged from that to take in the rest of the world (Lyndon Johnson, the Joint Chiefs of Staff), I lost interest. I went out and bought a copy of the video, and I watch it right up until Donald Sutherland appears—then I turn it off.

I haven't been to a movie in a year and a half. Helen and I went to see *The Fugitive*, which was a big influence on me as a kid. I was running wild, and I was obsessed with that show in a way I've never been obsessed with any show since. Here's this tormented fifteen-year-old kid, and his stand-in is handsome David Jannsen who's bopping around from one town to the next, all of which look like L.A., cops are in hot pursuit, and the grooviest woman in town falls in love with him wherever he goes. Then I saw the movie, which is this hyperkinetic piece of shit, culminating in a fistfight between two fifty-year-old cardiologists. That pretty much burned me out on popular culture.

Interviewer: What do you think the future holds for the relationship between you and your fans, as you begin to pick up critical acclaim from the mainstream reviewers? Do you see your reputation moving beyond the "gory crime writer" image?

Ellroy: I'm getting a wider circle of fans now. More women, more middle-class people, more people outside the regular "Ellroy combine" of journalists, rock and rollers, and movie biz people. If you have to have a bunch of fans marked off demographically, those are the kinds of fans to have. Journalists will write about you; movie people are opinion makers to one degree or another, they can influence the media; rock and rollers can get you the youth buzz, and younger people are fanatical readers. But when people are digging you for the wrong reasons, you start thinking, "What have I spawned? Don't they understand the moral of *White Jazz*, the way that Dave Klein crumbles under the weight of his own evil, how he's just flailing at acts of decency like a man dying of thirst reaching for a glass of water?" As critical acclaim and response has built up, every interview I give is a chance to puncture the myth I've created about my work and refine it.

Note

1. American scholar, urban theorist, historian, and left-wing political activist. He has strongly criticized Ellroy in his book *City of Quartz: Excavating the Future in Los Angeles* (1990), and in an interview with Marcus Frommer for the *Chicago Review of Books*.

James Ellroy: Barking

Paul Duncan/1996

From *The Third Degree: Crime Writers in Conversation*, edited by Paul Duncan, No Exit Press, 1997. © Paul Duncan, all rights reserved. Reprinted by permission.

WOOF. WOOF. HEAR THE DEMON DOG BARK.
HE'S GOT A TWELVE INCH WANGER THAT GLOWS IN THE DARK.
HIS BRAIN IS BIG, BUT HIS DICK IS BIGGER.
HIS RIGHT WING FINGER'S ON THE NUCLEAR TRIGGER.

Interviewer: Hello, Mr. Ellroy.
Ellroy: Call me Dog.

Interviewer: Okay, Mr. Dog.
Ellroy: No . . . just "Dog."

If there's one thing you have to admire about Dog, it's that he puts on a good show. He swears. He digs up his past and shoves it in the faces of his adoring public. He simulates masturbation on stage. He howls like the Demon Dog of American Crime Literature that he is. What's even funnier is that so many people take this stuff seriously.

I have this vision of Dog arriving home after a hard month or two touring, slipping off his shoes, falling into a chair and hissing with laughter as he recalls the shocked faces of his audience. A sort of tall, gangly Muttley who caught that dastardly pigeon.

Besides, what do people expect after reading one of Dog's novels? From Brown's Requiem *to* American Tabloid, *they're full of swearing, racism, drugs, bodily functions, violence, fluids, sleazeballs, and hairballs. How could you expect Dog to be anything other than rabid in real life?*

The fuel which keeps Dog up nights writing his fever dreams is the unsolved murder of his mother in 1958. His books are full of mother-substitutes,

61

the most famous being Elizabeth Short, the Black Dahlia, a celebrated un-solved murder which occurred in January 1947. It is as though he is trying to deny his mother's reality by treating her as fiction. However, Ellroy has shown a greater maturity with his last novel, American Tabloid, and with the publication of My Dark Places, which details Ellroy's search for his mother's murderer, he hopes to acknowledge his mother, to recognize her for the person she really was.

Paul Duncan talked to James Ellroy.

A Dog's Life

Lee "the Big Armando" Ellroy, born 1898 in Germany, came to America with his parents, who died in a hotel fire when he was aged six. He was sent to an orphanage, where he was taught by sadistic nuns fresh off the boat from Ire-land. He claimed to have had an affair with Rita Hayworth.

Jean (Geneva) Hilliker was born 1915 in Tunnel City, Wisconsin, and had a strict Dutch Calvinist upbringing. Aged nineteen, and a nursing-school stu-dent, she claimed to have seen John Dillinger gunned down by the Feds.

They met in 1939, married, lived in West Hollywood, Los Angeles.

James was born March 4, 1948, in Good Samaritan Hospital. He learnt to read aged three and has been a prolific reader ever since. In 1954, Lee and Jean divorced. Lee drank Alka-Seltzer for his ulcer and chased women. Jean drank Early Times bourbon and chased men. James drank what he was given and did some middle distance at school. Result: James lived with his mother during the week and his father most weekends.

Jean worked as a nurse at the Packard Bell electronics plant and went out with men on a regular basis. One, Hank, was fat and had a thumb miss-ing. She was always pissed. James preferred his father. When he turned ten, he was given the choice of living with mother or father—he chose father, his mother slapped him, he called her a drunk and a whore.

Three months later, he arrived back from a weekend with his father to find cops at his mother's house. They told him his mother was dead, a cop gave him some candy, a news photographer snapped him at a neighbor's work-bench holding an awl—they didn't use the second picture of him clowning, showing off.

James begged off the funeral. Moved in with father, freelance accountant, womanizer, minor hero in the war, bullshit artist, a history of heart disease. Briefly, Rita Hayworth's business manager in late forties.

Ellroy: I grew up very poor with my father, after my mother's death, right on the edge of Hancock Park, a ritzy WASP enclave. Okay, I had the WASP pedigree but the flipside of WASPhood is white trash and that's what we were basically.

James wondered whether his father was going to be murdered as well. The following year, his father gave him a copy of The Badge *by Jack Webb, which included a summary of Black Dahlia case—Elizabeth Short, a starlet tortured and mutilated, found naked and in two halves, reminded James of his mother, neither case solved.*

James used to ride over to the spot on Norton Avenue and 39th Street, where the Dahlia's body was dumped, to feel her presence. He had nightmares about her, saw her in daylight flashes. Read crime novels from that time on. True crime too. He talked about the Dahlia case with Randy Rice, childhood friend. Kicked out of school for truancy. Years later, he went to Black Dahlia's grave, felt that he knew her, loved her.

1965, aged seventeen, into the U.S. Army, then father became gravely ill, so James faked nervous breakdown, stammered, to get kicked out. His father died. James was virtually penniless and homeless.

Dog became a peeper around Hancock Park, breaking and entering, sniffing women's panties in South Arden. Bought amphetamines from Gene the Short Queen. When no money, Dog drank cough syrup, or swallowed cotton wads in nasal inhalers to get high. Dog spent nights in Robert Burns Park taking speed and masturbating. This was Dog's life for eleven years, drinking, stealing food, drinking, dropping acid, drinking, shoplifting, stealing drink, smoking Maryjane, living on the streets, lifting wallets, sleeping in dumpsters, flophouses. In and out of county jail more than a dozen times. Had odd jobs, once minded till at a porn shop until his hand was found in it.

Dog caught pneumonia and told abscess on a lung. Coupla weeks later he was hearing things from the drink. He knew he'd die if he didn't quit the life. Dog quit. He joined Alcoholics Anonymous.

Today, Ellroy doesn't drink, doesn't smoke, goes to bed early. He's very neat, meticulous, keeps a neat house, is disciplined. He presently lives with his wife, feminist author and critic Helen Knode, in Mission Hills, Kansas.

Ellroy: It's the Hancock Park of the Mid-West.

Interviewer: You don't have to break in anymore.

Ellroy: I own a house like those, now. The surroundings are restful and physically beautiful, and they underscore the silence that I need to work. I abhor outside stimulation.

Brown's Requiem (1981)

1977, Dog caddying at the Hillcrest and, after punching another caddy, the Bel-Air Country Club for $200–300 a week, whilst living in a $25-a-week room at the Westwood Hotel. Dog got the idea for a private eye novel in 1978 and began writing it January 26, 1979.

The story: Fritz Brown, ex-cop turned repo man, who uses the P.I. moniker as a tax-dodge on his illegal activities, is approached by super-caddy Freddy "Fat Dog" Baker to watch his sister and the old geezer she lives with.

Interviewer: I've seen you put this book down in previous interviews, but it ain't no dog. I think it's great and much underrated.
Ellroy: I think it's a good book.

Interviewer: It contains all the Dog trademarks: corrupt cops; excessive violence; the Black Dahlia case; our hero getting beaten to a pulp; Tijuana; dogs; wine, women & drugs; and the bittersweet conclusion. The unobtainable woman was a major feature of your early novels.
Ellroy: I wrote that book shortly after I got sober. I hadn't been with a woman for years and years and years. I'd had scant experience with women prior to that and I was looking for the woman. I was a big grrr, grrr, grrr, kinda guy and women were afraid of me. I hadn't refined my social act at the time. I was working as a caddy and sober and writing my first book. I wanted a woman, I wanted sex, I wanted all that stuff and I wasn't getting any, and that's what really informs that book.

It was autobiographical. Here's a guy who looks exactly like me, has a German-American background, likes classical music, came from my old neighborhood, gets involved with a bunch of caddies. All that's me. He was a private eye and an ex-cop and I was neither. I did repos very briefly in 1968, so I know a little about that.

Interviewer: What was caddying like?
Ellroy: It's lowlife, basically. Ninety-nine percent of all country club caddies in America are drug addicts, winos, compulsive gamblers, ex-cons, and generally shitbirds. I remember—I got sober in August 1977—the first winter of my sobriety was 1977/78 when we had tumultuous rains in L.A. You couldn't

putt on the golf course for rodents, so we were only getting five bucks a day rain money and these caddies were spending all their money on cheap wine and cigarettes and jungling up in the two restaurants at the golf course, sleeping in the cars in the parking lot, stealing steaks and barbecuing them. I wasn't because I had a place to stay—I was sober.

Caddying was good tax-free cash and allowed me to get home by 2 p.m. and write books. I caddied right up to the sale of my fifth book. I can afford to join the best country club in town now. There are three nearby, but I'd only want to join Kansas City Country Club because it's the oldest and most exclusive. But they wouldn't let me in because you need six letters of recommendation—you really have to be established in Kansas City society.

Interviewer: Are you interested in getting involved in society?

Ellroy: No. They don't let Jews or blacks in and that's no good. I wouldn't want to be part of some place that does that. I just think it'd be a kick to join a country club. My mother-in-law's boyfriend is a member so we get to go to the grill room every coupla weeks for dinner.

Besides, I've never taken a golf lesson so I can't really justify joining the Kansas City Country Club, never mind the fact that I can't get in.

Interviewer: I'd just join to cut up the golf course, but that's me.

Ellroy: I'd like to get two bull terriers and walk them across Kansas City Country Club and let them shit on the greens. I know how appreciated that would be.

Interviewer: It's good fertilizer, isn't it? Top quality shit.

Ellroy: From celebrity dogs, no less.

Interviewer: You're often photographed with your bull terrier, Barko.

Ellroy: He lives with my ex-wife in Westport, Connecticut, but I see him occasionally. Barko is both immortal and cross-species heterosexual and throughout history Barko has been the lover of some of the world's most beautiful women. As a matter of fact, for any year of the twentieth century, I can tell you the woman he was with chiefly.

1924: Gloria Swanson.

1958: Brigitte Bardot. People have wondered for years why Brigitte Bardot became an animal rights activist.

1963: people have been wondering for years what was that little white speck on the grassy knoll in Dallas on November 22. Now, was it smoke coming out of a gun barrel? Wrong! It was Barko, the hit dog. Barko assassinated John F. Kennedy. He was having an affair with Jackie K. and he wanted her all for himself. Now Barko, fickle hound that he is, dropped Jackie about a year and a half later for the beautiful British actress Julie Christie.

Also, Barko, currently: Emma Thompson. Grrr. Grrr. Grrr.

Barko is a very British dog, a pit bull terrier. Have you ever petted one?

Interviewer: I've never attempted to.
Ellroy: They're very friendly to people. They love 'em. They don't like other animals for shit.

Interviewer: Well, I'll be happy to test that one out when you bring him over to the U.K.
Ellroy: I don't think so. I'd never subject him to quarantine or anything like that.

Clandestine (1982)

Story: This is a thinly veiled, chronologically altered account of James's mother's killing. Freddy Underhill, rookie L.A. cop, plays golf, has one night stands. One of the women ends up dead, so Freddy uses this as an opportunity to propel himself up the ladder of ambition. Dog used many of his father's attributes when describing the killer, and doesn't know why he did this. There's a young boy in the novel, just like James, but this boy flashes the local girls. This is Dog's first historical novel, set in early fifties L.A., and it introduces us to Dudley Smith, who later played a crucial part in the L.A. Quartet.

Blood on the Moon (1984)

First Lloyd Hopkins novel. Story: Hopkins is an intelligent right-wing bastard contemporary cop who is often more dangerous than the criminals he hunts. In this novel he sees the link between a series of over twenty murders over the same number of years. The detection, suspense, and action are good. The film, Cop, starring James Woods, was based on this novel—watching it you realize how conventional the novel is, but also how extraordinarily compulsive and obsessive Dog's prose style is. (The film title was changed to Cop because Robert Wise directed a western called Blood on the Moon in 1948 and objected to it being used again.)

Because the Night (1985)

Second Lloyd Hopkins novel. I read this one in Austria—dark, brooding, oppressive—the book was like that as well. Story: A deranged psychiatrist, John Havilland, is responsible for manipulating the weak-willed to do his bidding. Sex and snuff-snuff are on the menu.

Suicide Hill (1986)

Third Lloyd Hopkins novel. Story: Bank robbers find managers with illicit affairs, hold the bit on the side hostage, and steal the money. Simple, until one of the robbers gets randy and goes berserk. Lloyd leads the manhunt and, in doing so, discovers not all is as it seems within the police force he knows and loves. Edward Bunker has done a screenplay for this one so it may, or probably won't, be coming to a multiplex near you.

Silent Terror (1986)

Also published as Killer on the Road. *Story: This is the first person narrative of serial killer Martin Michael Plunkett as he travels across America killing all and sundry. It's different from Dog's other books, and far better than some, so it doesn't deserve to be ignored, which is what some critics seem to have done. In fact, it's one of the best serial killer books you're likely to come across. About halfway through Martin is caught—then Dog delivers a twist which had me gasping.*

Of other serial killer books, Dog reckons By Reason Of Insanity *by Shane Stevens is "a great big beautiful comic book. It's absolutely preposterous, but great fun," and that Thomas Harris* (Red Dragon, Silence of the Lambs) *is "about the only guy who can do them and I think even he should grow beyond them now."*

I figured that Ross Macdonald would have been a big influence on Dog—Macdonald's books are all about people with hidden pasts, just like Dog's characters.

Ellroy: Yeah, he is. Raymond Chandler was also an influence early on. He's diminished in my mind now. A lot of his writing is flat-out bad. A lot of the construction is spotty. And I don't think he knew people anywhere near as well as Dashiell Hammett.

Interviewer: Dashiell Hammett is my fave.

Ellroy: Yeah. He's the great realist. Joseph Wambaugh, the L.A. cop turned novelist, is a big influence too.

Interviewer: He wrote big, sprawling, irreverent novels like you do now. Do you talk to many crime writers?

Ellroy: I'm not real close friends with any crime writers. I know Edward Bunker and Joseph Koenig, who wrote *Little Odessa*, quite well. I'm not friends with writers, period. Most of my friends are colleagues, basically. Some cops.

Interviewer: Are the cops normal?

Ellroy: Yeah. They're not like my characters! Bill Stoner's an amazingly great guy.

Interviewer: Do you read non-crime books?

Ellroy: I don't really read outside of crime and true crime.

Interviewer: I would have thought you'd like some of the Russian authors, Dostoyevsky especially.

Ellroy: I tried to read *Crime and Punishment* once but it was so drearily written; I had to put it down.

Interviewer: I think it depends on the translation you get but, also, you have to be prepared to get into the rhythm of the language. I find that your books are the same way, you have to work to get into the rhythm and cadence of the words and speech and, once you have, it's very evocative, mesmerizing even. Do you think in this style now? Is it a natural process?

Ellroy: The style of the book is always set, directly linked, directly derived from, the story. *White Jazz* is a frenetic first-person fever dream so that constant staccato be-bop riff style is applicable. *American Tabloid* is a more fully explicated full of odd syncopations and repetition of phrases. It's a big book of outrageous events. It's a very funny book, I think, too.

Interviewer: I think your books are very funny, but it's a dark humor that a lot of people don't see. For instance, many people won't think Jim Thompson is funny, but I find him so. He's so ironic, you have to laugh.

Generally, people in America don't understand irony—saying one thing but meaning another—whereas it's quite common in speech in the U.K., and it's also in your books. Do Americans have difficulty reading your books on that level?

Ellroy: There's a genre ghetto and people want the sympathetic character, the easy-to-identify-with character. People want that rebelliousness, the one person against the system book. Raymond Chandler created a very easy to adapt style which is why so many people have adapted to it with such great success. In America, you're up against a genre ghetto all the time. I've broken through that—I'm the darling of the deconstructionists, college professors, homosexual media mavens, people in the movie biz, the cognoscenti. These media hounds are capable of digging on irony but American writers take on an almost perverse pride in being simplistic, in being proud of their genre roots.

Interviewer: What you see is what you get.

Ellroy: Yeah. Editors, publishers are all in business to sell books, so accessibility counts for a lot.

Interviewer: Do you have to write?

Ellroy: Yeah. That's why I'm here. I love telling stories. I love doing it. I love the result of seeing the book in print. I love the glory. I love the money. I love the acclaim. But, mostly, I love doing it. I've always forced myself to live in the craft. I'm a perfectionist, and, the older I get—I'm arguably ten to twelve years away from my prime—a writer's real prime seems to be their early sixties.

Interviewer: You think of Leo Tolstoy, George Bernard Shaw, Rudyard Kipling, H. G. Wells all doing great writing past sixty. Painters are the same.

Ellroy: Symphony orchestra conductors seem to hit their peak in their late sixties, early seventies, and I hope that's the way it is with me.

I've always postponed the thrill of recognition. I've always stood aside from it. I like to perform. I'm a powerful character, and I've had a colorful past which has been mythologized, and I've attempted, to some degree, to demythologize it. My past is tremendously pathetic and really anything but melodramatic. So, I design the books very carefully. I know how to rest whilst writing a book, and how to rest between books. I like to think a lot, I like to brood. I've got absolutely no taste for popular culture. Parenthetically, it's very odd that on the past few trips to Britain, I'm continually questioned about Quentin Tarantino, who I think is a fatuous child. I think *Reservoir Dogs* is garbage and the forty minutes of *Pulp Fiction* that I saw is most excruciatingly naïve shtick, boring tedium that I've ever endured. I stand outside popular culture.

My wife is the most brilliant human being I've ever met. We have a disciplined but quiet home life together and I like to think, to brood, to listen to classical music, Beethoven, and it replenishes me, it puts me back in the book.

I write books that I can honestly say nobody else is writing. You've read a million private eye books—there may be some pretty gifted people out there writing private eye books. I've got no time for it. Serial killer books, thrillers, police procedurals . . . I have to set out to write the books that nobody else would write, to take the risks that nobody else would take, and to write the books that nobody, frankly, would have the patience to write, and it's paid off for me.

I'll write fewer books, develop less of a hard readership, than other big-name writers in my lifetime and probably earn less money, but it's okay. I'm earning quite a handsome living doing the thing I love. So, I'm always looking ahead, looking to the next book, looking for ways to refine the craft.

Interviewer: The object is not the money but the work, to express what you think, to channel all that into a form other people can understand. When I sit down to read your books, especially the last few, I can look up from the page and think a half hour has gone by, but it's only been ten minutes. The information is so dense, the brain activity so intense that reading your books distorts time, which is ironic considering the way you distort history. Do you have a vision of the reader and their reactions when you write, or do you see the reader as yourself?

Ellroy: As myself. I write the books that I want to write, and I haven't compromised on that level of complexity or of brain work. More traditionally minded editors have warned me about losing the reader with the density and complexity and I figure, if I lose 'em I lose 'em. I'm lucky that I've got some great editors in the U.S., the U.K., and in France. My American editor, who cut his teeth in Great Britain, is not interested in my reinforcing the genre qualities of my work. He's only interested in what makes me different, which is why he's publishing me in the first place.

Interviewer: Condensing everything down into a solid block of information, you're obviously spending a lot longer writing the book than the people who read it. Is the writing of it as intense as the reading?

Ellroy: It's a very intense experience. Ideally, the books should be read in decent blocks of time, over as short a period of time as possible, so that the reader can retain the information.

I start with a hugely detailed outline—the outline for *American Tabloid* was 275 pages. It's a very, very intense experience, very difficult work. I like density and complexity. Every word in *American Tabloid* and the L.A. Quartet means something. It's all there to advance the plot. There's no rambling. There's no unnecessary scene-setting. If there are discourses, they are essential to the plot. It's why people can't read the book. I'm sure it's why I don't get stratospheric sales numbers despite all the great publicity that I get. My sales are quite substantial on their own, but I doubt that they'll ever be staggering because most people don't have the discipline or the intelligence for the books. If you blink you'll miss something. If you want an intense reading experience, great, I'm for you.

The Black Dahlia (1987)

First of the L.A. Quartet. Now, we get serious. Story: Set against the fictionalized account of the hunt for the true-life murderer of The Black Dahlia in January 1947, this is really the story of two death-obsessed cops, Bucky Bleichert and Lee Blanchard. This was the first Dog I read, and it really shocked me. I remember reading it on a train and, after one passage, heart pumping, mind racing, looking up at the other passengers, who were totally unperturbed. For a second, illogically, I couldn't understand why they were unmoved by the book.

Ellroy: After I had established some sort of readership with my first six novels, I wrote the novel of the Black Dahlia case. It tapped into the deepest aspects of my unconscious. It is a book I had been waiting almost thirty years to write. Rather than go back to my tired-ass series character that I was writing at that time, which is what my publisher and agent wanted me to do, about mid-way through *The Black Dahlia*, I realized that I wanted to create a quartet about Los Angeles (my own smog-bound fatherland) between the years of 1947 and 1959.

The Big Nowhere (1988)

Second of the L.A. Quartet. Story: Moving to 1950, using the Red Scare commie-bashing investigating team as background, Dog shows us Danny Upshaw, ambitious death-obsessed deputy with a string of mutilated victims on his hands, Mal Considine, ambitious D.A. creep who wants power to get custody of his adopted kid, and Buzz Meeks, loveable ex-cop pimp for Howard Hughes. Death, deceit and double cross. Lovely.

Interviewer: What is your attitude towards violence? I think because some of your books are obviously violent, and you sometimes go into great detail, people assume that you like violence.
Ellroy: Violence is always very short, swift and to the point in my books. I rarely dwell on it.

Interviewer: Perversely, that makes it more violent. My assumption has always been that people who don't like violence, who are afraid of it, tend to write it better.
Ellroy: That's exactly right. I've never been a violent person. I'm appalled by it. I'm shocked by it. I'm a big advocate of gun control. Violence is at the root of all intrigue, it's the basis of all threat in history, which makes it so great to write—I enjoy it. My personal relationship to it—I'm attracted to it because I understand it's relation to history, but I'm appalled by it because I know what it costs.

Interviewer: There is a physical violence, which we can all see, experience in your work. There is also a mental violence in the way politicians mess with society, or people conduct their relationships. There's this unseen violence, which is felt just as keenly, if not more so. Are you interested in that?
Ellroy: The books will become more and more about that as they become more and more about politics. The basic theme for the Underworld U.S.A. trilogy is the private nightmare of public policy. It's mostly psychological.

L.A. Confidential (1990)

Third of the L.A. Quartet. From an enormous cast of characters, about eighty, Dog focuses a beady eye on three cops: Trashcan Jack Vincennes (media cop for hire), Ed Exley (overshadowed by his famous father) and Bud White (the toughest of tough L.A. cops, he's haunted by a wife-beating father). The elements: a Disneyland-like theme park under construction, a series of grisly murders, a cop Christmas party that goes horribly wrong and the cover-up that follows, and HUSH-HUSH magazine—sleazesheet to the slags with no end of sinuendo. Dog delivered 809-page manuscript which his agent Nat

Sobel advised to cut by taking out unnecessary words. Resulted in clipped cadence style which sounds like a rhythmic psycho-beatnik rap.

Ellroy: I am a fiend for darkness, sleaze, groovy twisted sexuality. I'm especially interested in this around the late fifties, early sixties, at the time of my emerging sexuality. I recall being holed up with a copy of *Confidential* magazine looking at a picture of Clorine Calvey for about three hours on a hot summer night before I even knew what masturbation was. And I like to go back and relive those times, the time of darkness in my life and explicate it.

I don't like to practice these things, but I'm curious about them. I like to retain an immunity from it which is why I live a very quiet, blissfully monogamous life in Kansas. I love to watch boxing on the TV—my wife has turned into a tremendous boxing fan. I go to the movies occasionally. I love the old film noirs. I lift weights. I like to think.

I haven't lived in Los Angeles in fourteen years. I have enough crazy shit going on in my imagination to last me the next forty-seven years of my life. Believe me, I need no outside stimulus whatsoever. But I grew up in L.A. and my father was a sleazebag on the edge of the movie biz. I knew that Rock Hudson was a fag in 1959—it was no newsflash when he finally caught AIDS and died eight or nine years ago. I like movies as cheap entertainment. To me, they're like hamburgers. I've ate about ten profound hamburgers in my life and I've probably seen about ten profound movies. I'm voyeuristically curious about people's sex lives, about their inner moral workings, and here you have a whole cast of—usually very good-looking—characters, both women and men, and all I want to know is who's a homosexual, who's a nymphomaniac, who's a sader, who's got the biggest wang in Hollywood, who's got the smallest, who's impotent, who's underhung, who's the snapdiver, who's the sword-swallower, who's the peeper, who's the prowler, who's the pimp, who's the pederast and who's the panty-sniffer? Don't put me in some fucking Martin Scorsese/Quentin Tarantino symposium—contemporary movies don't interest me that much. I don't want to know about that. I want to know about the stars, what they're up to: Tom Cruise, Nicole Kidman, Keanu Reeves, Brad Pitt, Liam Neeson, James Woods, Willem Dafoe . . .

Dog entertains and shocks by saying libelous things about various well-known movie personalities. He says he's got some well-placed sources in Hollywood, but anyone could say that.

Ellroy: It's true.

Interviewer: You're saying that these are things which everyone knows but no-one can print. Recently I was sitting around talking to friends who work in the media and they were talking about stories involving various personalities and events that they couldn't print, and outright lies they had to print. This is another secret history, only it's social rather than political or criminal.

Ellroy: Whatever story needs to be told will find itself into my imagination.

White Jazz (1992)

Fourth of the L.A. Quartet. Star: Lieutenant Dave Klein: lawyer, bagman, slum landlord, mob killer . . . a very bad lieutenant indeed. Quartet's Rollovers: Dudley Smith; Ed Exley; Mickey Cohen. This book has to be experienced, not explained.

Ellroy: *White Jazz* is definitely a one-off. It's a first-person narration of a very bad man, a cop named Dave Klein, whose life is running down in Los Angeles in the fall of 1958. The book is a fever dream—it's a stream of consciousness style—there are no tricks in it—everything is quite literal but, if you blink, you will miss things. You have to get into the rhythm of Dave Klein's head or you won't get the book at all. There are many people who didn't understand the book. The book did not sell as well as the three previous volumes of the L.A. Quartet. It was a risk I took—I think the risk is worth it. The important thing with me is always the book, not the sales. I did it for that one book, and I returned to a more fully developed style for *American Tabloid*, and I will never go back to *White Jazz* again. I've done it.

Each book, I think, is darker, more dense, more complex, and more stylistically evolved than the previous book. I have finished the L.A. Quartet. It is considered a monument of some sort—I consider it a great monument, like Mount Rushmore, and so does my dog, my wife, my agent and my current publisher. Others are not so charitable, but fuck 'em because they don't have to be. The bottom line is this: if you don't like my books you can kiss my ass.

Interviewer: Doing a series based in the past, even the recent past, a past you lived in, must have involved some research.

Ellroy: I did extensive research on the Black Dahlia murder case because it is fully the historical case laid out, in detail, before I digress fictionally. On *The Big Nowhere*, which is about the Red Scare in Hollywood in 1950, I read half a book on the subject, realized I could make the rest of the shit up, and threw the book away. *L.A. Confidential*—I only researched the Bloody Christmas police scandal of 1951 and tossed the rest of the books away. *White Jazz*—no research.

Essentially, for a long, long time. I had been obsessed with L.A. during that era, and if a person has talent and brains and some kind of self-knowledge and insight, then the chances are that the things you are obsessed with will be the things you will be good at. It all comes down to: can I make the public believe it? And I could.

Dick Contino's Blues (1994)

A collection of short stories set during the L.A. Quartet. Title novella—serial killer wants Dick as partner in crime. Stories: Lee Blanchard; Buzz Meeks; Stan Klein.

Ellroy: The short story form does not interest me. I wrote short stories at the behest of editors that I owed favors to and, luckily for me, because I'd recently been divorced, I saw that I had collected enough short stories to sell a short story volume and make some very quick cash with minimal effort. So I wrote a novella to stand as the frontispiece of this collection, called *Dick Contino's Blues*.

Dick Contino was a big star in America in the late forties and early fifties. He was a handsome Italian guy who played the accordion like this motherfucker. He humped it, he wolfed it, he waggled it, he gyrated with it, he orbited it like a fucking dervish flying on Benzedrine, Maryjane and glue. He was a handsome guy. He really banged that box. He had four hundred fan clubs nationwide. And five thousand fan-letters a week. But he was a fearful young kid, and in 1951 his handsome ass was about to get drafted and sent to Korea. He told the draft board that he was really scared and didn't want to go to Korea. This was the wrong thing to say at the height of the Red Scare in America. The draft board and Hearst newspapers throughout America took the stand "Hey Dick, you're getting more ass than a toilet seat, you're making five G's a week and you're twenty-one years old—we're gonna draft your ass." So, Dick's ass was drafted. He was sent to basic training at Fort Ord, California. So Dick ran for twenty-four hours, went home to his mom and dad, turned himself into the Feds, got slammed, took it right up the rump-ramp for this one in the worst way. Got six months in the federal penitentiary at McNeil Island, Washington and was then drafted and sent to

Korea, where he served with distinction. He came back to find the accordion somewhat passé and his career completely derailed. He went from being a big star and a main room guy, to a lounge act and the star of a very sleazy B-movie called *Daddy-O*.

I have some very dim recollections of Dick Contino from the late fifties, and after finishing the L.A. Quartet I was suffering some separation pangs from Los Angeles, so I decided to do a picaresque, light-hearted farewell to L.A. in the fifties, hence the novella.

Dick and I are still in touch. Dick is presently undergoing romantic troubles. He's sixty-five and is going out with the daughter of one of the members of his original fan club. There is only a thirty-seven-year age difference between Dick and this woman. She's an Italian woman from upstate New York. She's divorced. She has had several kids by several different men. I think Dick has picked a black marble with this woman. I think Dick is still, many, many years after his great fame and a few years after his resurgence via me, perpetuating the same patterns with bad women. So, in his way, Dick Contino is a noir character.

Interviewer: When you talk about rewriting history, and the whole glitzy fifties era, it reminds me of *Crime Story*.[1] I thought it was great the way they rewrote history, Vietnam, the A-bomb, the Kennedys, etc., and had the characters interact with history. It's one of my favorite TV shows.
Ellroy: Mine too. I'm very good friends with Anthony Denison—he played the villain, Ray Luca. I never saw the show originally, but Anthony Denison and Jeff Stein, who directed a couple of episodes, optioned *Dick Contino's Blues*. They've written a brilliant screenplay from it and are trying to get it made. I've since got all the *Crime Story* episodes on video. The show is great in Chicago, when it's a serial with a continuing storyline, but it goes to hell in the Las Vegas episodes when it becomes discursive and episodic.

Interviewer: I liked the Las Vegas stuff. It was over the top, camp, outrageous. It was great fun.
Ellroy: Yeah, a lot of people liked the outré design.

Interviewer: The characters and design seemed like they were from the fifties, but the plots were from the sixties. It was a weird mix.
Ellroy: Anthony and I discussed this and he said it actually started set in 1963, but it seemed like 1958. I kept waiting for references to the Kennedy assassination to set things in perspective but it never occurred.

I think Dennis Farina as Lieutenant Mike Torello is just a force of nature. When the hatred between him and Anthony Dennison fuels the plot, it's great, it's epic, but after a while it just goes to hell.

All Dog's books have been optioned for film, including his nonfiction memoir My Dark Places, *except* White Jazz, Killer on the Road *and* Because the Night. *They are in various stages of development—Edward Bunker has done a script for* Suicide Hill, *for example—but will any of them be filmed? Dog doubts it.*

However, the short story "Since I Don't Have You," which is in the Dick Contino's Blues *collection, was adapted for the* Fallen Angels *TV series. Was it the Dog's delight?*

Ellroy: It was interesting. I thought Gary Busey was a bad Buzz Meeks, James Woods an ineffectual Mickey Cohen, and Tim Matheson was great as Howard Hughes.

American Tabloid (1995)

First of the Underworld U.S.A. Trilogy. The legal: Kennedy; Hoover; CIA. The illegal: Trafficante; Marcello; Giancana. The legbreakers: Pete Bondurant; Kemper Boyd; Ward Littell.

Ellroy: Everybody has written about the Kennedys, but I hadn't done it.

When I finished the L.A. Quartet, I realized that that was then and this is now. I never wanted to do another novel that could in any way be categorized as a thriller, a mystery, or a book based around police work or, specifically, police investigations. I realized, what I wanted to do was write a trilogy—three books with fifteen years of American history broken down into five-year increments. I wanted one theme to pervade these works and that is politics as crime and the private nightmare of public policy. The genesis of all this is reading Don DeLillo's novel *Libra*, a brilliantly fictional take on Lee Harvey Oswald and the Kennedy assassination.

Now, I was fifteen when Jack "The Haircut" Kennedy got whacked in 1963. I was never fond of the Kennedys—I never loved them nor hated them. I was unmoved by Kennedy's death even though he was very much of my youth. But now, all of a sudden, after reading *Libra*, I was obsessed by the Kennedy assassination and the events which I viewed to be the harbingers of it.

I began to see that *Libra* precluded me from ever writing a novel specifically about the assassination, but what I could do was write a novel wherein the assassination was but one murder in a long series of murders. I decided that this book would be my first novel that would, in no way, be driven by psychosexual plots. Some of the action would take place in L.A., my chief locale, but most of it wouldn't. I would go one-on-one with history and re-create that era to my own specifications, so I did.

I hired a researcher; a magazine editor friend of mine. She compiled chronologies and factsheets for me so that I couldn't write myself into factual error. I extrapolated from those facts. I show all the real life characters in the book—the Kennedy brothers, Jimmy Hoffa, Howard Hughes, and the key gangsters of the era—Santos Trafficante, Carlos Marcello, Sam Giancana—in a totally fictional context. You don't need to show Kennedy giving his inaugural speech or having his brains blown out. We've seen it eight million times. Lee Harvey Oswald does not appear in the book. The assassination is 12 to 15 percent of the overall text. If you have the stones to say I can rewrite history to my own specifications, I can populate this book with fictional characters, the minor minions of the time, and make them more interesting and more perversely sympathetic than the Kennedys, J. Edgar Hoover, Howard Hughes, and the rest, then you can get away with it.

I have stopped writing psychosexual driven plots. It's the covenant of consciousness. I think writers can get better and better and better and better. I think good writers can bring a thematic unity, an innate talent, and a certain native intelligence embedded in his/her unconsciousness and that can see you through any number of books. Three, four, or five. There are then the implications of editors—write a series character, a sympathetic private eye, British inspector, innocent person who keeps getting caught up in violent intrigue, so that readers can have somebody to come back to and come back to and come back to. I have decided to ignore that rule and forge my own territory.

For me, my big thematic journey is twentieth-century American history, and what I think twentieth-century American history is, is the story of bad white men, soldiers of fortune, shakedown artists, extortionists, legbreakers. The lowest level implementers of public policy. Men who are often toadies of right-wing regimes. Men who are racists. Men who are homophobes. These are my guys. These are the guys that I embrace. These are the guys that I empathize with. These are the guys that I love.

Now, parenthetically, a number of critics have called me a fascist, a racist, an anti-Semite, an anti-papist because my characters are like that. These are the characters who are portrayed as multifaceted human beings. The reader, on some level, is meant to empathize with them, and I certainly do. I think what angers critics is that the racism, and homophobia and anti-Semitism and everything else that these characters express is not fundamental to their character—they are just casual attributes that they possess because they are men of the time.

So I write books of the time, in the language of the time in the first and third person, refer to Jews as kikes, homosexuals as faggots, and blacks as niggers. People don't know how to take it. I love the American idiom. If I can dip into the American idiom, I would rather use it, as profane and ugly as it sometimes is, than so-called normal King's English.

The bottom line is that twentieth-century American crime fiction is the story of bad white men, and I'll go to my grave thinking that.

With all these bad men to play with, Dog does find time for one good one in American Tabloid.

Ellroy: As much research as I've done, one fact stands fast—I think Robert Kennedy was a great man, perhaps the chief crime fighter of the twentieth century in America, and a paragon of moral rectitude. Parenthetically, he did not play bury the brisket and pour the pork with Marilyn Monroe. He did not dip the schnitzel with her.

I used to be friends with Shakedown Freddy Otash, private eye to the stars in L.A. circa 1955 to 1965. God bless him, Freddy died recently at the age of seventy-one. He was having a heart attack and called a cab rather than an ambulance.

Freddy Otash was the guy that you saw in 1955 to 1965 L.A. if you wanted to hotwire a homosexual bathhouse, if you wanted to pull a sex shakedown, get your wife's lover's legs broken, get your wife an abortion, get a dope cure, fix a drunk/driving, or get a picture of Rock Hudson with a dick in his mouth. You went to see Freddy Otash.

Now Freddy Otash was too cool to drool. Freddy Otash would leave you reamed, steamed, and dry cleaned, tied, dyed swept to the side, screwed, blued, tattooed, and bob-gung-gooed.

Shakedown Freddy was the guy hired by Jimmy Hoffa in the fall of 1961 to hotwire Peter Lawford's fuckpad where Jack was playing bury the brisket with Marilyn Monroe. Now, hepcats, again, parenthetically, off the record, on the QT, and very hush-hush, Jack Kennedy was a two-point-four-minute man. Shakedown Freddy timed a half-dozen Jack Kennedy/Marilyn Monroe assignations and averaged them out. A couple times Jack couldn't make it to two minutes and he was always citing his bad back, which is why in *American Tabloid* he's known as Bad Back Jack.

Freddy told me he is convinced that Bobby Kennedy never had an affair with Marilyn Monroe that, at the time of Marilyn's death, Bobby was interceding on Jack's behalf, trying to get this crazy fucking woman to quit calling the president of the United States at the White House. She just kicked off coincidentally.

Dog nips at the heels of historical figures and manages to tear chunks out of them. Doesn't this, er, lead to certain legal . . .

Ellroy: I have never gotten into trouble using real people in my books because they are dead and can't sue me. In America, their surviving families can't sue. I don't get feedback. The Kennedys, for instance, would never sue. So much is written about them that, if they were to sue, they'd be in court all day, every day, and that way they wouldn't have time to [text deleted].

America likes history because it has so little of it. It likes to define itself by history, its ancestry, its battles, its fights for truth, justice and the American way. Like most countries, it rewrites history from the winner's viewpoint. Dog rewrites from the point of view of the losers.

America seems very self-centered, like a child in some ways, reacting to what happens without considering its actions first. It also thinks it's a moral leader, as though it can dictate what others think and say and do. It has no myths it can call its own—myths are based on history and are an extension of the consciousness of the society—so America mythologizes the near-present. Systematically, Dog demythologizes the near-present, his world is closer to Bad Lieutenant *than* Dragnet.

Ellroy: As a kid, I always sensed history going on all around me. I knew I was part of it in some odd way. And I knew there were human stories to be told within it, but I didn't know what those stories were.

I remember, for instance, harkening back to *American Tabloid,* the Cuban missile crisis. I remember going to the store to get some canned goods because the old man thought the atom bomb might drop and we should be well supplied, and finding the shelves stripped clean, and running into our neighbor, Big John Kilbright, a notorious drunk, stocking up on liquor.

It's wonderful to be able to go back to rewrite history to your own specifications, to fill in the human stories within the real context of history, and link them to actual historical events.

I have the real-life characters doing things they didn't do in real life. The one question I never answer specifically about *American Tabloid* is what's real and what's not. You have to keep things ambiguous for the reader. You don't want them to know specifically where the dividing line between fact and fiction ends, or you destroy your verisimilitude. One of the ways I accomplish this in *American Tabloid* was to show the real-life historical characters in fictional situations. *American Tabloid* is historically valid. The real-life events happened similarly to the ways they did. Beyond that, it's all fiction.

Interviewer: Do you see the real-life people as people or as characters?
Ellroy: As characters. Characters to be manipulated.

Interviewer: Good. People tend to think that what's printed is the absolute truth, that if it's in black and white it must have happened. They don't seem to think beyond that.

Ironically, Dog uses newspaper, magazine, radio, and TV broadcasts to explain things that happen, but also to give his fiction a feeling of reality, of truth.

Ellroy: One of the themes of *American Tabloid* is the disparity between reported historical fact and what really happened. You've got *Hush-Hush* magazine in there distorting the truth in a hilarious fashion I think, and you've got the outward Kennedy front which is complicit of everything even though you don't see them advancing that front too much, and then the real-life Kennedys, Hoover, and Howard Hughes. Basically it's a secret history.

Interviewer: But it's *your* secret history. Although, as you said earlier, you're not going to say what is and isn't real, you're appealing to the idea of the conspiracy theory people, tapping into the idea that people are afraid of big organizations, whether they be political, commercial, or criminal.
Ellroy: I'm not afraid of the corporations, specifically. I think my central theory is valid—John Kennedy's murder is a conspiracy between renegade CIA men, crazy Cuban exiles, and organized crime. This is hardly novel. I

got the idea from *Libra*. I think something like this happened. Did it happen specifically in this way? It couldn't have—I invented it.

Interviewer: From the perception of the other characters, Bobby Kennedy is the villain.
Ellroy: That's a good point. I think he's a good guy, basically.

Interviewer: I'm not denying that. What I'm saying is that you write your bad guys as sympathetic and they hate Bobby Kennedy. If you sympathize with the bad guys, then you hate Bobby Kennedy too.
Ellroy: Exactly right, I want my readers to have a vigorous response to some of my characters, to identify with them on the basis of some of their hidden agendas. Bobby Kennedy was a man, heavily compromised by his family situation, and morally upright in many ways. I think he had essential Oedipal problems that got his brother Jack killed. Bobby recognized Joe Kennedy Sr. for what he was, and took his vengeance, once removed, on organized crime. This is what cost John Kennedy his life. Arguably Bobby Kennedy himself—I don't know much about the Robert Kennedy assassination. Robert Kennedy has ideals, and that's what these very tainted men can't stand.

Interviewer: The bad men can't stand someone standing up and making themselves heard and willing to die for their ideals.
Ellroy: The specific tragedy of this book is that it's Bobby who gets Jack killed.

Interviewer: Brother killing brother is the theme of *American Tabloid*—Pete Bondurant and Kemper Boyd accidentally killed their respective brothers. You've made a career of getting inside the heads of unsympathetic characters and making us understand them. It's terrible and it's exhilarating. This conflict of emotions brings out things in people that perhaps they didn't really want to feel. Are you trying to get inside people's heads?
Ellroy: I'm trying to get them on that level. I didn't realize that that's the course of my design until I'd written the L.A. Quartet.

Interviewer: Do you know the unsympathetic characters that are in your books?
Ellroy: They are all in my head. Other than a couple of characters in *Brown's Requiem* and *Clandestine*, nobody's based on real-life characters. I invent the stuff—even the characters based on historically real characters. It's all a work of imagination.

Interviewer: You're moving from the crime of the forties and fifties to the politics of the sixties and seventies. This reminds me of the way films stopped being film noirs and started to become counterculture political conspiracy/suspense/paranoia films. Is there a link there, since you grew up in that era and may be emulating its concerns and culture?

Ellroy: I think there is an obvious need to explicate your past. What are you, thirty-five?

Interviewer: Thirty-one.

Ellroy: Right. You get to be my age and you're in no way old, but you've been around for a long time. It's an interesting age. I remember the early sixties, just before you were born, quite vividly. I was not in any way moved by the tumult in the sixties. I had long hair because everyone else did. All I wanted to do, basically, was use drugs. I was so inept as a human being that I couldn't get laid during the Summer of Love. Now I get to go back and re-create it.

Interviewer: Are you reliving it because you didn't live it properly the first time around?

Ellroy: No. I think, to one degree or another, the more curious we are about existence the more curious we are about the past. Not necessarily our own past, but the historical past because it's a codified means of saying that this is who I am and this is how I got here. So, to be able to go back to the past and decode it is tremendously seductive.

Interviewer: But it's all about bad men and bad things. You're saying, in your books, that America is built on corruption. Do you actually like America?

Ellroy: Yeah. I love it, whatever corruption is inherent there. Again, I'm not entirely sure how factually valid my books are. My L.A. Quartet books are certainly a hyperbolized view of police work in the 1950s.

What I write about are the worlds within worlds. This is the insider world.

Interviewer: The *Hush-Hush* world.

Ellroy: Yes. Politics meets show business meets the paramilitary meets the big money meets organized crime. This is the world of the next two books. It's a tabloid sensibility, which is why *American Tabloid* is called just that and why, the whole trilogy is called the Underworld U.S.A. trilogy. (I'm also a bit of a Samuel Fuller fan—his film *Underworld U.S.A.* came out 1961.)

Interviewer: I've been to America a few times: L.A., San Francisco, San Diego. It's such a positive place.

Ellroy: America is a very positive place. I'm very optimistic about America's future, too. We only learn the hard way, so we've some hard lessons to come. They are often the best, most viable lessons, so I hope we learn from them.

Interviewer: But all the things you talk about in the books are the bad things about America.

Ellroy: Yeah, but the bad things are tremendously exhilarating to me. It annoys me when people say that my books are depressing because they're not. I think they're exhilarating. I think they're easily the most passionate crime books ever written, and I'm a relentlessly positive, hopeful, optimistic, almost utopian person and I have a great laugh. I'm happy for it, and I'm grateful for it. I think noir, in many ways, is dead for me. And I think the dividing line, for me, will be the nonfiction books that I'm doing next. After that, I think my books will express a greater diversity of character and motive.

Interviewer: All your books have conspiracies at one level or another. Is this your world-view, or does it just make good copy?

Ellroy: I enjoy connecting events. I enjoy filling in the blanks of history, and I enjoy plotting. This is very satisfying for me. Do I think conspiracies exist? Yes. I love writing the psychology of men in packs. I am a laureate of bad men and I enjoy the shifting cabals of bad men and putting them together.

Interviewer: My view is much more of a chaos theory of life, where each person does their own little bit and doesn't know the whole picture, and the whole picture sometimes naturally creates a form no-one has any control over. People don't have the ability to stop it or the power to control it. Your characters are completely driven to do the things they do, and they have no control over the big picture.

Ellroy: They are extremely willful, obsessive men, self-serving men, selfish men, and they don't understand that there are forces at work which are very much bigger than them, unless they know something specific. Pete Bondurant, for instance, knows you don't fuck with organized crime. He's a man who wants out of the life—he's getting older, he's met a woman—but self-destructively he forces himself out of the life by pulling a drug heist, and it's only by the grace of God of organized crime that, at the end of the book, he's left standing.

The single thing I hate most about crime fiction is the Raymond Chandler sensibility—*"Down These Mean Streets a Man Must Go."* Down these mean streets the single man who can make a difference must go. There is an institutionalized rebelliousness to it that comes out of a cheap liberalism that I despise. It's always the rebel. It's always the private eye standing up to the system. That doesn't interest me. What interest me are the toadies of the system.

Interviewer: The people who have to do the dirty work.
Ellroy: That's right. The unsung legbreakers of history.

Interviewer: You write about willful people, people who go out and do things. These are the people you need to drive plots. Specifically, their willfulness make them crime-orientated books. Have you ever considered writing about other types of people?
Ellroy: It's their willfulness, their tormented psyches, which makes the books unpredictable too. The characters' actions are linked to their psyches. If there was no history, they would still be valid as characters. Books of violent intrigue, books of men doing things are the only types of book I want to write for the foreseeable future.

Interviewer: What about women doing things?
Ellroy: I can't add it. I think, perhaps, again, the dividing line between one phase of my writing and another will be attempting to recognize my mother in *My Dark Places*. I think it all keeps coming back to her. My women are aggressive, they're intelligent. My men are attracted to them on the basis of their strength. When you set this in a pre-women's liberation time, where there's no established dialogue for that type of woman, you get some interesting stuff. My wife thinks my women characters are great and I think she's right.

My Dark Places (1996)

Saturday, June 21, 1958, 8pm, Jean Ellroy was drinking at the Desert Inn (11271 East Valley Boulevard, El Monte) with a man (dark-haired, fortyish, swarthy Caucasian, thin, between five feet nine and six feet tall) and a woman (white, blonde hair tied back in ponytail, in her late twenties). A drunk at the bar was told the man's name but could not remember it later. The three left together at approximately 10pm. Jean's car (1957 Buick, registration KFE 778) was left in the parking lot.

10.20pm, Jean and Swarthy Man, in man's car (1955–6 dark green Oldsmobile), arrived at Stan's Drive-In. Jean had a grilled cheese sandwich. Swarthy man had a coffee. They ate in the car, talked, obviously had had a few drinks, left at 10.50pm.

Sunday, June 22 1958, 2am, Jean and Swarthy Man, in man's car, arrive at Stan's Drive-In. Swarthy Man, quiet, sullen, bored, had a coffee. Jean, happy, chatting, was disheveled and looked as though they had been petting. They left at 2.45am.

Jean was attacked at an unknown locale. She was hit on the head several times. Blood, skin, and beard fragments under her fingernails indicated she clawed at her assailant's face. She was strangled to death. After she died, her killer took off one of her stockings and tied it loosely around her neck. She was dumped by bushes besides the Arroyo High School, a mile and a half from the Desert Inn.

11am, Geneva Hilliker Ellroy's body discovered by children. Her murder remains unsolved.

Ellroy: Early in 1994, a friend of mine, a newspaper writer in Los Angeles said that he was going to write a piece about the five unsolved, uncelebrated St. Gabriel Valley homicides and that he was going to the office of the L.A. county sheriff's homicide bureau and review the open files on these five homicides—my mother's among them. He was going to see my mother's files, something that I had never done. I decided, shit, I have to see this file myself.

There had to be, of course, a reason for it, a carrot. So I talked to Paul Scanlon, my editor in America for *G.Q.*, and said I want to go out and read my mother's homicide file and write about the experience in 5,000 words for *G.Q.* Paul Scanlon said "Go Big Daddy, do it." So I flew out to L.A. and saw the file and it was just as shocking an experience as you would think it would be. I saw the pictures of my mother nude on the morgue slab. I saw pictures of her dead, a nylon stocking around her neck, where her body had been dumped. And a little click went off in my head, and it meant that this wasn't over. Also, there was a little sub-click that meant "oh." And what that "oh" means is "You've exploited the similarities between your mother's death and the Black Dahlia murder case for many years, you've exploited your mother's death because it made you a crime writer, and now you have to come back and embrace this woman for the first time, you have to acknowledge her, you have to pay the debt, you have to find out who she is, and to do this you have to find the man who killed her, as unlikely as your success in this endeavor could ever be."

The man who showed me my mother's homicide file was a brilliant, very humane, soon-to-retire L.A. county sheriff's homicide detective named Bill Stoner. A man who'd been a homicide cop for fourteen years. A man who had nothing to do with my mother's case. In fact, wasn't even a cop at the time of my mother's death. We got to be good friends. I wrote the piece for *G.Q.* in America and in Britain and it was a finalist for the National Magazine Award in America. I spoke to my editors and said that I wanted to expand this piece into a full-length memoir. The book would be my autobiography, Bill Stoner's biography, my mother's biography, and Stoner and I would attempt to find the man who killed my mother thirty-seven years after the fact. So that's what I've been doing for the past ten months, looking for the man who killed my mother.

We've been getting a lot of publicity for it. There was a significant incident in the case—my mother was seen leaving a bar with a man who presumably killed her, and a blonde woman. That blonde woman as well as the man have never been identified. Chances are that the blonde woman told numerous people that she was out with a couple of people and that man ended up killing the woman. In these bar-scene, alcohol-fuelled, lust-killing milieus this often happens. The material witnesses often talk. Chances are there are a number of people out there who either know the entire story or elements of it and can help us put it together, especially as we garner all this publicity. So far, we've been unsuccessful.

What's daunting about this, more than anything else, is not any inherent emotional danger, but not being able to make it up. The basic dramatic thrust of the book is first I re-create the investigation of the death using records and the testimony of the surviving witnesses, then Bill Stoner and I reinvestigate the case.

We've interviewed many old people, many of them with faulty memories. They hem and they haw, they digress off the point. It's not linear. It's not like the bullshit homicide investigations you read in my books and the books of crime writers good, bad, and indifferent. One thing does not lead to another. It's one dead end after record check after unsatisfying interview after another after another. But facts about my mother and her life are being gleaned en route. Stories and sub-stories are weaving themselves into the tapestry.

Interviewer: Like other authors before you, your life story makes great copy and you've used that for publicity purposes and to get attention. Do you regret that?

Ellroy: It's true. It's a true story. I've always tried to deflate myself as a dangerous persona. Maybe to some crime writers, most of whom are notoriously wimpy, I am a dangerous guy. But I've never been a dangerous guy except maybe to myself. I've never been violent. I was basically self-destructive and pathetic. I go to great pains to explain this to interviewers and it somehow comes out different when I read the pieces written about me. So now I can set the record straight with this memoir and basically never answer any questions about my past life again, I hope.

Interviewer: You'll just refer them to page so and so of the book.
Ellroy: Yeah. Buy the book. So, no I don't regret using my past.

Interviewer: I was going to ask you questions about your family life, but if it's going to be in the book . . .
Ellroy: I never had a family life.

Interviewer: That was going to be my point. You didn't have a mother, and your father was an absentee. It must have been a very traumatic time.
Ellroy: It was. I learned self-sufficiency very early on because I did not expect people to take care of me. There's a cold side to me, a tremendously ruthless side to me. But, really, I only try to be ruthless with myself.

I want to sum my life up in this memoir, and I want to pay homage to my mother, and I want to recognize her. I want to find out who she was as much as I can and the way to do this is to attempt to locate her killer. I will never stop looking for her killer, but I will not let it run my life. Bill Stoner and I have become very close friends—he is easily the best friend I've ever had and, outside of my wife, the person I will love the most in this life. He's morally, spiritually committed to this case but we're not going to let it eat up our lives. I think that if we do not find the guy by the end of the year; when I go home to write the book, then it's highly unlikely that we'll find him for the rest of our lives. After that, we'll get together for a couple of weeks every year and run down leads.

Interviewer: Did you find her old friends?
Ellroy: We haven't found any yet. We found my old landlady from the late fifties. My mother was an alcoholic and a very secretive woman. She'd be eighty if she was still alive. We're up against the passage of time—she was killed thirty-seven years ago.

Interviewer: Do you feel as though you've missed out?
Ellroy: I feel like the luckiest man in the world.

Underworld U.S.A.

Ellroy: After *My Dark Places* I will return to finish the Underworld U.S.A. trilogy of which *American Tabloid* is the first volume. That book runs from 1958 to 1963. The two subsequent volumes will run from 1963 to 1968 (Howard Hughes's Las Vegas, Vietnam War heroin deals, Jack Ruby and Lee Harvey Oswald—it starts five minutes after Jack gets the bullet in the head), and from 1969 to 1973 (Nixon and Watergate). Thus, fifteen years of dark American history broken down into three books.

At the end of *American Tabloid* you get two of the three main characters surviving however tenuously. I want to show these men getting older as they interact with history, and becoming humanized, and becoming frailer, and becoming more morally easy to show the first tumultuous meeting between a man and a woman and a lot of hot sex early on—that's easy as dirt.

Interviewer: It's lust, not love.
Ellroy: Yes, it is. But, to show Pete and Barb sticking it out over the course of five years in the next novel is something else.

After I finish the Underworld U.S.A. trilogy, I'm going to jump around a lot. I'm going to write a very long, *a very long*, novel about the Wisconsin State police and my German-American roots. After that, I don't know. I'll never write anything again that can be categorized as a straight thriller or crime novel.

Interviewer: I'm very interested in America's involvement in the Mexican war back in the nineteenth century, where America basically held Mexico to ransom and, as a result, got the cattle, oil, and gold it needed to finance and feed the nation to become a major world power. It's a very dark period of American history. Does this interest you at all?
Ellroy: No. I'm an urban man. I'm interested in the intrigue. It's the clash of wills. It's the pitting of one man against another and then in packs against each other, more than anything else. It's the changing cityscape. It's the forces of greed and lust that shape a city. It's growing up in Los Angeles during a time it underwent a lot of change.

I don't like noise. I live in Kansas City, in the ritziest enclave in Kansas

City, in Johnson County, Kansas. I like peace and quiet. I like quiet, affluent surroundings and well-behaved people. I got enough craziness in my own mind to last me the rest of my life. But my curiosity still rages and continues to rage.

Interviewer: Do you haunt the places where you used to live?
Ellroy: I go to L.A. a lot, especially recently to do *My Dark Places*. It's a real memory bank for me. It's got a lot of force, a lot of power, but I can't live there anymore.

Interviewer: Where does this power come from?
Ellroy: I've lived an extraordinary life, and I've done some amazing things. I've been around for forty-seven years and seen a lot of history, and I've been introspective from the gate. I've had a very impoverished life and a very full life, and I'm grateful for it, and you'll see this as you get older, and your curiosity gets richer and richer, and you can become haunted by your own past and the way that it relates to the overall past. It's just fascinating to touch the fabric of the physical places.

Interviewer: Do you see yourself linked with history? In your novels, everyone has a past, something that drives them on, something they want to keep hidden, that they don't want to face. You talk as though you're directly linked to your own history, and that your own history is directly linked to the history of America. Do you feel that way?
Ellroy: Yeah. I feel that way and, I think, in many ways, my mission in life is to explicate it through the writing of the novels.

Interviewer: Is the writing of the novels a way for you to define your own identity?
Ellroy: Yes. I see it as therapeutic—not in the sense that it's something I want to overcome, because I don't think this curiosity, these drives of mine, are neurotically derived. As I get older, I divide humanity into two camps. There are the people who are neurotically derived and there are the people who have transcended the fearful aspects of their personality and the aspects which are holding down their imagination, holding them down from enjoying life to the fullest. My greatest teacher, the only person I've ever met who has a bigger fucking hard-on for life as I do, is my wife. I'm having a blast. People, especially in France, expect me to be fucking tormented. And I have to say, *"Au contraire, Froggy."*

I'm still choked up from last night—I was in a room full of smokers. I can't believe I'm picking my nose in a fucking interview.

Interviewer: Just be pleased we're not being filmed.

Note

1. NBC Television crime drama which ran for two seasons from 1986 to 1988. The show was created by Gustave Reininger and Chuck Adamson and the executive producer was Michael Mann.

Dead Women Owned His Soul

Jesse Sublett/1997

First appeared in the *Austin Chronicle* (February 14, 1997), vol. 16, no. 24. Reprinted by permission of the *Austin Chronicle* and Jesse Sublett.

He should have known he'd have to go back. Not just part of the way. All the way. That's where the answers are. He should have known because that's the way it is in noir fiction. He should have known it like Robert Mitchum knew it midway through *Out of the Past*. He doesn't just write noir fiction, he's lived it. He's James Ellroy.

Ellroy began devouring crime novels at the age of ten. Growing up in L.A. in the fifties and sixties was a long walk through hell. He was a voyeur, petty thief, burglar, wino, Benzedrex addict. He became obsessed with true crimes, especially the Black Dahlia case of 1948. The victim's real name was Elizabeth Short, a wannabe Hollywood starlet. After torturing her for several days, the killer cut her body in half, scrubbed it clean, rearranged her internal organs, and dumped the remains in a vacant lot. The crime was never solved.

By his late twenties, after several near-death experiences, Ellroy cleaned up his act but his fantasies continued. Dead women owned him. He started writing his fantasies down on a legal pad. Ten dark crime novels later, he still uses the same method.

In *The Black Dahlia*, published in 1987, James Ellroy channeled his fascination with the case to produce his first best-selling novel. The next four were bestsellers, too: *The Big Nowhere, L.A. Confidential, White Jazz*, and *American Tabloid*. But with this giant leap forward in his writing career, Ellroy also took tentative first steps on a journey that would eventually take him back to the genesis of his fascination with crime, to the terrible event that warped his future and spawned his consciousness: his own mother was murdered in 1958, when he was ten years old. Her body was found dumped near a schoolyard in El Monte, a suburb of Los Angeles. At the time, Ellroy hated his mother. She made him go to church. She hit him occasionally. She told him lies (he thought) about his father, a small-time Hollywood hustler. He lusted for her. She hot-wired him to sex and death. Her death set him free—he thought. Like the Black Dahlia, Jean Ellroy was a woman who had bad taste in men and liked to party—a redhead. As with the Dahlia case, the murder of Jean Ellroy was never solved.

In 1994, a friend of Ellroy's called him and said he was working on a story about unsolved murders in the San Gabriel Valley. He was going to look at Jean Ellroy's file, he said. Did Ellroy want to see it for himself? He did. He had to go back. All the way back. To know her. To know where he came from.

The moment Ellroy opened the file and saw the photos and read the detectives' notes, "a little gear clicked." He knew he had to investigate the crime for himself, if not to find the killer, to finally get to know his mother. *My Dark Places* is Ellroy's account of the original murder case, his own investigation with retired L.A. County Sheriff's Detective Bill Stoner, an autobiographical memoir, and four decades of homicide in Los Angeles County. It is the darkest and most explosive of all of Ellroy's work. At the same time, it is easily the most readable.

I've known James Ellroy for six years or so. I've seen him do his psycho-hipster rap at bookstores a dozen times ("If you buy a thousand copies of this book, you'll be able to have unlimited sex with the partner of your dreams for the rest of your life . . . It's a book for the whole family—if your family's name is O.J. Simpson."). People who only know him for that shtick might be surprised to hear that he's a genuinely nice guy who remembers to ask about your spouse and child, who has an incredibly deep love of canines. In his own way, he's one of the least self-absorbed writers I know.

Knowing all these things, I wasn't shocked when I learned that he finally realized he had to go back. I was also a little worried at the effect it might have on his mental health, and further, on his desire to continue writing crime fiction. I spoke with him during his recent trip to Austin. He said not to worry about that stuff.

Interviewer: What do you expect readers to come away with after reading *My Dark Places*?
Ellroy: I would want people to be thrilled, moved, appalled, horrified by the book. I would want them to see my mother as the complex and ambiguously defined woman that she really was. That's the biggest thrill about the book,

giving my mother to the world. I wouldn't have wanted to write a full-length memoir at the tender age of forty-eight that was just about me. It's so much about her, and women in our society, and violence. That was the density that I was going for, you know, all the woman-killings that were woven in along with my mother's story.

Interviewer: After your mother was murdered, you began your fantasy life, breaking into houses, stealing women's undergarments, things like that. In the book, it appears that the seed was planted after your parents separated, when your father asked you to spy on your mother when she had you on weekends.

Ellroy: Yeah, that was the beginning, really, of voyeurism, and toward the ending of the book, Joe Walker, Bill Stoner's colleague, found my parents' divorce records, and there's my father breaking into her house, and I'm letting him into the house, through the French windows. Then, ten, eleven years later, here I am doing this shit myself, breaking in places. I mean, you can really see the arc of my life and hers in this book.

Interviewer: Was there a sexual thing connected with your voyeurism and breaking and entering from the very beginning?

Ellroy: It was imagination and a sexual thing pretty early on. We were right on the edge of Hancock Park. If we were out in L.A., Jesse, even though you were a Valley guy and I'm a city guy, I could show you the pad. It's right on Beverly and Irving. It's a dump. If you walk a block south from 1st Street, you're in Hancock Park. There's all these nice Tudor and Spanish and French Chateau houses, and girls, and cars, baseball gloves, and Ivy League clothes. I grew up right on the edge of that and I was hungry.

Interviewer: I can picture it. I can picture El Monte, too—the way you describe it back in the fifties. Why do you think your mother moved there after the divorce?

Ellroy: She was a big one for starting over. I think that's probably what she was doing in El Monte. And man, when you're starting over in El Monte, you're at the end of the fucking line. And you know my father, who was a stone low-life, called El Monte "Shitsville, U.S.A." And he was right. I mean, this was dulled-down, pre-breakdown-America-Shitsville, U.S.A. There were only four murders in El Monte in the entire decade of the fifties—the two lesbians who killed that guy, the head job, the guy who drove his car through the window, and the guy who killed my mother.

Interviewer: I was really fascinated with your blow-by-blow account of the original investigation, the difference in the witness accounts, and how they described the "Swarthy Man" [the suspected killer]. Margie was the one who had the incredible memory for the kind of hair people had, for example.

Ellroy: Yeah. We interviewed Margie's daughter. Margie bellied-up from a cerebral hemorrhage in '72. He slipped through the cracks. The guy slipped through the cracks. My feeling is the guy killed Bobby Long, as well [a waitress murdered in early '56, with the same *modus operandi* as the Jean Ellroy case]. But he just . . . he freaked out twice in seven months and didn't do it again. And he got away with it. And the way that it can be cracked is, you know, the blonde woman probably told people. In these bar milieu lust killings scenarios, the material witnesses that don't come forth for fear of reprisal usually tell people, and the more publicity we get, the better our chance. But you know what? If I don't find the killer, who gives a shit. I got my mother back.

Interviewer: That's the important thing, right?

Ellroy: Yeah, I honored her in this book.

Interviewer: Do you have any unresolved feelings about your father?

Ellroy: Not really. You know, he lived in my purview for another seven years. I had plenty of time to get disillusioned with him over time. And I treated him badly; I deserted him when his health was failing. I just wanted to get the fuck out of town.

Interviewer: Before reading this memoir, I had no idea you were in the army.

Ellroy: Yeah, very, very briefly. I mean, I wanted to join the Marine Corps because they had cooler uniforms, but my dad wouldn't sign for it. And that's good. I might not have been able to fool them in the Marine Corps. I might have gone to Vietnam and got my ass shot.

Interviewer: Do you think you'll ever get past this?

Ellroy: I think I've gotten past it. I think I've looked at my craft consciously and tried to improve. I mean, as much as I've understood the importance of this event, I have—first intellectually and then emotionally—confronted my mother. After a while, you know, it just becomes consciousness. You're not just reacting to stimuli because your mother got whacked out thirty-eight years ago.

Interviewer: But that's been your shtick for so long. What can you see ten years from now? What's the James Ellroy Show going to be in the future?

Ellroy: I've got another eight days to tour for the book here in the States, and I'm going to France, Japan, Germany, and Sweden, and after that, I will never answer another personal question. I figure that's it, you know. This stands as the text. That's how I got here. Now ask me questions about my new book.

Interviewer: And what's the next book going to be?

Ellroy: The next book is going to be the sequel to *American Tabloid*. It picks up five minutes after *Tabloid* concludes. It's going to cover 1963 to '68, John Kennedy's assassination to Bobby's. It's going to be bigger than *American Tabloid*, and more evil, and I think it's going to show a greater diversity of character and motive as a result of my having confronted my mother.

Interviewer: When are we going to see a James Ellroy novel on the big screen?

Ellroy: *L.A. Confidential* was filmed. It'll be out early next year. Curtis Hansen directed it, the guy who directed *The Hand That Rocks the Cradle* and *The River Wild*. Danny Devito, Kim Basinger, James Cromwell—who was the pig farmer in *Babe*—and Kevin Spacey are in it. I've seen about half an hour of that and it looks good.

Interviewer: I look forward to that. It's sure taken awhile. I thought the *Fallen Angels* episode adapted from your short story was really good.

Ellroy: Yeah, for what it was, a doofus-y little short story, that was it.

Interviewer: I was pleased to see your reference to *Macao* in the new book. That's one of my favorite movies.

Ellroy: Yeah, starring Robert Mitchum and Jane Russell.

Interviewer: You know, the back story for Mitchum's character is such a mystery at the beginning. Finally, it dribbles out, and it just boils down to a couple of lines: "There was a hassle with a redhead . . . There was another guy, and a gun. The gun went off . . ."

Ellroy: No kidding? "It was a hassle with a redhead"? Oh that's the best. Well, you're a real romantic, Jesse, I can tell you really liked the thing with the redhead.

Interviewer: Well, yeah, Mitchum's always been my hero, too. And I was thinking, if you were going to cast your past, with period actors, Mitchum would be in there somewhere, wouldn't he?

Ellroy: He'd be one of my mother's low-life boyfriends, yeah. Denzel Washington as me. Jesus, I can't even think. Maybe Danny Devito as me. I'll have to think about that and tell you later.

Interviewer: You aspired to be a great crime writer in your early teens. Have those aspirations changed?

Ellroy: Yeah, fantasy was my big thing. My one great hero was myself. Finally I outgrew that shit. Now I just want to write great novels. I'm trying to tone down my act, Jesse, be a little less flamboyant. I mean, I'm forty-eight.

Interviewer: Now you can just start being eccentric. You've already got the rep.

Ellroy: Yeah.

Interviewer: What was the moment you decided you had to investigate the case for yourself and write this book?

Ellroy: It was after I went back and wrote that piece for *G.Q.* The gears clicked when I looked at my mother's file. It was an amazing moment. Then I met Stoner, and Stoner impressed me. I think I examined myself. It was really when [my wife] Helen got that picture of me as a kid, and that got me thinking. Then a friend of mine called and said, have you seen your mother's file. And the die was cast.

Interviewer: "Dick Contino's Blues" (in the collection *Hollywood Nocturnes*) is a great novella. Are we going to hear any more from Dick?

Ellroy: Maybe if I can find a venue, a place to write a novella-length story.

Interviewer: You told me once before that blues and rock and roll is just noise to you. Do you still feel that way?

Ellroy: I don't care for popular music. I don't know why. I haven't the vaguest idea. It's just one of those instincts that I just trust.

Interviewer: What about O.J.?

Ellroy: He's guilty. We all know that. He's a piece of shit.

Interviewer: Are there any modern crime writers you admire?
Ellroy: No, I haven't read a book in I don't know how long.

Interviewer: Who's your number one favorite from the old school?
Ellroy: I was always a Dashiell Hammett guy.

Interviewer: Do you think it helps to have a little psychic damage to write good crime fiction?
Ellroy: Doesn't hurt, yeah. But it's about consciousness, it's about getting better.

Interviewer: Has the adventure of investigating your mother's death and writing this book changed you in any way? How do you suppose it will affect your writing?
Ellroy: I want to show greater diversity of character and motive in my books. I want to be less dark but no less powerful. And I think that's my mother's gift to me in the course of this investigation. It was an astonishing journey, and it's not over yet. My mother and I are a continuum and we will continue. We may never find the swarthy man, but I will learn more things about her.

"Confidential" Commentary

Rob Blackwelder/1997

From *SPLICEDwire* (September 3, 1997). Reprinted by permission.

"I think that if a writer options a novel to a studio or to film makers in general, then he has an obligation to keep his mouth shut if the movie gets made and it's all f----- up."

So opines James Ellroy, the gruff and sardonic author of the 1950s crime and corruption bestseller *L.A. Confidential*. So why is he making press appearances to promote the film adaptation?

Quite simply, he's taken with the movie. "I am in the wonderful position of actually wanting to open my mouth and extol *L.A. Confidential* the film."

In San Francisco for a day with the film's director Curtis Hanson, Ellroy could be straight out of the 1950s himself, with his wire-rim glasses, a policeman's mustache, and very short hair that wouldn't be mussed by a handsome fedora.

He speaks dryly, often with the tips of his fingers tapped together in front of his face, and at first seems a little abrasive. Like your favorite aloof college professor with a little Sam Spade thrown in.

The author sold the film rights to *Confidential*, the third in a quartet of novels about 1950s Los Angeles cops, just before the book was published in 1990 and thought nothing of it.

"(Selling) the option is to a finished movie what the first kiss is to the fiftieth wedding anniversary," he shrugged. "I figured, thanks for the money, now go away and write when you get work."

But director Hanson (*The Hand That Rocks the Cradle*) was driven in adapting the confoundingly layered, 500-page novel. A daunting task, to be sure.

The story is told from three points of view, those of a trio of rival LAPD detectives. Two of them, the politically savvy Boy Scout Ed Exley and the temperamental vigilante Bud White, are played in the film by relative new-comers Guy Pearce and Russell Crowe. Detective Jack Vincennes, a very Hollywood narcotics cop whose life revolves around his perk job advising a TV police drama, is played by Kevin Spacey. The cast also includes Kim Basinger, Danny DeVito and James Cromwell.

Half a dozen plots orbit around centerpiece investigation of a seemingly random coffee shop massacre and eventually weave together into a complex conspiracy (which is even more complex in the book).

Because of Ellroy's detailed but staccato stream of consciousness narrative style, one can become submerged in his labyrinthine layers without getting lost. But he had to be worried about how that would translate to film.

Interviewer: Did you ever imagine that somebody could whittle down that 500-page book into a 140-minute movie, what with all the interweaving plots and all the characters?

Ellroy: I didn't think they'd succeed. I didn't think it would be made into a movie . . . (but) lo and behold several years later Curtis Hanson, a man whose films I had seen and admired, called me, and I read the seventh draft of the script.

I saw that they had done a good job of compressing my story while main-taining the overall dramatic thrust of it, and I saw that they had contained the narrative structure of the three men. Of course when I saw the film I was very, very taken with it.

Interviewer: Did you have any input after you read the script?

Ellroy: Yes. Curtis Hanson, Brian Helgeland (co-screen writer) and I talked. I pointed out anachronisms in the script, deviations from 1950s vernacular. I gave them advice. Some they took, some they didn't.

Curtis Hanson and I became friends, and we would meet periodically when I happened to be in L.A., and discuss points of police procedure, points of LAPD lore from back in the '50s.

We discussed the '50s in general. Curtis is three years older than me, and he remembers the actual year 1953, in which the film is set, much better than me because I was only five and he was eight, and that's a big difference.

Then New Regency flew my wife and I out to Tacoma, Washington to see a focus group screening of the film in February. I saw it, and I was blown away.

The most startling thing about it is seeing a work of art that I created out of thin air, metamorphose into a compatible work of art that is recognizably my work, yet is something that I couldn't have imagined in a million years.

(Ellroy says there were minor things he would have changed had he been given a hand in the scripting, but after seeing the finished film he implies many of those changes would have been mistakes.)

Hanson proved me wrong on a couple of things. When I read the script, I thought the shoot-out (the adrenaline-packed finale) was preposterous. And you know what? In the movie it's preposterous. Two guys holed up in a room where they kill fifteen guys—it's bullshit. But you know what? It's inspired bullshit.

Interviewer: A lot of the plot that was left out of the book to pare it down was the stuff that might be hard to take for your average Peoria Joe American—you know, there's pedophilia, rape, child murders that are alluded to. I was wondering if you have any feelings on the stuff that was left out.

Ellroy: The Dream-a-Dreamland plot (a twisted take on the underground goings on at a Disney-esque theme park) had to go because so much of it was backstory. The entire Wee Willie Wennerholm-Loren Atherton story is backstory, so of course that had to go. There's only one action scene that I would have enjoyed seeing. The shoot-out at Kikey Titlebaum's deli.

Interviewer: What did you think of the casting?

Ellroy: I was thrilled with it. I never see actors as my characters when I write books. I think about it afterwards (with) my wife, an ex-film critic and feature writer for the *L.A. Weekly*. It's fun to do. It's a fun game.

It was wonderful to see relative unknowns in two of the lead roles. I go back and forth in my admiration for those two performances. Some days it's an Exley day and some days it's a White day, a Russell Crowe day or a Guy Pearce day.

The greatest character in the book is Ed Exley. He's the most complex man. He goes on the greatest journey. And there's that calculating intelligence that Guy Pearce has—the glasses and the beady eyes—he's always thinking, he's always calculating. He was terrific.

Basinger (playing a Veronica Lake look-alike prostitute) was terrific. She's markedly older than Russell Crowe, and there's almost a maternal aspect to their relationship.

One of the most startling things was seeing James Cromwell as Dudley Smith (the imposing and crooked police captain) the first time. Dudley Smith is a character in four of my books . . . and I love him. He's immensely articulate and charismatic, brilliant and draconian.

The first time I saw James Cromwell enter the screen—it was in an editing house when Curtis was editing the film—and here's this imperiously tall, he's about 6'6", skinny man glide onto the screen and say, "Call me Dudley," with that brogue, I felt the hackles on the back of my neck hop.

Interviewer: How about Spacey?

Ellroy: Spacey is so deft. He is so controlled, is so subtle, is so good at suggesting a character's inner life with a minimal of outward action.

He glides. There is something amorphous about the guy. I met him a couple of times. I don't have any kind of rapport with him, you know. I like him well enough, he's not a bad guy, (but) there's a mask that's up when you meet him personally, and I imagine that this helps him when he immerses himself in a character. And this is a deep immersion performance. It's some of the best self-loathing I've ever seen on screen. He's only on screen I'd say half as much as Pearce or Crowe, and he steals every scene he's in because there's something going on internally, and your eyes automatically shift to him.

But I think it's a great ensemble piece. I think it's rich in implication and I think it's a passionate film.

Interviewer: Has anybody been beating down your door about the rest of your L.A. books now?

Ellroy: They're all optioned. All the L.A. Quartet books are optioned. Two of them have been purchased outright. Will they be made? I don't know. I don't think you can predict that.

Interviewer: I wanted to ask you about how you created that language you use in the book. The staccato sentence structure . . .

Ellroy: I created that in *L.A. Confidential* as a result of having to cut the manuscript by about a hundred pages. I didn't want to alter the dramatic thrust of any of the scenes or take out chunks of the book, but I needed to do some cutting and that's how I built that style.

Cutting the expository language down to the bare minimum gave the book a phonetic feel that made it read very excitingly. And it got you back and forth between Ed, Jack, and Bud very fast.

Interviewer: It felt to me like some of the narrative is from the charac-ters' point of view, and the reason it was staccato like that was because one doesn't think in full sentences. You think in ideas and flashes . . .

Ellroy: Well, that's part of it. And of course every chapter in the book is from either Ed, Jack, or Bud's point of view.

Interviewer: What do you see as the biggest difference between the film and the book?

Ellroy: The book is black type on white paper and the film is visual. That's it. It's a brilliantly compatible visual form of the novel.

Lunch and Tea with James Ellroy

M. G. Smout/2001

From *The Barcelona Review* (May–June 2001), no. 24. Reprinted by permission.

1. Lunch: Easter Sunday, April 15, 2001. Marítimo Restaurant, Barcelona.

Jeez, the man's a giant. The person towering over me and shaking my hand looks nothing like the photo commonly found in his books—the one where he looks like a squat, chubby, neofascist British politician circa 1950. "Great hair. If I had hair, I'd have it like yours." The man is a charmer and I am won over in one sentence. He then asks about my background and says how much he likes the north of England, Manchester and so on. Americans are like that, they can go on autopilot extracting basic social information, but Ellroy's probings seem genuine. He loves meeting people and our arrival (myself and *TBR* editor Jill Adams) has sparked an interest, maybe even revitalized him a little. Barcelona is the quiet start to the Spanish leg of his massive book tour, but he still has to speak slowly and carefully as he and his hosts—Spanish publishing house Ediciones B—can only communicate in ponderous English. On our arrival—a Brit and a Yank without a tape recorder—Ellroy relaxes and, not performing for journalists, is off, every pent up sentence let loose in a flood of rapid-fire speech, vitriol, slander, and wonderfully sick humor. In a lull, Santi, on my left, says sadly, "I could understand him until you two came along."

We are in an ugly, crowded, box-like all-window restaurant whose saving grace is an incredible view of the old port and the dockside, and good food. An added bonus for Ellroy are the German shepherds in the boatyard below. Their presence often draws his attention. Ediciones B editor Susana Andres asks for a menu in English, but it is a wasted effort as Ellroy is the world's fastest chooser of food. He doesn't eat meat so goes straight to fish and from there anything with the word "cod." He starts off with a raw salt-cod salad—a Catalan specialty—and follows it with a huge cod steak in a cream sauce. It is very rich and defeats Jill, but Ellroy is a hearty eater and scoffs the lot in minutes. He also has a frightening array of vitamin pills and supplements lined up on the table. These he washes down with copious amounts of green tea which he has brought along for the tour, producing bags from his pockets to plop in hot water after testing the temperature with his finger. The fear of illness, the upheaval of traveling (alone) and being on a tight tour schedule, calls for strict cautionary measures to help combat a persistent apprehension over health matters which leads to nervous check-ups in hotel mirrors. Every blemish, mark on his skin, wheeze, or whatever urges him to seek transatlantic phone help from his wife, writer Helen Knode. Her name crops up a lot. It is mid-April and he won't finish this tour until July, and although he actually enjoys it, you can tell he desperately wants to be back in Kansas City. The vitamin pills, the no-booze and tobacco, working out in hotel gyms (if they have them—no such luck in Spain) all speak of worries other than just surviving a tour. He is worried about getting old. This worry has added extra depth to the characters in his latest novel, *The Cold Six Thousand*, but it also serves as a reminder that Ellroy has quite a few "missing" years which he fully intends to recuperate in some way. And looking at the very fit and bouncy man opposite me, wolfing down cod like it was going out of fashion, waxing lyrical on all things and being very in love with Helen and life in general, I see a hyperactive teenager without zits and not someone in his early fifties. The only way James Ellroy is going to grow old gracefully is if someone sedates him. The man is all energy—he must have been one hell of a drinking buddy.

The Spanish contingent are the only drinkers at the table (and the only smokers, although they kindly refrain). We touch on the subject of alcohol abuse and the effects it has on one's character. He has recently finished a documentary for a TV station that shows a bunch of his "colleagues" slowly getting drunker and therefore more stupid around a table.[1] He knows they are going to shit from embarrassment when they see themselves as others saw them. He quit booze and his self-destructive lifestyle in order to survive, to create a whole new person, and knowing what he was is all the fuel he needs to keep from the bottle. He is not really tempted but tells of being on an airplane where there is a Johnny Walker promotion of some sort and the whisky is flowing freely. The guy next to him is throwing the stuff back, and Ellroy is inhaling the wonderful fumes and enjoying it until "the motherfucker passed out."

The past sometimes catches up with him. An ex-girlfriend, now married and living down in Valencia, once tried to get in contact with him. Ellroy's response was to hide behind his (genuine) tight schedule and say no. His dilemma is not because he is married—he only has eyes for Helen—but because he doesn't know and doesn't want to know what this woman wants. Now that he has some money, is she going to try and hit him up? Fame and bucks make you a target and though a meeting could have just been two old lovers nattering over green tea, Ellroy prefers to play it safe and keep the past at a safe distance. Fame and being a target: he hadn't heard about Boris Becker's run-in with the girl in the broom closet who supposedly impregnated herself with his semen from a blow job. Ever the practical storyteller, he wonders how she kept the stuff alive or was she just very lucky to get it right the first time. Thinking about it kind of put people off their food and the subject was quickly changed.

We also hit on Hollywood. Ellroy loves to scuttlebutt and one of the secrets he divulges has Susana nearly in tears, "No, not him, I don't believe it!" It is a hilarious roll-call of names and vices, with Jill egging him on. Whether the stories are true or not there is a certain joy in having these untouchables reduced to corruptible flesh and blood. Ellroy points out that just being a Hollywood actor has got to warp you in some way. The pressure and surreal nature of the whole scene has to have a wounding effect on the psyche. I ask him who then is normal. There is silence, then a few names are bandied about and I realize that even to name the normal ones automatically points a finger at the hundreds not on the list. What a freak show. Ellroy has a new piece of scandal that he heard the night before and you know that even if the rest of the trip to Spain is a disaster the nugget he heard was worth it. A Spanish writer the night before confirmed that Ernest Hemingway *did* have a homosexual relationship while in Spain. This leads into the less slanderous area of debating whether or not Hemingway's *The Nick Adams Stories* wasn't thinly disguised gay writing in the first place.

He tells us that he is very pissed off with the selling of his manuscripts and galley proofs of *The Cold Six Thousand* for vast amounts of money over the Internet. It isn't the loss of money that's the problem—those who paid for them will buy the book anyway—but the fact that people are reading versions with typos and errors. That is not the Ellroy he wants people to read, obviously. He put a message up on the Net expressing his displeasure and in explaining this it became apparent he was not very computer savvy. I somehow didn't see him with the latest, all-flashing-lights PC and imagined him being, like many Americans his age, an Apple user banging away on a Mac

Classic or, the cutest CPU ever built, an LC111. It was jaw-dropping then to discover that he writes *by* hand and faxes the pages to someone—the same person for about the last twenty years or so—to type out and send back. There can't be many authors in the twenty-first century writing such vast tomes as the Underworld U.S.A. Trilogy by hand. Ellroy has a fierce reputation while on these tours, and we were told to be early and that lunch would be short as he likes to get back to the hotel in the afternoon and do all his transatlantic phoning. It was this latter necessity that eventually forced the issue. Ellroy appeared to be having fun, was actually chilling out, and I think we could have jawed away for another two hours or more. We were in a quite privileged position and on hindsight I wonder if we would have clicked as well if there had been a tape recorder present or if we had been on "native" soil. I think so, because he likes people anyway. And I liked him a hell of a lot: I liked his vulnerability about his age, I liked his honesty and genuine interest, and I liked that the fact that even as a fanatical dog lover he also likes cats. I also like his books. Lunch over, we felt a bit guilty as our Spanish hosts had been pretty much left out of the conversation. We asked him to sign a book for our quiz winner, and when he asked the rest of the table for things to sign, a library of Ellroy in Spanish immediately appeared and we realized that we hadn't brought a copy of an Ellroy from our collection for him to sign. Boo-hoo. But that was a minor disaster. They start to get bigger. Not wanting to detain him, I fired off a few photos on a digital camera that only records images at 72 dpi. The quality left a lot to be desired, but Montse Gurguí, his Spanish translator (along with Hernán Sabaté), was going to take more photos in Madrid the next day, so no problem. She did . . . and then her traveling companion left the camera on a bench in a small village where they stopped to sit on their way to Segovia. Ellroy had also kindly granted Montse some time to interview him while he was in Madrid, but by the time her allotted time came he was tired and a Madrid journalist had pissed him off royally. She hadn't read any of his work and was only interested in the websites dedicated to him. He told her in no uncertain terms that a man who writes by hand has doodly-squat interest in websites. Listening to the tape that Montse bought back, it was obvious that Ellroy had had enough. He answered some questions with a "No" or a "Yes" when just the day before he was spinning circles and only a large blow to the head could have shut him up. One could feel his irritation. Then, just when he was slowly warming to the task, Fabio Vericat, who is reviewing the book in Spanish, asked about the film version of *L.A. Confidential*. We had covered this topic in Barcelona, and Ellroy—though very willing to talk about it—made it plain that what he had to say about it was "off the record." Anyway, when Fabio unknowingly asked the question, Ellroy answered but turned the recorder off first . . . and it was never turned back on.

2: Tea: April 16, Hotel Alcala, Madrid

A very noisy hotel lobby. James Ellroy has just spent all day promoting the Spanish translation of *The Cold Six Thousand.* He is at first very chatty with Montse Gurguí, Hernán Sabaté, and Fabio Vericat but admits to being very tired and sleeping badly; he asks about over-the-counter sleeping pills. It is safer that nobody points out that even green tea has caffeine. He tells them about the journalist and biting her head off (Dog bites journalist—that's news) and then laughs off the whole sorry incident, but not before slagging off Madrid and stating that the next time he is in Spain he is only going to go to Barcelona. Seeing that he appears to be his normal self, Montse decides it's time to switch on the tape recorder. Ellroy stiffens. He had hoped his day was over. He is not a happy bunny.

Interviewer: This is a long tour. How do you cope?
Ellroy: I go back to my room and I do deep breathing and a little bit of yoga and . . . you know . . . try to calm down. Travel fucks your brain. I don't enjoy it.

Interviewer: So this is a new habit, yoga . . .
Ellroy: Yeah, my wife Helen taught it me . . .

Interviewer: I try it myself when I get to the point . . .
Ellroy: When you get stressed out, you mean? It works, doesn't it?

(Ediciones B, a P.R. person, reminds Ellroy of his appointment to get a haircut.)

Interviewer: If we can begin by going back to the distant past. . . You once said that you couldn't get laid in the Summer of Love [1967].[2] Is that right?
Ellroy: I was trying in the worst way. I had short hair in the Summer of Love—that's how fucked up I was. Nobody wanted me.

Interviewer: Then later as you were discovering the writer inside you, you were getting laid regularly as well as working as a caddy . . . how did you do that?

Ellroy: Well, I wrote in the afternoon. Caddied in the mornings, wrote in the afternoons and early evenings and had the affairs later on.

Interviewer: How many hours a day is that?
Ellroy: It was a full day.

Interviewer: At the time did you have any contact with the publishing industry . . . how did all that come about?
Ellroy: I knew a woman in . . . well, I knew a woman who had published a novel and she told me that she found an agent in *Writer's Market,* which is a literary reference book. I bought a copy of *Writer's Market* in 1980 and there were about four agents who would read unsolicited manuscripts, so I sent four copies of the manuscript to them and they all wanted to represent the book. And I went with the guy who sounded the most intelligent and aggressive.

Interviewer: When did you start living off the money from your books?
Ellroy: I was paid for my books from the beginning. I actually hung up my caddy cleats when I was living in suburban New York, in the early fall of 1984. I started making a couple of grand here and a couple of grand there to where I didn't have to caddy.

Interviewer: So you kept it all together, pretty much.
Ellroy: Yep.

Interviewer: Is it true that your publisher made you edit *White Jazz* down from 900 pages to 400?
Ellroy: No, *L.A. Confidential* was 800 pages, I cut it to 635. I had developed a "telegraphic" style that I later used in *White Jazz.*

Interviewer: By "telegraphic style" you mean . . .
Ellroy: I am talking about the fractured sentence style *only* in *White Jazz.* I am not talking about the more concise style of *American Tabloid* or *The Cold Six Thousand.*

Interviewer: Is your telegraphic style modeled from or used by any other writer?
Ellroy: There is *no* one else.

Interviewer: It seems you are using fewer and fewer words to explain the most intricate stories. Many writers and artists when they reach their maturity tend to dispense with all that is superfluous and go straight to the essence. What is your process towards this minimalism?

Ellroy: It is actually more and more words. Secondly, the style is not minimalistic, it's anti-minimalistic. It's highly stylizsed, it's extremely literal, it's a direct expression of the language of the characters, their inner and outer lives, and the language of the base narrator, but there's actually more physical description in this than there has been in my last few novels, it just doesn't seem like it because it's so stylized. It isn't minimalistic at all.

Interviewer: What are the implications of minimalism for you?

Ellroy: Small lives, neurosis, an unromantic way of looking at the world, an absence of moral ardor or rigor and the denial of the fact that people have free will. If you have free will, and you know something is wrong, and you act upon it in the wrong way, you are a bad person. I heard somebody once say that there are no bad people, the forces that have made them force them to make their decisions—and I don't believe that.

Interviewer: Do you believe in God?

Ellroy: Yes.

Interviewer: After writing the L.A. Quartet why did you then pick the vast subject of modern American history?

Ellroy: I wanted to write bigger books, I wanted to write books that can never be categorized as a thriller, mystery, or police and I wanted to get out of L.A. as a strict locale for my books. I wanted to become a more mainstream, less generically derived, novelist.

Interviewer: You speak about being up against the "ghetto genre" all the time in America. Can you elaborate on that?

Ellroy: Well, you know, who wants to be a mystery writer? Who wants to be a crime novelist when you can be a plain old novelist with a capital "N"? You are known by the company you keep. I mean, do you want to be in the same . . . mentioned in the same breath as Agatha Christie and a bunch of people like that?

Interviewer: How about being in the same category as Dashiell Hammett?

Ellroy: That's dandy, I mean I certainly don't want to morally be Dashiell

Hammett but, I'll take that. But the truth is he wrote crime novels. They subscribe to a formula; he largely invented the formula and invented the language. But there is a big difference between writing *The Dain Curse, The Maltese Falcon, Red Harvest, The Thin Man,* and *The Glass Key . . .* establishing the genre, taking off the genre then doing something different, completely different, as he did with his last two books. Also, he was finished very young in his career.

Interviewer: You are moving away from crime and physical violence to psychological intrigue and politics. In what essential ways has the White House changed in the last fifty years? Where is America heading?
Ellroy: I don't know and I would never comment for attribution on the current political scene today. I'll tell you, I voted for George Bush because I wanted to repudiate Gore and Clintonism and nobody hates Bill Clinton more than me unless it's a wonderful American pundit, Bill O'Reilly,[3] or the wonderful author of the *Book of Virtues,* William Bennett, or Christopher Hitchens, the writer for *Vanity Fair.* My only recent political occupation was hating Bill Clinton; now that Clinton's out of office, I don't have much to do.

Interviewer: Well . . . best politician in the last fifty years?
Ellroy: Harry Truman?

Interviewer: One thing you'd say to George W. Bush.
Ellroy: Sign the Kyoto Accord.

Interviewer: Why?
Ellroy: To protect the animals.

Interviewer: Your thoughts on gun control . . . You are an advocate, aren't you?
Ellroy: No, I own thirty guns. I have a commemorative firearms collection. I think responsible people should be able to own guns for sporting purposes and home protection. I think *assault* weapons should be banned. I mean, you're not going to go hunting with a machine gun. There's no reason for that.

Interviewer: But some people do . . . Would you ever consider moving to Europe for a time?
Ellroy: No, I only want to live at home, Kansas City.

Interviewer: And this is where you want to spend the rest of your life?
Ellroy: Absolutely.

(Ellroy is brought some hot water for his green tea.)

Interviewer: Female characters are becoming more prominent in your books, would you care to comment on this?
Ellroy: I'm getting older; I'm seeing a broader base of humanity. I made a conscious effort to do this as a direct result of having confronted my mother in *My Dark Places*, and I want to write more profound books. I mean *The Cold Six Thousand* is largely about gangmen getting older and this book is intimate in a way that none of my previous books have been.

Interviewer: By rediscovering your mother then reconciling yourself with women, how . . .
Ellroy: No, no, I am not reconciling myself with women; it was reconciling myself with *this* woman and realizing that I had to do this.

Interviewer: And the consequences for the rest of the women are . . .
Ellroy: The rest of the women are just fiction. There's only one woman in my life, my wife. The rest of them are just fiction.

Interviewer: In what way did writing *My Dark Places* mean a turning point in your life as a man and as a writer?
Ellroy: I learned . . . as a writer I learned a great deal about myself. I plumbed my origins and this gave me a greater resolve to show the larger diversity of plot and motive in my next novel and to give more time to work with characters, and I think this all comes to fruition in *The Cold Six Thousand*.

Interviewer: What are "Wet Arts?" It's a term I'm not familiar with.
Ellroy: Wet Arts are killing arts as defined by intelligence agencies: strangling, neck-slicing, obviously . . .

Interviewer: And these things really go on?
Ellroy: Oh yeah!

Interviewer: Is it true you don't eat meat?
Ellroy: No, I don't eat meat. I'm an animal lover. You're an animal lover, right?

Interviewer: Isn't it a bit of a contradiction? In your books there is so much blood and guts and then you don't eat meat . . .
Ellroy: Yeah, but it's human, human blood. I'd never hurt an animal. I am very soft-hearted about animals.

Interviewer: You're like a surgeon; you cut but repair rather than eat it afterwards? (laughs)
Ellroy: Yeah.

Interviewer: You have said that you want to write in a vacuum, you don't want to make references or have another author in mind when you write. Isn't there a denial, in a sense, of the influences of the real and literary world?
Ellroy: I've learned from Don DeLillo. I discovered Don DeLillo and I credit him every chance I get, but I am not in competition with Don DeLillo nor with any other writer and I am my only frame of reference.

Interviewer: But you acknowledge an influence from DeLillo?
Ellroy: Yes, absolutely, every chance I get. Specifically *Libra*. I have only read two books of his, *Libra* and *Underworld*. I write journalism, and I went to the Republican and Democrat conventions, and I went to the Eric Morales and Marco Antonio Barrera boxing match, so I partake of the real world as far as journalism goes. I have no desire to go see current movies; if something moves me, I'll go see it. Contemporary music doesn't interest me.

Interviewer: What did you think of *L.A. Confidential*?
Ellroy: I'll talk off the record. Is that on?

Interviewer: Not now. (clicks off)

Notes

1. There have been at least six documentaries focusing on Ellroy's life and work up to this point. In the 2001 documentary *Feast of Death* directed by Vikram Jayanti, Ellroy is seen having dinner at the Pacific Dining Car with several LAPD detectives. Also present is *Los Angeles Times* journalist and Black Dahlia researcher Larry Harnisch, whose theory regarding the identity of the Black Dahlia killer Ellroy had endorsed at the time. Harnish receives a grilling from the detective regarding inconsistencies in his findings.

2. One of the defining moments of the Hippie Revolution of the 1960s when an estimated 100,000 people converged on the Haight-Ashbury neighborhood of San Francisco. Similar events or "Be-ins" took place in cities throughout North America and Europe.

3. American conservative political commentator and host of *The O'Reilly Factor*. Ellroy wrote the afterword to O'Reilly's book *The No-Spin Zone: Confrontations with the Powerful and Famous in America* (2001).

James Ellroy: The Tremor of Intent

Craig McDonald/2001

From *Art in the Blood: Crime Novelists Discuss Their Craft*, published by Point Blank Press, 2006. Reprinted by permission by Craig McDonald.

James Ellroy, circa May 2001: a crime novelist at the crossroads.

At fifty-three, Ellroy was three-quarters of the way through an international book tour that had taken him across France, Italy, Spain, and Great Britain. Ellroy was pushing across North America.

In September, he planned to return to Europe to kick off what he had dubbed, "the Axis Tour."

It was an unprecedented campaign conducted by an author renowned for audacious book promotion. Maybe the biggest tour ever conducted by an established American author.

Ellroy's extraordinary efforts were paying off:

The Cold Six Thousand, Ellroy's largest and most ambitious novel, became the first of his hardcovers to crack the *New York Times* extended list.

Reviews were running in his favor.

Ellroy was thrilled by his new novel's snowballing success.

However the public image and reputation for wild readings he had spent more than twenty years cultivating had begun to tire and trouble the author. Like Ernest Hemingway's Papa persona, Ellroy's craftily conceived and constructed public image attracted fans, reporters, and filmmakers (name another living author to inspire at least five documentaries).

That image—susceptible to misunderstanding—at times threatened to eclipse the art.

Ellroy, like Hemingway, had been a shrewd and tireless self-promoter.

Like Hemingway, Ellroy was finding his cultivated celebrity cut two ways.

In 2001, James Ellroy was determined to slip the collar of genre tags and stand as a "historical" novelist, sans any "noir" or "crime" prefixes. That assertion would rub some crime novelists, such as Ken Bruen, the wrong way.

Ellroy forged ahead, experimenting with language and narrative forms most contemporaries wouldn't contemplate.

He claimed to write his books for himself and felt blessed that they were finding an audience.

Cynical cracks regarding tax write-offs aside, Ellroy's decision to donate his original manuscripts, notes, and personal papers to the University of South Carolina tacitly underscored his determination to transcend the strictures of genre. Check out that heady company: The Ellroy papers were to be archived alongside those of Hemingway, F. Scott Fitzgerald, and Joseph Heller.

Ellroy's novels were already being taught in colleges.

But Ellroy increasingly remarked about the rigors of his world tour as the campaign ground on: "Really, frankly, when you're on a tour like this you're too busy staying alive. The logistics and prosaics of this kind of tour more than anything beats you down," he confided.

Ellroy's comments made in the following exchange proved harrowingly prescient.

Two days after this interview, he cancelled the balance of his tour. A few days later he issued a statement:

> *"It is with great regret that I have had to cancel appearances on my U.S. book tour. I have been on the road since March 12 and the effect of this global tour finally caught up with me in Chicago. . ."*

Eventually, Ellroy would write about the psychological and physical toll taken by his *Cold Six Thousand* tour in one of his last articles for *G.Q.*

Interviewer: Your biggest tour?
Ellroy: Oh yeah, it's my biggest tour by far.

Interviewer: How are you holding up?
Ellroy: I'm holding up. I'm holding up . . . The book's doing great. And that thrills me. It's all about getting a good night's sleep. If you can sleep, you've got it made. If you can't sleep, you're fucked.

Interviewer: You have an international reputation and following. Why this scale of tour at this point in your career?

Ellroy: It's a huge book. It's a daring book. It's the whole of the 1960s—five years of it and the great key events. There has never been a book like this about the American 1960s. It's the centerpiece of a trilogy. This seemed to be the book to do it for.

Interviewer: You were out promoting translations first. Is the translation ever really the book—particularly with this book? The language in this novel is very specific.

Ellroy: The style is very specific. The story and plot of a book always mandate the style. I became aware of style when I was writing *L.A. Confidential* and had to cut it down 150 pages. The story was thematically and dramatically inviolate but too long. I started removing words. I shaved 130 pages. When I began to write *White Jazz* in the conversational first-person style it felt flat to me. I cut and cut and cut. I saw that I had developed a style directly consistent with the character, Dave "the Enforcer" Klein, a white racist cop in 1958 L.A. whose life is burning down and who gets hooked, inexplicably, on black bebop jazz. From that point, I became aware of language and all its implications. The style of *The Cold Six Thousand* is a direct representation of the violence of the American 1960s—the violence of the inner and outer lives of the three main characters. It is comprised of shorter rather than longer sentences and a good deal of racial invective because it is a novel of racial hatred and attempts to derail Martin Luther King and the Civil Rights Movement. The next book will be in an entirely different style. It may be a style that stresses concision. It may not be.

Interviewer: If you are not reading *The Cold Six Thousand* in English, I'm not sure what you're getting.

Ellroy: My wife speaks fluent French, and they say the French translation is great. The Spanish translation is supposed to be great. Ditto Italian. Dutch? You know, who knows?

Interviewer: Do you manage, or even attempt, to write when you are touring?

Ellroy: I try to sleep. No, you can work and you can travel and you can sleep and make a few phone calls and that's the extent of it.

Interviewer: *The Cold Six Thousand* has gone through five drafts. If one were to look at draft one and number five, what would stand out as the big difference?

Ellroy: You'd see how much more precise the language is. How much more stylized. The style of this book, which some critics love and some critics hate, is extremely coarse and vulgar. It's full of racial invective. It is full of odd riffs on Yiddish, French, and Spanish. It's a direct representation of both the violence of the events that I describe and the violence of the inner and outer lives of the three main characters. I wanted a perfect ordering of words. I wanted a perfect reworking of the American idiom, and I think I achieved it with this book.

Interviewer: Positive reviews seem to be running about three-to-one over the negative. It is the voice that seems to be singled out by a lot of the critics who haven't been charitable to the new novel. Does that affect you at all in terms of the third volume?

Ellroy: No. Just kiss my fucking ass. No. There's a couple of reviewers—and you're right, it's about three-to-one—the negative reviewers say the book is sloppy. Well, there's not a word out of place in this entire book. There is not a plot thread that isn't buttressed. There isn't a thread of incident or circumstance or character that isn't layered-in seamlessly. You have to develop this tack: If you don't like my books, kiss my ass. Or you'll write books for other people. Or you'll write books for the critics. Or you'll write books for a perceived readership. You know, I've written every book I've written for myself and I've developed a readership and that says something. This book scares people.

Interviewer: From sentence one.

Ellroy: That's it. In paragraph one, the word "nigger" is a warning.[1]

Interviewer: It seems like people on this tour are really trying to pin you down in terms of getting you to delineate between the fictional and nonfictional elements of the novel.

Ellroy: They want to know, and I try to head them off at the pass and say the one question I never answer is what is real and what is not. What thrills people about this book is the combination of complexity, the language, the style, the scope, and the ugliness of it. You are in the minds and the souls of these horrible guys who are nevertheless empathetic on some levels. You love these guys. When Pete Bondurant kills those guys in the middle of the heart attack, you love the guy. My wife came up to me, put her hands on my shoulders and said, "Do not fuck with Pete Bondurant, or Pete Bondurant will fuck with you." Women love Pete Bondurant.

Interviewer: He's the first character of yours I can think of who actually has a committed relationship.

Ellroy: Well, yeah. I know, I know. He doesn't even look at other women. And he loves his cat.

Interviewer: This current series was a trilogy from the get-go.

Ellroy: It was a trilogy from about two-thirds of the way through *American Tabloid* when I realized, "Oh shit, it's three books."

Interviewer: When you were writing *American Tabloid*, how locked-in were you regarding the arcs of the characters that continue on through the subsequent books?

Ellroy: Everything was set up in *American Tabloid* from the outline stage to be continued on through *The Cold Six Thousand*. If you look at Littell, his Jesuit background, his liberalism, his relationship with Mr. Hoover, it's all there. Pete Bondurant's reflexive yet committed anticommunism . . . his longing for a woman early on in the book . . . his sentimentality toward animals. He's always trying to avoid hitting stray dogs . . . and stray 'gators, when he's down in the Everglades.

Interviewer: In between hits.

Ellroy: In between hits. Yeah. Littell assumes the psyche, the manipulative qualities of Kemper Boyd of *American Tabloid*. He gets stronger and stronger and stronger throughout that book, yet there is still a bumbling quality to him. And, of course, he miscalculates egregiously as far as Mr. Hoover is concerned.

Interviewer: Let's talk J. Edgar Hoover.

Ellroy: Gay Edgar Hoover? I just gave him the best lines in the fucking book. I don't believe for one iota that J. Edgar Hoover ever had sex with man, woman, or beast. I do not believe that he went in drag to the Waldorf Astoria. He was much too extreme, much too ugly to ever successfully impersonate a woman. It's my wife's theory that Clyde and Gay Edgar were an old Victorian gay couple that enjoyed their antiques and their rare dogs and never did the dirty dog deed.[2] That's the way I have portrayed him. All of J. Edgar's sexuality, in fact all of his personality, because he only appears in telephone transcripts in this story, is sublimated into language.

Interviewer: Between *American Tabloid* and *The Cold Six Thousand*, it's been five, six years?

Ellroy: It's been six years. Of course, I wrote *My Dark Places*.

Interviewer: Right, you put a hell of a memoir in the middle there. But has that—combined with the *G.Q.* articles and the TV and movie scripts—contributed to the uncharacteristically long period between novels?

Ellroy: Film work is stuff I do for the money, and I go into it with the assumption it will never be made into a movie. I'm good at it, and it's very fast for me. I do a lot of journalism, and I love feature journalism. I also published the book, *Crime Wave*, a collection of my *G.Q.* pieces. There will be a second book of *G.Q.* pieces, I would think between this novel and the next.

Also, I like to *think.* It's my biggest book, *The Cold Six Thousand*, and I like to think and I like to brood and I like to plot and plan. And I like to deliberate. I've never read this book, parenthetically, but there's an Anthony Burgess book called *The Tremor of Intent.* I remember seeing a *Reader's Digest* condensed version of *The Tremor of Intent* and the title stuck in my head. I like to savor the tremor of intent where I think of how the next several years of my life will be eaten up by the creation of an epic novel where I will live with the characters.

I'm to this day in awe of the fact that I can do what I do as well as I do it and write books on the scope that I write. I love big things. I love an epic film. I love an epic piece of music. A great symphony or concerto. A sustained work for solo piano. That I can do this . . . it continues to blow my mind and I savor it. What I am savoring now in the odd moments when I'm not thinking this book tour is going to kill me—and fretting over every new little dot on my arm and thinking it is a malignant melanoma and I have six months to live even though I know it is not—is the tremor of intent. My mandate now is to re-create 1968 to 1972 America. To create a new language. To live with the three characters who will carry the story in the next book and that takes a lot of time.

Interviewer: You're thinking of doing something about Warren G. Harding. In the interest of glimpsing the creative process, how did that idea come to you?

Ellroy: I've wanted to write about the ascent of a political figure for a long time.

Interviewer: There's a lot there for you to work with. Alleged poisoning. The occult . . . all that scandal.

Ellroy: There is. Yeah, there is. Also the rumor that he was black or that there was black blood.

Interviewer: Now, you mentioned earlier, in a joking fashion, your skin and your concern over new marks or blemishes and so forth. A number of journalists in your recent interviews seem fixated on your perceived fixation regarding your own health.

Ellroy: No. No. I've said at this time in my life I am concerned about being healthy and everything else. This is what they don't understand: No psycho could write these books. Nobody who isn't superbly disciplined, who doesn't attempt to lead a healthy, moderate, well-contained, decent life would have the energy to write books like this. My health is fine. What happens is you don't sleep for a couple of nights in a row, you're out there, you're drinking too much coffee, you're a little bit whacked (looking at his arm) and you're going *"what's that?"* and "Aaaggghh." Or as a journalist said to me, "Jesus, man, you're doing that in Europe? I don't have to go to Europe to do that." But no: There are these people who expect me to be a certain way. Are you coming to the gig tonight?

Interviewer: Oh yeah.
Ellroy: I know how to talk in front of an audience.

Interviewer: Do you get stage fright at all?
Ellroy: No. I love it. I love it. I know how to talk in front of an audience. I know how to read. There are secrets, inherent. For one thing, the shtick that I do tonight—the introductory shtick—sounds off the cuff? I do it every night. It's grooved. The reading I'm going to give tonight? It's grooved. Yeah. You groove one reading so that you can maintain audience eye-contact and you can read for emphasis. And you get better and better at it. I started it in Great Britain—I picked these two excerpts that I read. Also you never tax your readers with long readings. You *don't* do it. *Forty-minutes? Oh-my-God.* And how many people who can't read? You should read something funny. Something fast. Something engaging. A little bit shocking and profane. Get the fuck *off.* I read for ten or twelve minutes (snapping fingers): It's over. Yeah.

Interviewer: [Gesturing at a stack of Ellroy profiles] Has anyone caught you yet? Caught James Ellroy, circa 2001?
Ellroy: [Long pause] I'm tired of myself, if you want to know the truth.

Interviewer: You mean your public image?
Ellroy: Yeah. I'm tired of myself. I'm tired of the story of my mother's mur-

der. You know: You haven't asked question one about my mother's murder. You read *My Dark Places* and you don't need to. That is the word on that. This book goes on the *New York Times* bestseller list on Sunday. It's on the *Publisher's Weekly* list and the *Book Sense* list. I've never had a hardcover on the *NYT* list before.

Interviewer: *The Black Dahlia* didn't?
Ellroy: In paperback, for one week, at fifteen. So that's fourteen years ago. The thrill—not so much the anointment of the *New York Times* bestseller list and the other ones—but the thrill behind it, is a shitload of people are buying the book and reading it.

Interviewer: It's a testament to something that *The Cold Six Thousand* is the book that's going to crack the list for you. It's challenging literature. It's also the middle book in a trilogy.
Ellroy: As Paul Gray said, "Pick it up if you dare; put it down if you can." You know, that's it more than anything else. When I get back home and I start brooding and thinking and looking at the beautiful dust jacket of this book, well, then it will all start coming into focus for me. But really, frankly, when you're on a tour like this you're too busy staying alive. The logistics and the prosaics of this kind of tour more than anything beats you down. Get to the airport. Get checked in. Curbside check-in. Tip money—carry the big roll of tip money. It's about logistics. I hate travel. I *hate* travel. I don't mind driving to the next town. But *fuck:* Travel in general . . . *noooo.*

Interviewer: This book is literature. It may therefore be a book that accumulates further regard, or respect, over time—some people may be a few years catching up to it.
Ellroy: Some critics, yeah.

Interviewer: You've stated, I think it's fair to say repeatedly, recently, a desire to shake off the mantle of "noir," or "crime writer." Particularly after the film, at this point you could probably rewrite and recast *L.A. Confidential* twenty times under twenty different titles and float a fine career. Will fans and critics permit you to move beyond genre?
Ellroy: Yeah. Yeah. It's odd. It's quite often the first question you get—*L.A. Confidential*. It's a great movie and did wonderful things for me. But as you know, the movie is 20 percent of the book, if that. It's a wonderful movie and a salutary work of art.

Interviewer: You're asked to weigh in a lot on topical matters—everything from politics to the death penalty.

Ellroy: Here's where we get to a point where I coin a phrase. Actually, my wife coined it: "The specious proximity of media." Why—this happens all the time, particularly in academic communities—should I comment on George W. Bush? This is like going to England and the little guy with a brogue says, "Hey lad, what do you think of the Troubles in Northern Ireland?" Or, you go to Berkeley and the androgynous human being asks, "What do you think of gay rights?"

Interviewer: You've written and talked *a lot* about your wife. In *My Dark Places*, you described your wife, Helen Knode, as a reporter who worked for "a lefty rag." Others have described her as a staunch feminist and have expressed shock she married someone who writes books like you do. How do the two of you blend, politically, philosophically? Based on what's been written, I can't quite visualize the two of you sitting down together to watch Bill O'Reilly.

Ellroy: Are you an O'Reilly fan?

Interviewer: In doses.

Ellroy: Men like him. And I guess some women, too. Helen is a moralist. I am a moralist. Bill O'Reilly is a moralist. That's what it is, there. Helen has that wonderful quality that you see in evolved people: She thinks personal honor and personal morality are the paramount human qualities and that's where we coincide. Helen worked for a liberal rag, a left-wing rag yeah, and it's not so much that I am right-wing . . .

Interviewer: It's partly self-evident, and you've written or said enough to allow someone to get a pretty good bead on how Helen Knode has changed you. How have you changed Helen Knode?

Ellroy: The shock of recognition when we met was huge. And she's fairer than me, in many ways, and not as fearful as me, in many ways. And not as volatile as me in some ways, and more volatile in others. But, when you find somebody like that who becomes your whole world, it opens up whole worlds and it recircumscribes the world that you have. We've been together ten years and these shocks of recognition are still coming.

Interviewer: The "James." Your given name is Lee Earle Ellroy. You changed it to "James." You've written that your father sometimes went by the pseudonym "James Brady." You don't explicitly say it: Is that where you got the "James"?

Ellroy: That's exactly right. That's exactly where it came from. It's just a simple name that goes well with "Ellroy."

Interviewer: You've met the Hilliker side of the family. Have you tried or thought about tracing your roots on the Ellroy side?

Ellroy: The old man's origins are pretty obscure. He was an only child who grew up in an orphanage. And he's not a pale-skinned redhead . . . what can I tell you? And he's a man.

Interviewer: He was part of the Pershing Expedition, right? Chasing Pancho Villa?

Ellroy: So he said. So he said. I saw a picture of him with his World War I outfit and, you know, there he is. I mean, that was him. It was taken on Armistice Day, so he was over there on Armistice Day. And there he is. That's him. You can tell.

Interviewer: Of all the breeds of dog in the world, why English Bull Terriers?

Ellroy: Bull Terriers have that wedge head. They're very friendly. They're very intelligent. They're very durable. They love humans. They're not wild about felines. They love to chew up a good cat. And they have a tendency to scrap with other dogs. But they're great. They're great kids' dogs. They're just beautiful, beautiful animals.

Interviewer: Your backlist of novels—I suspect you keep track of these sorts of things—what sells best in terms of your oeuvre year to year?

Ellroy: It comes and goes between *The Black Dahlia, L.A. Confidential*—because of the movie—and *American Tabloid.*

Interviewer: A rather recherché question about your oeuvre: How did *Silent Terror* become *Killer on the Road* in the U.S.?

Ellroy: I called the book *Killer on the Road.* Avon, who published it as a paperback original, wanted *Silent Terror*, which was their title. They foisted it upon me. When they reprinted the book—rejacketed the book—they wanted to be nice to me, so they called it *Killer on the Road*, which is *my* title.

Interviewer: You and L.A. in literature—quits forever?

Ellroy: I'm from L.A., so L.A. is in my books. I knew L.A. on a more conscious level, so I plumbed it first. I also knew the form of the crime novel intimately by the time I got to the L.A. Quartet. I wrote them and realized I had said everything I could in the crime novel and everything I had to say about L.A. So I made a conscious decision to move beyond it and write strict historical novels.

It is a question of studying history. It's a question of being able to create a human infrastructure for history—to understand history and to have the ability as a plotter to link perhaps disparate events and make them cohesive. For the race angle in this book (*The Cold Six Thousand*), I can only say that I can remember a different America. I was in the Army in Fort Bragg Louisiana in 1965 and saw Klan rallies and segregated washrooms. Being fifty-three years old is wild, because you've been around a long time, but you're nowhere near old and can recall a different world.

Notes

1. The first two lines of *The Cold Six Thousand* read "They sent him to Dallas to kill a nigger pimp named Wendell Durfee. He wasn't sure if he could do it."

2. Anthony Summers alleged that J. Edgar Hoover was a secret transvestite and was being blackmailed by the Mafia as a consequence in his book, *Official and Confidential: the Secret Life of J. Edgar Hoover* (1993). Clyde Tolson (1900–1975) was associate director of the FBI and Hoover's long-time companion. Upon Hoover's death he became acting head of the FBI, but was replaced when President Nixon appointed L. Patrick Gray.

Interview: James Ellroy

Keith Phipps/2004

From *The A.V. Club* (December 1, 2004). Reprinted by permission of Keith Phipps.

James Ellroy is a man with few secrets. After spending his early years drifting from one sordid situation to another following his mother's still-unsolved 1958 murder, he beat back a handful of addictions in the '70s, found steady employment as a caddie, and began writing. His autobiographical work—most memorably *My Dark Places*, his 1996 memoir/true-crime account of his mother's death—is unflinchingly honest, and he brings the same unblinking directness to the bad guys and the clay-footed heroes of his crime fiction. Early efforts like *Brown's Requiem* and *Killer on the Road* earned him a cult following, but he didn't truly find his voice until 1987's *The Black Dahlia*, a fictionalized account of a famous Hollywood murder that bore similarities to the death of Ellroy's mother.

The Black Dahlia initiated an overlapping series Ellroy dubbed his L.A. Quartet. *The Big Nowhere, L.A. Confidential* (adapted as a hit film in 1997), and *White Jazz* followed, advancing Ellroy's shadow history of postwar Los Angeles and further paring down his prose to a telegraphic essence. With its completion, Ellroy launched the still-in-progress Underworld U.S.A. trilogy with 1995's *American Tabloid*, which blew his often-nightmarish vision of a world driven by brutish men and shady assignations up to a national scale with a story that culminated in the J.F.K. assassination. Between that book and 2001's equally massive *The Cold Six Thousand*, Ellroy filled his time with screenwriting projects, the occasional piece of short fiction, and short pieces of nonfiction, mostly for *G.Q.* While working on the final Underworld U.S.A. installment, Ellroy recently released *Destination: Morgue!*, an anthology of autobiographical sketches, three linked novellas, and journalism that revisits unsolved murders, celebrity trials, and his own past, topics touched on in a recent conversation with *The Onion A.V. Club*.

Interviewer: Apart from autobiographical work, what opportunities does nonfiction present to you that fiction can't?

Ellroy: I get to go back to Los Angeles, my smog-bound fatherland, and indulge my curiosity in unsolved murders of women, and do things like read the Stephanie Gorman file for that [*Destination: Morgue!*] piece, "Stephanie." Ilena Silverman, now at the *New York Times Magazine*, got me to write the piece on Gary Graham. She wanted me to write a piece on the death penalty and explore the case of someone who might have been dubiously convicted, although 85 percent of me thinks that Gary Graham was guilty. Art Cooper suggested "I've Got the Goods," about tabloid journalism. I've utilized tabloid journalism in the '50s in my fiction. There was also the piece on the creative process, "Where I Get My Weird Shit," and the further autobiographical piece, "My Life as a Creep," originally entitled "Beaver Man." Can't get everything you want, kid.

Interviewer: You're back in California now, right?

Ellroy: Yeah, I live on the Monterey Peninsula.

Interviewer: You've effusively praised Kansas City. It seemed to suit you. Why leave?

Ellroy: The fuckin' heat drove me out of there. Very hot a third of the year. Monterey's beautiful: It's temperate, right on the ocean.

Interviewer: It was never the need to flee L.A. that drove you out?

Ellroy: I wanted to be somewhere else. At the time, I wanted to move east. That was in '81, around the time my first novel was published. I had never been anywhere but L.A. It was time to move.

Interviewer: Do you think having been born and raised there, and not having left for so long, gives you a perspective that other L.A. writers don't have?

Ellroy: I can write about L.A. wherever I happen to find myself, but I made a conscious decision after my L.A. Quartet books that I wouldn't utilize L.A. as the strict locale of my novel-length fiction. Hence *American Tabloid* and *The Cold Six Thousand* were set throughout all of America. I was lucky to be born there, I stayed there for many years, and I like going back periodically, but I couldn't live there.

Interviewer: Do you find yourself at a disadvantage when you're writing about New York, or Chicago, or another city?

Ellroy: No, but I trust the old Joan Didion line. She said something like, "A place belongs to the writer who claims it most obsessively." In that case, L.A. is mine. The three novellas in the back of *Destination: Morgue!* are all set in L.A.

Interviewer: The last time we spoke with you, you described yourself as "an uptight, rich, square-ass, WASP motherfucker." Does that description still fit?

Ellroy: Well, of course, there's a little bit of the tongue-in-cheek in there, given the kind of shit that I write about. That's the persona that I've adopted, and there are great elements of truth in that. But I sure as hell have a wild imagination for a motherfucker like that.

Interviewer: The "uptight" tag seems least appropriate, given where you come from and what you write about.

Ellroy: I think what I was commenting on there was the fact that I despise sordidness and low-life and avoided it at all costs. I like wholesome, homogenous, peaceful surroundings and amenable people. In that case, L.A. is out, Chicago would be out, New York would be out. The Monterey Peninsula suits me just fine.

Interviewer: You said that you coldheartedly decided to use your mother's murder to promote *The Black Dahlia*. Did you ever fear that your life story would detract attention from your fiction or change the way people read it?

Ellroy: No. The books are inextricable from me, and I repaid my debt to my mother when I wrote *My Dark Places*. I copped to exploiting her death to sell books for *The Black Dahlia*. Still, *cherchez la femme*: Look for the woman. There are always these unsolved murders of women coming back to bite me on the ass.

Interviewer: Looking at your work, it's tempting to draw a line between *The Black Dahlia* and the L.A. Quartet and what came before it. Do you feel that's when your writing started to come into its own?

Ellroy: Yes, *The Black Dahlia*, *The Big Nowhere*, *L.A. Confidential*, and *White Jazz*; there was a huge dividing line, as the two more recent novels, *American Tabloid* and *The Cold Six Thousand*, are political novels. It was rising to the occasion of *The Black Dahlia* that haunted me for so many years, that got me to write a book that fine. When I finished that book, I saw that I only wanted to write epic-length period fiction, and I've been following that lead ever since.

Interviewer: There's a shift in prose style, too. Is there any influence you can attribute that to, or was it just a matter of material, changing the way you write?

Ellroy: It came about accidentally, in that I needed to cut 150 pages of *L.A. Confidential*. It was plot-inviolate, but it ran too long. Thus I began to trim individual scenes, so that there's a telegraphic quality to the prose that fits the story I'm telling: the violence of the action and the violence of the language. I utilized that to a greater degree, stream-of-consciousness style, in *White Jazz*, which is written in the first person. Then I went back to a more standardized, more explicated style in *American Tabloid* and *My Dark Places*. The style I developed for *The Cold Six Thousand* is a direct, shorter-rather-than-longer sentence style that's declarative and ugly and right there, punching you in the nards.

It was appropriate for that book, and that book only, because it's the 1960s. It's largely the story of reactionaries in America during that time, largely a novel of racism and thus the racial invective, and the overall bluntness and ugliness of the language. And the book that I'm working on now, which is a sequel to *The Cold Six Thousand*, is a different style entirely.

Interviewer: You've been working on a lot of film projects lately. How does that differ from the publishing industry?

Ellroy: The movies will never be made. And I understood that going in. I exploited my reputation as a novelist to take rest periods between novels. A novel is very taxing. To earn money writing movies . . . I don't disdain the process—I don't condescend to the process—but I know full well that the motion-picture business is largely dysfunctional, and that the majority of all commissioned screenplays fail to be filmed for one reason or another. So I go at it to the best of my ability, but I honestly don't care if any of these screenplays I work on ever get filmed. I don't think about it.

Interviewer: You don't mind the work being lost?

Ellroy: It's all collected in my drawer, and it'll all end up in my archive at the University of South Carolina.

Interviewer: In your essay "I've Got the Goods," you allude to possibly becoming a Lutheran minister. How seriously should we take that?

Ellroy: Not seriously at all. But for all my dark curiosities and profane shtick, I'm a moral guy, and the books are moral, and I think I'm a moralist.

I've said this before, so if you see this quote on the Internet, don't be surprised: Morality in literature is largely the expositing of moral acts and their consequences, the karmic price of the perpetrators of the immoral acts, for having committed them. In that sense, I think the books are very moral.

Interviewer: You're on the record about hating the notion of closure, but you believe in redemption, correct?
Ellroy: It happens for individuals, yeah.

Interviewer: How does that come about? In your books, it seems like it's a process of plunging into the depths before you can come out the other side.
Ellroy: It is, and there's redemption in love. Generally, in my books, some bad men will find some strong women. I once told an interviewer that the subtitle for the L.A. Quartet should be "Bad Men in Love with Strong Women." There's the fact that my guys ultimately come to see the futility of their evil ways and learn the value of self-sacrifice.

Interviewer: As a moral individual, does it ever disturb you to spend so much time with men doing bad things?
Ellroy: No, and this sounds cold-hearted, I realize, but the people don't exist. They just reflect my moral concerns and my curiosities and my overall obsession with history, with re-creating it.

Interviewer: Do you have any theories as to why the public latches on to some murder cases and not others?
Ellroy: Generally, more than anything else, it's sex. There's a good sex quotient, like the Laci Peterson[1] murder: good-looking woman victim, good-looking woman girlfriend . . . I haven't followed this one.

Interviewer: How long does it take to research your big novels, versus the time it actually takes to write them?
Ellroy: Three-to-one, the actual writing of the text . . . maybe four-to-one. I hire researchers to compile fact sheets and chronologies. I give them their marching orders; I know what I want, going in. Then it's a question of putting together all my notes on character, plot, milieu, style, historical events. I start connecting them, and then I write a huge outline, a formal outline. For example, the outline for *The Cold Six Thousand* was 350 pages. The novel itself is 672 pages. It was a 1,100-page typed manuscript.

Interviewer: When you're researching these stories, you encounter all kinds of conspiracy theories. Is sorting the bullshit from the real stuff a priority? How watertight do you need these to be, factually?

Ellroy: They need to be factually valid. When I state a historical fact, it needs to be correct chronologically and in detail. Beyond that, what I'm giving you is a secret history. My themes often express the private nightmare of public policy. We all know that attending every great violent, seismic, public event, there must be small minions out there doing their dirty, ant-like work. These are my guys. You have to be able to extrapolate off the bigger events the lower-level implementation of the bigger events. Then you've got the books that I write. I think the books are factually valid that way, yes.

Interviewer: During this year's election, Slate.com polled novelists about their political leanings, and they were overwhelmingly for John Kerry. Why are most novelists Democrats?

Ellroy: Because they're misguided humanists. I would never say whom I'm voting for. I actually don't like that whole "Let's weigh in because we're a name" sensibility. I avoid that question.

Interviewer: That must be partly due to the rarity of encountering an author who doesn't toe the liberal line on most issues.

Ellroy: Oh, I'm not a liberal. People have figured that out. The third novella in *Destination: Morgue!* is called "Jungletown Jihad." It starts out with [an appearance by an] informant, Habid Rashad, a male Arab. This has got "Rhino" Rick Jensen, the narrator, and his cop partners knocking on the door of the informant. When he opens up, I describe him as a "full-drag dune coon" in a "Hussein-esque house smock" and a "boss burnoose from Bin Laden's Boutique." One cop laughs, and the other says, "Hey, Ahab the A-rab, where's your camel, motherfucker?" The walkouts I get from reading this are hilarious. I was just at a book fair in the South. I knew I'd get ten liberals and ten Christians walking out, and I did.

Interviewer: That must be something you deal with all the time: people confusing your characters' racism for your own.

Ellroy: You know what? Call me racist, and call me a xenophobe, but I'm not wild about Arab terrorists. I think they're a bunch of camel-fucking motherfuckers. And I want to make fun of them, because I'm a bad guy. And anyone out there who doesn't like it can kiss my ass. It's saying it that's so much fun. I'll admit, in some ways, even though I'm fifty-six years old, and dare I say a great artist and a wonderful human being and all that, and reasonably sensitive, there's just some part of me that's immature, that likes fucking over people and pissing them off.

Notes

1. American substitute teacher who disappeared on December 24, 2002. She was expecting her first child with her husband Scott Peterson at the time of her disappearance. Her dismembered body washed ashore in the San Francisco Bay area on April 14, 2003. Scott Peterson was convicted of first degree murder of Laci Peterson and second degree murder of the unborn child. At the time of writing he is currently serving his sentence on Death Row, San Quentin Prison.

James Ellroy: To Live and Die in L.A.

Craig McDonald/2006

From *Rogue Males: Conversations & Confrontations about the Writing Life*, published by Bleak House Books, Madison WI, 2009. Reprinted by permission of Craig McDonald.

In May 2001, I sat down with James Ellroy in the lobby of an Ann Arbor, Michigan hotel to discuss the second volume of his Underworld U.S.A. Trilogy, *The Cold Six Thousand*. The novel, the sequel to his hugely successful and much acclaimed *American Tabloid*, had just become the first of the author's hardcovers to crack the *New York Times'* best-seller list.

At fifty-three, Ellroy was three-quarters of the way through an international book tour that had taken him across France, Italy, Spain, and Great Britain. Ellroy was starting to push across North America.

It was an ambitious publicity campaign far exceeding all previous junkets attempted by an author already renowned for the most audacious of book promotions.

But Ellroy was racing toward a wall he would later write that friends and family couldn't stop him from slamming into.

As the time for my 2001 interview with Ellroy neared, I started noticing strange and ominous comments Ellroy made to interviewers in the days leading up to our exchange. He increasingly remarked about the rigors of his world tour as the campaign continued. "Really, frankly, when you're on a tour like this you're too busy staying alive. The logistics and prosaics of this kind of tour more than anything beats you down," he confided to me. He talked of his inability to get sleep, and his growing obsession with his own health.

Eventually, Ellroy would write about the psychological and physical toll taken by his *Cold Six Thousand* tour in one of his last articles for *G.Q.* (Ellroy's long-standing gig with *G.Q. Magazine* abruptly ended when he and a host of other authors were booted following the ousting of revered editor Art Cooper.)

But his ordeal was far from over.

What followed was a five-year struggle that stalled the author's writing of the final installment of his ambitious Underworld U.S.A. Trilogy and changed his life forever.

Ellroy, who had many years before beaten back addictions to alcohol and drugs, found himself increasingly reliant on sleep medication.

As he would later describe it, his remarkable brain turned in on itself. "My mind looped obsessively . . . I could not cut myself off from the world. All my compartments were sieves . . . My work habits were megalomaniacal . . . Anxiety drove me back to my desk at all hours . . . I did interviews with cold sweats . . . I was at the height of my public recognition and going insane."

As he would reveal in a long, blunt, and candid essay published in *Los Angeles Times Magazine* in the late summer of 2006, in the summer of 2003, Ellroy overdosed three times. He enrolled himself in a rehab program, and, eventually, endured the end of his marriage to novelist/journalist Helen Knode.

The following exchange consists of two interviews conducted with James Ellroy. The first took place in autumn of 2004, when Ellroy was starting his climb back. He was promoting *Destination: Morgue! L.A. Tales*, an omnibus of his uncollected nonfiction and essays penned for *G.Q.*, as well as three new novellas featuring L.A. homicide detective "Rhino" Rick Jenson and his alliterative inamorata Donna Donahue—a thinly disguised version of actress and Ellroy friend Dana Delaney.[1] (Delaney was also the author's choice to portray his mother in any adaptation of his memoir *My Dark Places*.)

Jenson is obsessed by the unsolved murder of Stephanie Gorman[2]—a particularly brutal unsolved sex crime that also receives nonfiction treatment in *Destination: Morgue!*

James Ellroy had recently resettled from Kansas City to Carmel, California, when we spoke in 2004.

He had also made news when he penned an introduction for the book *Black Dahlia Avenger* in which retired LAPD detective Steve Hodel claimed his own father, George Hodel, killed Elizabeth Short—the woman at the center of Ellroy's breakthrough novel, *The Black Dahlia.*

While Ellroy questioned some aspects of the case as laid out by Hodel, he expressed his belief that Hodel's solution was likely as close to the correct one as can ever be expected.

Ellroy had also recently taken a more active role in a different medium, serving as executive producer of the documentary *Bazaar Bizarre* about now-dead Kansas City serial killer Bob Berdella.

The second interview was conducted in August 2006—a quick, rat-tat-tat exchange as Ellroy was poised to board a plane for Venice for the premiere of a lavish film adaptation of his 1987 novel, *The Black Dahlia*.

In September 2006, director Brian DePalma unveiled his film adaptation of Ellroy's novel starring Josh Hartnett, Scarlett Johansson, Aaron Eckhart, Hilary Swank, and Mia Kirshner as Elizabeth Short. Ellroy was sufficiently pleased with the adaptation to hit the road in support of the film and the special movie rerelease of his novel incorporating a new afterword.

Ellroy was newly single, and had recently moved back to L.A., vowing to write only Los Angeles-centered novels after completing the final volume of his ambitious trilogy.

Ellroy's self-revealing essay about his five-year trauma appeared just a few days before I spoke with the author.

In that piece, Ellroy asserted the essay would stand as one of his last autobiographical statements and insisted his publicist would be instructing future interviewers that Ellroy would "walk" if confronted with any further personal questions.

If Ellroy holds to that sentiment, our brief conversation conducted before Ellroy flew to Venice may stand as one of James Ellroy's last unfettered interviews . . .

October 2004

Interviewer: Do you miss the outlet/platform of *G.Q.*? I had the sense you had great latitude in terms of subject matter and the topics you focused on.
Ellroy: Great question. Wonderful introductory question. The answer is *yeah*, I do. A bunch of events interceded last year in June of '03. They fired Art Cooper—a legendary magazine editor, inducted in the Magazine Editors' Hall of Fame. They brought in a fella who wanted to reshape the magazine. Astonishingly, I got the boot. Odd.

Interviewer: Given the fact that you'd won, at least twice I think, the *G.Q.* novelist of the year award, yeah.
Ellroy: Their award for literature, yeah. And, you know, I'm a man in my fifties. They fired all the mature guys.

Interviewer: I noticed there are some pieces that you wrote for *G.Q.* after

Crime Wave (the first *G.Q.* collection) appeared, that aren't in *Destination: Morgue!* Any particular significance to that? I know there was the last piece on Anne Sexton and Dana Delaney . . . something on 9/11, that was very short.

Ellroy: It was a short piece that was part of a larger piece on the terrorist bombings.

Interviewer: And the presidential piece, on the 2000 Bush/Gore race isn't here.

Ellroy: The presidential piece, which was a hilarious piece, didn't make it. It wasn't timely. Sonny Mehta thought it wasn't timely. And my piece on Bill O'Reilly isn't there. They wanted to keep it to crime and keep it to L.A.

Interviewer: Anything happen recently that you'd particularly like to have sunk your teeth into as a journalist or essayist?

Ellroy: Actually? No. I don't follow politics. I don't watch news. I went to Vegas for a couple of fights and I didn't find them moving or explicative in any way. What I love about this book here, is that it is such a primer on me . . . on my obsessions . . . on my interests . . . on my fixations. And, then, those three wild-ass novellas at the end.

Interviewer: Let's jump ahead to those. I remember in your last piece for *G.Q.*, you were talking about maybe writing some things with actress Dana Delaney as a protagonist. And you have a "Donna Donahue" here, and they are, for the most part, a contemporary set of stories, so I'm wondering, is it okay to read anything in there?

Ellroy: Well, you certainly can. Dana and I are friends. I wanted a thinly disguised Dana Delaney. I wanted a Dana Delaney stand-in. Did you enjoy the novellas?

Interviewer: I liked the last one ("Jungletown Jihad") the best. And in a way, it's funny, I wish that one had been first, because it kind of contextualizes the other two.

Ellroy: Well, keep in mind, there's chronology there. The first one where Donna and Rick meet, it's '83. Then you go to '04 and to '05.

Interviewer: And you go way out into the future.

Ellroy: Oh yeah, because Rhino Rick narrates this from heaven.

Interviewer: You've made some statements about the "crime novel" being "dead" or moving away from crime fiction. I really thought after the Lloyd Hopkins books you probably wouldn't write another contemporary cop and I think you had even indicated that that was the case. And here we are.

Ellroy: These are novellas, keep in mind. And keep in mind these are also deliberately comic. They are comic novellas. This is as dark as humor gets, I think, in many ways. You look at the last one—it's a comedy about Arab terrorists, you know. Half of whom want to blow up buildings and half of whom want to go to lap-dance layers and get blowjobs.

Interviewer: All factually accurate, if I remember the facts surrounding Atta and company prior to September 11, 2001.

Ellroy: All factually accurate. And each of the three stories ties to a sex killer from the 1950s L.A. scene.

Interviewer: Right. In the novellas, you use something you write about elsewhere in the collection in nonfiction form—the murder of Stephanie Gorman. That's an obsessive case for your detective in the novellas, Rick Jenson. What is it about that case, particularly, that keeps bringing you back around to it in this book? I guess in terms of age, she'd have been roughly a peer of yours . . .

Ellroy: She was one year and three months younger than me. We grew up four-and-a-half or five miles apart. She grew up more affluently than I did. We went to adjoining high schools. I recall the case very, very dimly from "freedom summer" for me, 1965—the year that my father died and I got kicked out of high school . . . got kicked out of the Army. It's a particularly horrible crime that should have been a signature L.A. crime had the Watts Riots not intersected. Also, it's a one-off sex crime. They were never able— and I read the file, many times—they were never able to link that killer to any other existing crime, pre or post.

Interviewer: That's a little like your mother's murder in that sense, too.

Ellroy: Yeah, but this was a deliberate, planned sex crime. My mother was a date rape that went bad.

Interviewer: You wrote an introduction recently for the book *Black Dahlia Avenger*. You don't necessarily really endorse its author's theory, but you seem to accept it as a real possibility.

Ellroy: I think it's more than that. I think he did it. I say that with some reluctance. I think a lot of the underpinnings of the story don't work. He posited a great and far-reaching LAPD cover-up and conspiracy and can't prove any of it. Here's the thing that gets me about it: When I read the book in hardcover, I wasn't convinced.

Interviewer: The alleged pictures of Elizabeth Short, alone, threw me. Those clearly were not pictures of Elizabeth Short.[3]
Ellroy: Well, here's the thing: Here's what you have to believe—this is the jump between hardcover and paperback—at the very least, George Hodel was a psychopathic libertine. He was tried for incest with his fourteen-year-old daughter. A very bad guy. He had eleven kids by various women. One kid grew up to be a homicide detective in the LAPD—odd, in itself. Okay, dad dies. Steve Hodel sees his personal effects and comes to the conclusion, erroneously, I think, that those pictures are of Elizabeth Short. He becomes convinced and posits in a very well-layered, circumstantial case, his theory that his father killed Elizabeth Short. I'm unconvinced.

In the lag-time between the hardcover and paperback publications, an *L.A. Times* reporter named Steve Lopez unearths the D.A.'s bureau file on the Short case. George Hodel, Steve Hodel's father, was the number one suspect. They had bugged and hotwired all his telephones and his house. They have him on tape in a certified transcript from February of 1950 saying, "So what if I killed the Black Dahlia? They can't prove it. The only one who knows it is my secretary and she's dead."

So, reluctantly, given that, I'll buy that. This feels to me, almost, like divine intervention. If indeed, as I suspect, that those pictures are not of Elizabeth Short, but he (Steve Hodel) investigates the case at great length, puts together a finally unconvincing case, but it turns out his old man was the number one suspect and admitted it on a tape. That's enough.

Interviewer: Have you had any feelers about replacing the *G.Q.* gig, at all? I seem to remember *Vanity Fair* courting you at some point.
Ellroy: They came around while I was working for *G.Q.* six or seven years ago. You know, what I do is very specific, and Art Cooper was behind it 100 percent of the time. I'm more or less convinced that the magazines that are out there right now have other agendas. I don't know American culture very well. I'm uninterested in the war on terrorism. I write about a very specific number of things. I have a very limited imagination. I think prudent magazine editors know that.

Interviewer: You've moved back to California—has that sparked anything in terms of wanting to write about L.A. again?
Ellroy: Naw. I just like the central coast here. It's amenable. It's very rarely hot.

Interviewer: It beats a Kansas City summer?
Ellroy: Boy . . .

Interviewer: The Robert Blake⁴ case is addressed in one of the pieces in *Destination: Morgue!* Have you had any more thoughts about that case since your treatment first appeared in *G.Q*?
Ellroy: I haven't followed it at all. The murder occurred in May of '01. We're in October of '04. That's three-and-a-half years.

Interviewer: Any loud, current crimes you'd like a crack at or are tracking?
Ellroy: I retain very strong friendships in LAPD. I'd bet you could cut me loose—I have several friends on the LAPD Cold Case unit—I would love to just take a walk through . . . to read some old files. I'm sure I could make it happen. But then of course I'd get obsessed like I did with Gorman. My life would get disrupted again and I can't afford that right now.

Interviewer: It really became that big an investment of your time working on that piece?
Ellroy: Yeah. Yeah: There were five boxes of files and memorabilia and miscellany to read through. And you better read through 'em all. In a way you have probably eight pages of reconstruction down to the most-minute detail in essential chronological order (in "Stephanie"). In order to get that, I had to read five file boxes and take notes.

Interviewer: That's a bigger investigative record than you went through for your entire book-length account of your mother's murder for *My Dark Places*, isn't it?
Ellroy: Yes.

Interviewer: I recently watched a screener of *Bazaar Bizarre*, about Kansas City serial killer Bob Berdella. You're executive producer for that film. Did you know much about that case before the documentary?
Ellroy: No, (director) Ben Meade is a good friend of mine, and I was presented with material by Ben. You know, we're doing a *Destination: Morgue!* documentary together later in the year. Regarding Berdella, Ben presented me with specific pieces of film to view, and then I commented on them. I haven't seen the movie, but apparently, a lot of my comments are hilarious.

Interviewer: You haven't seen it?

Ellroy: No. But he's a good filmmaker. We're going to do that documentary, called *Destination: Morgue!* later in the year. It will be dramatized sequences from the book—not the fiction but the nonfiction. Dramatized pieces, my voice, to camera narration—interviews with Steve Cooley, district attorney of Los Angeles County and maybe even another dinner with my policemen friends focused on some crime. Then we're going to do a nonfiction segment on those three killers—(Stephen) Nash, (Donald Keith) Bashor, (Harvey) Glatman—who inform the text of the three novellas.

Interviewer: Now that you don't have that *G.Q.* outlet, I just wonder what you do when you're not working on a novel. Do you continue to write short stories and novellas?

Ellroy: No. I do film and TV work to earn money, and to bide my time between writing the novels, which is all-consuming.

Interviewer: There's a lot of pressure on people these days to write a book a year. Usually to pretty poor effect. You've resisted that and actually gone the other route. Are you under any pressure to put more out there?

Ellroy: No. I'm fifty-six years old and healthy. I have seven more novels that I want to write in my lifetime and I'll probably write more.

Interviewer: But you *do* have seven in mind? I know you were talking about a Warren Harding book.

Ellroy: Oh yeah, Warren Harding is right after this book (volume three of the *Underworld U.S.A. Trilogy*). I've got a book about Wisconsin—a generational novel about Wisconsin.

Interviewer: About a family of patrolmen, right?

Ellroy: I'm not sure yet. But, after that point, more will be revealed. Yeah. I think I write a great book—and they're huge. And that's the kind of book I like to read. I don't want some shit fucking generic motherfucker toadstool of a book. Oh, I can't wait for the latest, you know?

Interviewer: How is that going? Are you fairly deep into the writing of volume three now?

Ellroy: Yeah, yeah. I'm deep into it. I'm not promising a delivery date, but you know, it's *huge.* It's bigger than *The Cold Six Thousand.*

Interviewer: I know you've said you want the three novels, literally, to be successively larger. I'm wondering how you sustain your concentration and your interest across this many years.

Ellroy: The interest is *easy.* The concentration . . . you need a very, very strong superstructure. And you need the outlines that you and I discussed when we were in Ann Arbor that day (May 2001). You know, you need a big, big superstructure and the determination to make it work. Now, one of the big revelations for me, early on as a writer when I was into writing *The Big Nowhere*, was that I realized I could execute whatever I could conceive of.

Interviewer: That's . . . amazing. That's stunning. That puts pressure on you, though. If you have that ability, you've got to use it . . . not lay back.
Ellroy: *Yeah.*

Interviewer: Do you read a lot of poetry? You drop these lines of poetry into interviews, articles . . . and I've seen you do it across a number of years. Auden, particularly.
Ellroy: You know, I've read through Auden. A lot of the shit I don't understand, and I don't like and I don't *get.*

Interviewer: I know you read Anne Sexton.[5]
Ellroy: *Ohhh baby!* Oh man!

Interviewer: Hot but doomed.
Ellroy: Craig, you're brilliant. You've just defined Anne Sexton: hot but doomed. You'd do her, wouldn't you?

Interviewer: Well yeah, based on the photos I've seen of her in her prime . . . *yeah.*
Ellroy: Hah!

Interviewer: Have you written any poetry of your own?
Ellroy: Nah. But I do love Sexton. "Hot but doomed."

Interviewer: I know you say you don't read a lot of crime fiction, but have you read anything recently? And if so, what was it?
Ellroy: No. No. People tell me there are Ellroy manqués out there. I don't know who they are. I'm always getting some fucking 1950s-noir pastiche in the mail.

Interviewer: I'm sure. I've heard of a couple and I've picked up one or two to look at, but other than milieu, it's not doing what you do. Although I did run across a song recently by L.A.-born, Texas-based songwriter Tom Russell ("Tijuana Bible") about Johnny Stompanato that had to have been inspired by the L.A. Quartet . . .

Ellroy: Did you see the movie *Collateral*?

Interviewer: Nope.

Ellroy: Well, it stinks. But there is a scene where Jamie Fox and Tom Cruise were running around doing stupid riffs on life and death and Jamie Foxx throws out the phrase, "The Big Ass Nowhere."

Interviewer: Do you go back and reread your older stuff now?

Ellroy: No.

Interviewer: Don't look back?

Ellroy: No. I concentrate on what I've got in front of me.

Interviewer: You once started and never finished a novel, I think it was called "The Confessions of Bugsy Siegel."

Ellroy: Yeah. It was a dog.

Interviewer: It's a dog?

Ellroy: Yeah, it's in my archives at the University of South Carolina.

Interviewer: I suppose there's no possibility we'd ever get *The Confessions of Dudley Smith, As Told to Dave Klein*?

Ellroy: Hah! No.

Interviewer: It's over?

Ellroy: Dudley is, let's see, he's right at 100 . . . no, he's 102, or something. He's still alive. I'm the guy who created him, so I can say when he's dead. Twenty years from now: "Alright he's fuckin' dead!" Evil dies with him.

Interviewer: Is there anything on your mind that you'd particularly like to share with your readers?

Ellroy: I like this book a lot. I like the illustrations. Kaya Christian (*Playboy* Playmate November 1967): To go back and write about having the hots for Kaya Christian, and have a picture of Kaya Christian in there . . .

Interviewer: This is a big improvement over *Crime Wave* because one of the

things I like about the original *G.Q.* articles, you did get the photos, you did get the great original illustrations, but in *Crime Wave,* the first *G.Q.* collection, you didn't. Some of the art and illustration in *G.Q.* was so nicely done.
Ellroy: *Yeah.* You know what? I miss *G.Q.* God bless 'em. I miss Art Cooper, you know? I had wonderful editors there. I had Paul Scanlon, Ilena Silverman, and Michael Hainey. I had wonderful friends there.

Interviewer: I wish you luck with the tour—it looks like another big one. I guess you've done Europe already?
Ellroy: You know what, I did France.

Interviewer: You're huge in France. What's the appeal of your stuff there?
Ellroy: Well, you know, they were the early discoverers of the *roman noir.*

August 2006

Interviewer: Mr. Ellroy . . .
Ellroy: Mr. McDonald . . .

Interviewer: I'm grateful you're taking the time for this talk. I know they've got you on the wheel for this one . . .
Ellroy: *Fuckkk* . . .

Interviewer: You're along for the press junket for *The Black Dahlia* film. The implication would be that you approve or embrace the De Palma film adaptation of your novel.
Ellroy: Oh yeah. You know what it is? It's compression. It's reduction. He isolates the themes very well . . . the sexual obsession and the triangulation—the one man with the two women. You know the book, intimately: You've got Bucky Bleichert and Madeleine Sprague (who's called "Lindscott" in the movie) and Kay Lake. You've got Madeleine and the Dahlia. You've got Kay and the Dahlia. And you've got Bucky in the middle. And you've got the triumvirate of Bucky, Lee, and Kay. So all of that is there. And it doesn't look like any fucking movie you've ever seen before.

Interviewer: It was filmed in some European backwater, right?
Ellroy: It was filmed in Bulgaria and the only Anglo-Saxons in the movie are the four above the title. Yeah, a lot of Slavs in this one, you know. Overall, I'm well served by it. And it's going to sell me a lot of books.

Interviewer: In your new afterword to the novel, you venture that the film could expand your reading audience exponentially. The sense I got from that is that you regard this as a potentially bigger film phenomenon than *L.A. Confidential* proved to be . . .

Ellroy: *L.A. Confidential* was a very good film. What this brings to mind though is just the power of motion pictures to reach an audience and grab 'em by the nuts very fast. That's rather astonishing to me. I don't take movies as seriously as I take novels. I think the novel is a more profound art form, chiefly because it's indigenous to only one person. And that stated, I think a shitload of people are going to see this thing.

Interviewer: Guy Pierce as Ed Exley seemed to be the revelation for you in the film adaptation of *L.A. Confidential*. Who pole-armed you in *The Black Dahlia*?

Ellroy: Listen, Josh Hartnett is by and large very, very good. Here's one of the reasons why, just coincidental: He physically resembles Bucky Bleichert, unlike anyone else has in the film adaptation of one of my books. Which is to say, physically he resembles me. It's just coincidence—tall, lanky, dark-haired, pale. He's sort of youthful. He reads the voice-over narration very well, so that offsets his physical youth.

He's good at projecting cognition. Bleichert is a character who is always measuring and thinking, as I say in the afterword. And Mia Kirshner breaks your heart as Betty Short.

Interviewer: I've always liked her as an actress. She seems perfect for the part.

Ellroy: You know what my ex-wife said—my most recent ex-wife? She said, "I think you should go to the Venice film festival and fuck Mia Kirshner. Because it's the closest you'll get to fucking Betty Short and by extension your *mother*. *Oooh*, that's dark, huh?

Interviewer: That's *very* dark.
Ellroy: Helen Knode!

Interviewer: You pick your ex-wives well.
Ellroy: Helen Knode!

Interviewer: Have you revisited or reread the novel in preparation for the junket and so forth?

Ellroy: I'm doing a reading tour, Craig. I'm also going out with Bruce Wagner[6] and Dana Delaney, our friend. I'm reading from Bruce's new novel, *Memorial*. Bruce is reading from *The Black Dahlia*. And then Bruce, Dana, and I, at the Hammer Museum, are reading from both books.

Interviewer: In 2007, the Black Dahlia murder case will have its sixtieth anniversary. Your novel will be twenty years old. How do you assess the book now?

Ellroy: I'm a sixteen-book writer and I've got four signature books: *The Black Dahlia*, *L.A. Confidential*, *American Tabloid*, and *My Dark Places*. That's pretty great. It's my first signature book. It *may be* my signature book. It is the last gasp of my pure unconsciousness as a writer. I mean I just wrote that book on instinct—and no lack of skill, certainly. But that book is my heart. That book, and *My Dark Places*, that's my heart. *American Tabloid*, *L.A. Confidential*, *White Jazz* . . . *Cold Six Thousand*, especially, that's my intellect.

It's just an uncommonly obsessive book. It's an uncommonly obsessive book about a certain kind of unvarnished maleness.

Interviewer: The Black Dahlia case crept into your first novel, *Brown's Requiem* . . . it's in your second novel. In *Clandestine*, Dudley Smith describes his role in the Black Dahlia case. But his actions are given to another in the actual *Dahlia* novel.

Ellroy: Yeah, to Fritzie Vogel. You know what that is—that was in deference to John Gregory Dunne's *True Confessions*. Dudley Smith is an Irish immigrant and that was such an Irish book (Dunne's). And I know absolutely shit about Irishness. Or about *Catholicism*.

Interviewer: A number of books about Elizabeth Short's murder have been released recently, and more are set to come out around the time of the film . . .

Ellroy: We're trying to find a language for this horrible act—the murder of Betty Short. Imaginative people want to certify their language as authentic. I don't. I gave you the most psychologically sound, pathologically valid, lunatic language that I was capable of in describing Betty Short's death. And I have not the slightest idea who did it.

Interviewer: Some more has been revealed in recent years about Elizabeth Short and her past and her character . . . implications about her physical anatomy that may or may not have been true. Other novelists have revised early works . . . John Fowles did it with *The Magus*. Would you go back to

that novel and tweak it at some point?
Ellroy: Nah. I already wrote it.

Interviewer: Does this close out the Dahlia now for you?
Ellroy: It closes it out. After this interview I go to Venice tonight for the Venice Film Festival—it's a tough life, but somebody has to live it—then I have a junket day and the premiere on the sixth of September. Then I have bookstore appearances with Bruce and Dana and by myself. Then a court TV documentary. That's American crime writers on their favorite cases. Mine, though, is different. It's Michael Connelly, Lisa Scottoline, Jonathan and Faye Kellerman, individually. My case is my mother's case and I narrate and host it. And that's it.

After this November—roughly the ninth—I will never answer another personal question. I will never discuss the Black Dahlia or my mother ever again. *Ever* again. When I go out for the new novel when it comes out, the publicist will inform everybody no personal questions or Ellroy will walk out of the room, like *that*.

Interviewer: I read your long new essay in the *L.A. Times* . . .
Ellroy: Yeah, yeah, I've had a wild five years.

Interviewer: It's been a lot of water under the bridge, my friend. I grasped the essay's implicit and explicit assertion that it stands as your last autobiographical statement. Honoring the spirit of that piece, I will only say it's very bluntly self-disclosing. It reminded me of a similar wrenchingly confessional piece penned by F. Scott Fitzgerald.
Ellroy: "The Crack Up"?

Interviewer: Right.
Ellroy: Tell me about that—he cracked up and he wrote about it?

Interviewer: He did. He wrote a fairly lengthy piece, and then Hemingway, for one, absolutely reviled Fitzgerald for it publicly. Hemingway thought that was something that a fiction writer shouldn't do, or that it was some kind of breach of writing etiquette, so Hemingway mocked Fitzgerald in a short story.
Ellroy: And then Hemingway cracked up and blew his brains out . . .

Interviewer: Yeah. Yeah. Absolutely. I wonder what your feedback on that essay has been. Or have you been in a position to have feedback on the piece yet?

Ellroy: Oh yeah, yeah. The woman who edited the piece forwarded it. People were floored by it. You're always kind of humbled by that. I cracked up. I fucked up. I trashed my marriage. I'm back. I'm back and I'm really back, and if you don't believe it, *fuck you*. It's my best book yet—the book that I'm writing—and if you don't like it, shove it up your ass. And I'm happy to be back in L.A. If you don't dig L.A., or dig me, fuck you and kiss my ass. There was all of that.

Interviewer: It's an amazing piece.
Ellroy: I think it is too. I don't *ever* want to write about myself again after that. I got obsessed with a woman up in San Francisco, and I was going to mention that a little bit, but forget it. It was good, though.

Interviewer: You've moved back to Los Angeles. Do you have an eye on one of those Hancock Park big houses you obsessed over in your youth?
Ellroy: No! Shit no! Can't afford one, Craig. I can't afford one. I've got a two-bedroom apartment in a nice old building.

Interviewer: You state in that essay you will only write L.A. novels from here forward. So no Warren G. Harding novel?
Ellroy: No, I'm not doing the Harding novel. It was just a momentary thing. When I met you in Ann Arbor, that was the big plan. But I'm not.

Interviewer: Do you have a sense yet whether those L.A.-centered novels to come will be contemporary, or more books set in the twentieth century?
Ellroy: Not yet. Haven't the slightest.

Interviewer: Let me ask you then about volume three of the Underworld U.S.A. Trilogy and how that is coming along.
Ellroy: You've read *Cold Six Thousand* . . .

Interviewer: Absolutely. Couple or three times. Now volume three is—or was—to be titled *Police Gazette* . . .
Ellroy: You know, I don't know how that misinformation got out. It was just an idea for a title. Did you dig *Cold Six Thousand*?

Interviewer: I loved it.
Ellroy: Yeah. You know what, you're among the 30 percent and the brave.

Interviewer: It's a dense book. I know a few who have trouble with it. I've read it two or three times and love the book.

Ellroy: It's as fierce as literature gets. It's very difficult. It may be overly stylized for a book that complex. I'm going back and I'm finding a new language. It's every plot thread from *Tabloid* and *Cold Six* from '68 to '72. Some real narrative risks and a huge book.

Interviewer: Are you prepared to talk about the three characters who carry the book?

Ellroy: I'll tell you, Craig, off the record.

Interviewer: On the record, Pete Bondurant—back?

Ellroy: Pete Bondurant, on the record, is retired. He's still living in Sparta, Wisconsin, with Barb and the cat. The cat is still alive, though.

Interviewer: Betty McDonald's cat?

Ellroy: Yeah, Betty McDonald's cat—your namesake. It's the world's oldest fucking cat.

Interviewer: In your new afterword to *The Black Dahlia*, you assert that only you know whether Kay and Bucky still are alive. The last time I spoke with you, you asserted that Dudley Smith might still be "alive" in your world and that he will "die" at a time and place of your choosing. Ed Exley's fate also remains unknown. For a guy who's written many books regarded as noir, many of your characters' fates are left open-ended or ambiguous . . .

Ellroy: Well, Ed Exley never became governor of California . . .

Interviewer: I'm just wondering: Do your characters live on in your head to some extent, past the books? Are you still concocting private storylines or scenarios in your head for some?

Ellroy: Yeah. Ed is eighty-four and healthy.

Interviewer: The good die young.

Ellroy: The good die *hung.*

Interviewer: With *The Black Dahlia*'s release, two volumes of your quartet now have been adapted for film. Any sense of action on *The Big Nowhere* and *White Jazz*?

Ellroy: *White Jazz* is fairly far along in development with Joe Carnahan slated to direct—the man who did *Narc*. The script is good and needs some paring down. His brother Matt wrote it and it is a very faithful adaptation of my book. I think they're going out to actors now. But as always with this stuff, I'll believe it when I see it.

What I would really like to see is the three-hour *Big Nowhere*.

Interviewer: That book resonates for me a little more than some of the others in some funny ways.
Ellroy: You know what? It does for me, *too*.

Interviewer: Anything we can expect prior to volume three of the trilogy?
Ellroy: No.

Interviewer: Anything you'd like to share, Mr. Ellroy?
Ellroy: Let's see: What would I like to do? I'd like to find a woman. I need a woman, Craig. I need a woman.

Interviewer: You're on the road . . .
Ellroy: That's true. I'm on the road, so I'm keeping my eyes peeled. I'm a tall rangy guy. I look good in a white dinner jacket, and I've got one for Italy.

Notes

1. American actress. She has starred in television dramas such as *China Beach* (1988–1991) and *Desperate Housewives* (2007–2010)

2. Stephanie Gorman (1949–1965). American teenage actress who had uncredited roles in the films *Pollyanna* (1960) and *Bye Bye Birdie* (1963). She was raped and murdered by an intruder who had broken into her Los Angeles home. The case was never solved.

3. Steve Hodel discovered two photographs in his father's belongings that he believed to be Elizabeth Short. Through his research Hodel has since publicly discounted one of the photographs after finding a Filipino woman who recognized herself in the photograph.

4. American actor. Noted for playing Perry Smith in the film adaptation of *In Cold Blood* (1967). He was tried and acquitted for the murder of his second wife Bonnie Lee Bakley but was later found liable in a civil court for her wrongful death.

5. Anne Sexton (1928–1974). American poet. The epigraph to *The Black Dahlia* is taken from Sexton's poem "All My Pretty Ones": "Now I fold you down, my drunkard, my navigator, my first lost keeper, to love or look at later."

6. American novelist. Like Ellroy's mother he was born in Wisconsin but later moved to Los Angeles. Formerly married to the actress Rebecca De Mornay.

James Ellroy: *The Black Dahlia, L.A. Confidential*

Peter Canavese/2006

From *Groucho Reviews* (August 21, 2006). Reprinted by permission of Peter Canavese.

Though he has yet to have a screenplay produced, author James Ellroy scored big in Hollywood when Curtis Hanson filmed the much-lauded *L.A. Confidential*, adapted from Ellroy's novel. Ellroy's other books include *American Tabloid, The Cold Six Thousand, The Big Nowhere, White Jazz,* and the autobiographical *My Dark Places.* The documentary film *Feast of Death* retells the story of *My Dark Places* by following Ellroy around L.A. Ellroy came to San Francisco's Four Seasons Hotel to talk up *The Black Dahlia*, Brian De-Palma's film of what may be Ellroy's most celebrated novel.

Interviewer: In 1947, Betty Short was cut in half with bits of dug-out flesh and her mouth sliced wide. Brian De Palma chalks up the weird allure of the Black Dahlia case as coming from the imprint of those crime scene photos on people who've seen them. Why do you think the case has held people's imagination for so long? Is it the unsolved quality of it?

Ellroy: It's January 15, 1947. I defy you to think of anything that's happening in America, much less specifically Los Angeles, during that particular time. It's postwar years, boom economy—America is on a roll. We have no language for sexual psychopathy. We have a profound language for it today. Here's a young woman, horribly tortured, dumped in a vacant lot. It is the first media-manufactured murder. It is a primer on how certain women get dead. And it takes over the public imagination as no crime, truly, before or since.

Interviewer: In recent years, credible suspects have emerged in the Dahlia Case—

Ellroy: Hold on, Mr. Canavese. I do not talk about who really killed Elizabeth Short. Let me state for attribution: I don't know. I don't care. I wanted to create art out of the death of Elizabeth Short. That's what I've done with my book and what Brian De Palma has done with his movie.

Interviewer: I'm guessing you never made it out to the Bulgarian set?

Ellroy: I did not fly to Bulgaria to watch the movie being shot because Bulgaria's bulgarity. And I could drive five hours—I was living in San Francisco then—to L.A. So I did.

Interviewer: So were you involved at any stage in the development of the film? Did David Fincher [who abandoned the project in preproduction] or Brian De Palma ever approach you to discuss the material?

Ellroy: I had one discussion with David Fincher and one discussion with Brian De Palma. I was not an active participant in the movie.

Interviewer: You did take screenwriter Josh Friedman out to see the site of the crime scene, right?

Ellroy: Josh Friedman and I have since become good friends, yes. Josh and I had dinner at the Pacific Dining Car Steak House downtown and drove down to Thirty-Ninth and Norton to talk to Elizabeth Short.

Interviewer: What did you say to her?

Ellroy: "Betty, are you grieving/Over Goldengrove unleaving?/—you with your"—oh, shit. It's a Gerard Manley Hopkins[1] poem: "Margaret, are you grieving/Over Goldengrove unleaving?/ . . . You [sic], like the things of man, you/With your fresh thoughts care for, can you?" You know what? I didn't say that. I quoted Anne Sexton. And this is the epigraph from my novel, *The Black Dahlia*. "Now I fold you down, my drunkard, my navigator . . . to love, or look at later."

Interviewer: I know you been back to that site more than once. Do you ever hear her talking back to you?

Ellroy: No, because I'm sane, Mr. Canavese.

Interviewer: [*Laughs.*]

Ellroy: Yeah, when I start having auditory hallucinations, you know—you go out and you get the net for me.

Interviewer: Right. [*Laughs.*] I understand you were particularly impressed with Josh Hartnett and Mia Kirshner when you saw footage from the film.
Ellroy: Mia Kirshner especially. She breaks your heart. This is Elizabeth Short.

Interviewer: What does the film do best, do you think, in adapting your book?
Ellroy: It is a lush evoking of Dahlia mania. Of what Elizabeth Short's death was to people. How this obscure young woman tortured them in death. People didn't even know her, and she exerted a profound imaginative pull over them. There's that, which Mr. De Palma captures. There also is lush recapitulation of L.A. in 1947.

Interviewer: And he takes you in with that kind of manic, hellish scene with the riots at the beginning of the film.
Ellroy: Zoot Suit riots, June 1943. Do you know the story behind it?

Interviewer: Yeah. So, be honest now. There's got to be something about the film that irritates you—that you think, "Why couldn't they have gotten this right, from my novel?"
Ellroy: You always lose, in a full-length motion picture, interior monologue. No motion picture can capture all of your character's thoughts. My book is particularly ruminative. Thank God we had Josh Hartnett projecting cognition. You can tell that Hartnett's guy—he speaks the voice-over, and very well, I think—you can tell that he's always measuring and thinking. And that's important.

Interviewer: As I understand it, you're a bit of a control freak. Would you cop to that or not?
Ellroy: Sure.

Interviewer: That would seem to make you a bad fit with Hollywood be-cause—well, there's a line in the film: "Hollywood—"
Ellroy: "will fuck you enough—"

Interviewer: "when no one else will."
Ellroy: Right.

Interviewer: Have you ever attempted to obtain any, or more, creative control of your material in those films?
Ellroy: No. Here's why. Money is the gift that no one ever returns. Twenty years ago, when I was less well-heeled than I am now, filmmakers came forth and gave me twenty-five thousand bucks for the option of *The Black Dahlia*. Money's the gift no one ever returns. When's the last time someone gave you twenty-five G's for nothing? And the answer is "never." This happens to novelists. At that point, I realize well, the movie option is to the finished movie what the first kiss is to the fiftieth monogamous anniversary. Many called, few chosen. It's just a miracle that the movie got made after almost twenty years.

Interviewer: *Feast of Death* shows you shooting the shit with detectives who bestow you with an honorary badge.
Ellroy: Right.

Interviewer: And metaphorically, to me, *My Dark Places* is almost like an account of your rookie years as a detective with Bill Stoner, your experienced partner. Do you consider yourself kind of an honorary detective?
Ellroy: I'm not a detective. Many of my friends are police officers and homicide detectives. I can read and assess a homicide file fairly well, but I'm not a detective. One of the reasons I get along so well with cops is I've never wanted to be a cop. So there's none of that wannabe thing going.

Interviewer: How did you first get into that group? Or how did you first befriend a detective?
Ellroy: Well, what happened was—and you know this story—I saw my mother's murder file and decided to write a magazine piece about it. And I met Bill Stoner and we became great friends, and he introduced me to a lot of policemen.

Interviewer: In *My Dark Places*, you mention *Laura* and *Double Indemnity* as two of the ultimate cinematic projections of the detective psyche.
Ellroy: Well look at *Laura*. You've got a good-looking woman who's murdered. And a horny and lonely police detective played by Dana Andrews falls in love with a portrait of her and she turns up alive. C'mon. What's wrong with that?

Interviewer: Right. Right. And then the dark side is *Double Indemnity*. You've got the wishful thinking, and you've got the worst-case scenario.

Ellroy: Well, you know what? You meet a woman and maybe your lust for her will lead you to do things you wouldn't normally do. I've done it. I've done it recently. Can't wait to do it again.

Interviewer: What's your favorite film noir?

Ellroy: I think very few are truly artful. I think there's *Double Indemnity, Sunset Boulevard, Ace in the Hole*, Billy Wilder's three wonderful ones. *The Lineup*, Don Siegel's San Francisco, set-in-1958 film noir.

Interviewer: Ellroy fans and movie buffs will be fascinated to know that your father, for a time, worked for Rita Hayworth.

Ellroy: He told me he poured the pork to Rita.

Interviewer: Yeah, that's another unsolved mystery, right? You'll never know for sure.

Ellroy: I hope it's true. When I get to heaven, and I lock eyes with Dad— "Dad, did you really put the boots to Rita?" And I'll find Rita too. "Rita, did my Dad . . . ?" "Yeah, he was hung like a mule. He gave it to me like I never had it before. What a schlong. Had to be a yard long."

Interviewer: Yeah. [*Laughs.*] *L.A. Confidential, The Black Dahlia*, and *My Dark Places* are probably your most well-known works.

Ellroy: *American Tabloid! Time* magazine's Novel of the Year 1995.

Interviewer: I was just going to ask you: which of your novels do you feel is the most underappreciated, that you wish more people were going out and reading?

Ellroy: The early books—I think are good. There's *The Cold Six Thousand*, which is very difficult stylistically. It's the sequel to *American Tabloid*.

Interviewer: What do you think about the films of your early novels, like *Brown's Requiem*?

Ellroy: *Brown's Requiem*, no comment. *Cop*, no comment. *L.A. Confidential*, wonderful film. *The Black Dahlia*, wonderful film.

Interviewer: Very good. Did anything remain, in *Dark Blue*, of your original screenplay, *The Plague Season*?

Ellroy: No. Very little.

Interviewer: Is there any chance of ever seeing you publishing your original screenplays? I know you have several that are unproduced.

Ellroy: I may recoup publishing rights at some point. But the people—the studios that hired me to write the original screenplays—if they would prefer that I not publish them, that would be fine with me as well. I write motion pictures for the money. I don't condescend to the craft. I enjoy the work that I do. But I put no great stock in these scripts of mine being filmed. I do it for the money.

Interviewer: Can you tell me anything about the upcoming *Night Watchman* project? Did you write the screenplay?

Ellroy: I wrote a screenplay called *The Night Watchman*. I doubt if it'll be made.

Interviewer: Why is that?

Ellroy: Motion-picture dysfunctionalism trumps development every time. I would be insane to think that any original screenplay that I'm commissioned to write would ever end up as a movie. That stated, I don't condescend to the craft. I do the best work that I'm capable of, hand it to the producers, and it's up to them.

Interviewer: Yeah. It is an insane world—the amount of money that gets spent for things that never happen.

Ellroy: Yes, and there are beneficiaries, and I'm one of them.

Interviewer: [*Laughs.*] One of the funniest talk show appearances I ever saw was you and Dave Chappelle on *Late Night with Conan O'Brien*.

Ellroy: Well, Dave Chappelle is a lovely cat. And I think we discussed the creation of an equal-opportunity Klan, didn't we? Is that what we talked about?

Interviewer: Yeah, I believe so.

Ellroy: Yeah, I had a good time with him.

Interviewer: We also see in *Feast of Death*, this documentary that's about you—it's sort of the *My Dark Places* story on film—we see you working the crowd at a book event.

Ellroy: Right.

Interviewer: I think maybe people hone in on your angst so much that they don't give you as much credit for your sense of humor. Where does your sense of humor spring from?

Ellroy: I enjoy people. I'm in love with life. I've got a hard-on for life. I love to read in front of audiences. I love to perform, and I'm very good at it.

Interviewer: You have a distinct dialect both on the page, in your diction, and also in your readings.

Ellroy: Yes.

Interviewer: How did that develop? Did you consciously try to emulate any writers in your youth, or how did that come to—

Ellroy: I'm in love with the American idiom. I love profanity. I love big language. I love Yiddish. I love black hipster patois. I love racist and homophobic invective, and I know how to use it.

Interviewer: And there's a natural humor that evolves out of that?

Ellroy: Yeah. To me, humor is simply shit that confirms and thus explodes all racial and gender stereotypes. So outrageous black-pimp shit. For instance, I have a friend—black woman—who's a homicide detective who is the most—who addresses me routinely as "nigger." And in fact has recently conferred on me the status as her "main nigger." And she and I and a bunch of other cops went out to dinner Friday night—Pacific Dining Car—with a reporter from the *L.A. Times.* And we had a black gay waiter who waited on us, and my homicide cop friend addressed this guy as "Nigger, get your gay ass over here. I want a rare steak. Do not fuck with the meat. Cut that motherfucker's horns off. Wipe his ass and put him on my plate."

Interviewer: [*Laughs.*]

Ellroy: What's not to dig about that?

Interviewer: Yeah, well, there's no punches pulled. And that kind of outrageousness is just—it gets people.

Ellroy: And you know, people enjoy it and have fun with it. One of the things—a recent girlfriend of mine who was up here, who was very left-wing, thought I was full of hate because of all the language in my books. And she couldn't be more far from the truth.

Interviewer: You've said, "Closure is bullshit."
Ellroy: Yeah.

Interviewer: But has the hunger to pursue your mother's murder case dulled with time?
Ellroy: You know, listen. I was removed from the desire to solve my mother's murder case even as I actively investigated it. I knew it was an extreme long shot. I'm fine. Listen. It's not like I think about this shit all day, every day. I'm an insomniac, and the weight of my over-lived fifty-eight years on this earth traps me when I put my head down on the pillow and attempt to sleep. And, in a word, it's not mother, it ain't Dahlia, it ain't women, it ain't trauma, it ain't angst—the word is "everything." And I deal with it as best I can. And I try to be happy and, by and large, I am happy.

Interviewer: How would you describe your own prose?
Ellroy: Precise. Emphatic. They asked Ayn Rand[2] once to give—an interviewer asked Ayn Rand, "Give me an epigraph—give me an epilogue for your life." And she said, "My books are my life, and the epilogue is the four words 'And I mean it.'" That's what I would say.

Interviewer: That kind of detail, again, I think is reflective of what detectives do, right? Your precision?
Ellroy: What I tried to capture in *My Dark Places* is the metaphysic of the unsuccessful homicide investigation—leads that go nowhere. Implicitly, a narrative like that is the story of a detective's search for himself. And I did not find the man that killed my mother. I do not know who killed Elizabeth Short nor do I care. One book, *The Black Dahlia*, which is a novel, had to have a solution provided. The second book was more powerful—*My Dark Places*—for having no solution. In the course of both books . . . one fictional investigation and one real-life investigation—I got closer to myself.

Interviewer: Your father's last words to you were—
Ellroy: "Try to pick up every waitress that serves you." Yes.

Interviewer: And do you follow that advice?
Ellroy: It's a legacy I have fulfilled with mixed results.

Interviewer: Let's end it there. Thank you very much.
Ellroy: You're welcome.

Notes

1. Gerald Manley Hopkins (1844–1899) English poet and Jesuit priest. The quote is from the poem "Spring and Fall."

2. Ayn Rand (1905–1982). Russian-American novelist and philosopher. In the afterword to *Atlas Shrugged* she wrote, "My personal life is a postscript to my novels; it consists of the sentence: '*And I mean it.*' I have always lived by the philosophy I present in my books—and it has worked for me, as it works for my characters. The concretes differ, the abstractions are the same."

Engaging the Horror

Steven Powell/2008

This interview was conducted on June 12, 2008. Previously unpublished.

Interviewer: In *Killer on the Road* Martin Plunkett has a fantasy he dubs "Brain Movies" which bears some similarity to *The Big Nowhere* where Danny Upshaw uses a technique dubbed "Man Camera." Why the presence of cinematic techniques in your novels?

Ellroy: I love movies, and I'm a voyeur is the best and most direct answer. You know about my childhood. I was going around looking in windows and peeping and perving out here and there. And there's a great deal of this in this novel I'm writing now. And imagery, particularly when it comes to women and sexuality, is key to me, and thus you have a bunch of men with disordered personal lives, Martin Plunkett, Danny Upshaw in *The Big Nowhere*, and interestingly, you know both these guys are homosexuals, and they're going around looking to be eroticized by interceding in the big events, lives, and criminal cases because they have chaotic inner lives and they wanna countermand their internal chaos by imposing order on external events. That's Upshaw; it's not so much Plunkett, who's an out-and-out psychopath. But he needs to control external events, i.e. because he's eroticized by killing people.

Interviewer: Yes. I was just reading the novel *L.A. Confidential* next to *L.A. Confidential* the screenplay. I was interested to find that actually the novel seemed to be less descriptive and more visual than the screenplay at times, which appeared to be more descriptive, and I thought that's a unique thing within a novel to be that visual.

Ellroy: Yeah. Well for one thing the motion picture of *L.A. Confidential* is dramatically reduced. What is it, 18, 19, 20 percent tops of the entire story in a dramatically compressed timeframe? Different, entirely different fate for one of the three characters, Jack Vincennes. But in its concision and in its density the scenes have to be, in order to make that thing fly—it's a five-hundred-page novel, not quite five hundred pages. It needed to be very punchy. It needed to be set up visually very accurately and very quickly.

Interviewer: You mentioned that as a novel the outline for *L.A. Confidential* was originally the size of a small novel, so is it fair to say this sparse writing style that you've developed that it came about perhaps by accident or was there more design to it than that?

Ellroy: Well the outline for *The Black Dahlia* was 144 pages, slightly more than that for *The Big Nowhere*. And *L.A. Confidential* was 211 pages, and then the outline for *American Tabloid*, which was my longest novel to date—just under six hundred pages, was 250. And what happened was there was an editor at Warner Books who thought the book was too long in its existing form, *L.A. Confidential*, albeit dramatic and violent, and she wanted me to make cuts for the sake of publishing costs. And that's how I developed that style, and then subsequently when I wrote the concluding book of the quartet, the direct sequel of *L.A. Confidential*, *White Jazz*, I started the book out in a more normal, conversational first person style—it felt flabby to me. And then I realized that Dave Klein's voice, panicked, insomaniacal influenced—he's a racist cop in late 1958 L.A. His life is burning down largely as a result of bad karmic juju that he's created—and he gets hooked inexplicably on black bebop jazz despite his racism. And that's when I developed the fractured, dissipated style of *White Jazz*, which I'll never go back to. Big, big elements of it, and I think excessively so in *The Cold Six Thousand*, but the novel I'm writing now, the third book of this trilogy, it's a much more elegant, fully explicated style because it's what the story dictated. And I try to learn from the mistakes of the previous book.

Interviewer: Yes, that style in *The Cold Six Thousand* did put off a lot of reviewers, a lot of people. I think why I found it so riveting, for me a big draw of your work is it's so visual. It's action packed, never a dull moment. I didn't understand some of the criticism that it was too distancing.

Ellroy: I think the criticism is valid, Mr. Powell. I think that the book is too complex and somewhat too long and that the style is too rigorous and too challenging in its presentation of a very complex text. And so although I'm writing a book which will easily be as long as *The Cold Six Thousand* now, it is a more explicated style and a somewhat less complex story.

Interviewer: Yes. Please call me Steve by the way.

Ellroy: Steve, yeah. Call me Dog, Steve.

Interviewer: The excesses in your work, the excess of violence that puts a lot of people off. You also have this kind of Demon Dog persona where you have what you've dubbed "Dog humor," which is so offensive it becomes very funny because you know you don't really mean that kind of bigotry. Do you think there's a link between the excesses of language in Dog humor and the excesses of violence in your books?

Ellroy: That's a very, very good question. It's actually a brilliant fucking question! You know British people dig Dog humor. Especially British men! I don't have to tell you that do I. Sex shit! Animals and their crazy hijinks! Race shit! And you know that by and large my best foreign readers are British, and there's really a dumb reason for it: they speak English. So they get to read the books sans translation. You know what, put all that aside—I had dinner last night with some very nice people, and they won a raffle to have dinner with me, at the school, the progressive school of my ex-wife's sister. My ex-wife Helen Knode. Very best friend. And they're very, very nice but they're very liberal, and it was so much fun to give them a hard time and tell them that Senator Obama[1] looked like a Lima and the witchdoctor in all the old jungle flicks. And they were momentarily shocked, and then they realized that I don't hate anybody. And I was doin' pimp shit—YEAH BABY! And race shit. Shit about homosexuals and all kinds of shit. And after a while, they started digging it—but it really took a while! And what's more funny than depraved race shit and sex shit? And why not in alliteration and fucked-up tender fifty-year-old guys chasing women if they want love, and what's more funny and courageous and heart-wrenching than that shit and absurd? And grabbing it by the nuts? I mean have you read the novellas in *Destination Morgue*? I mean the whole thing there where Rick and Donna go to a porno bookstore and the titles of the homo movies. This to me is funny shit. And there's people who get it and people who don't. And I think there is a correlation in language and in theme because both violence and Dog humor deal with outrageousness.

Interviewer: Yes. It's interesting that I find I enjoy Dog humor and everything, and I don't think it's something to haul you over the coals about. But I also find that your portrayals of homosexual subculture in *The Big Nowhere* and *American Tabloid* are quite sympathetic and understanding of Danny Upshaw and his plight.

Ellroy: Right, and Lenny Sands. Yeah, Lenny Sands and his plight. Basically, when confronted with shit I'm rather a fucker for people. I like people across a wide, wide margin, and it's the idea of ingrained grievance. It's the notion of identity that bugs me. If somebody's going to be a pain-in-the-ass-Tory, pain-in-the-ass-left-winger, pain-in-the-ass-homosexual, and get up on their high horse about it as a group, and further institutionalize the grievance, and then you know what? Then I get pissed off. And bigotry crumbles when you meet individuals. And you notice this over and over again, you may be inclined to hate someone as part of a group, and then you meet them individually, and they're dandy. They're dandy, and all that shit serves to be coherent.

Interviewer: Which I guess in the L.A. Quartet and Underworld U.S.A. the likeability of Mickey Cohen as a person, even though his acts are despicable, gives the novel a very unique chemistry. I mean Pete Bondurant as a person is despicable, but on a one-to-one level has a kind of chemistry.

Ellroy: Yeah, you dig Pete Bondurant because you see the price that he's paid for his misdeeds: the accidental killing of his own brother and his parents' subsequent suicide. The tender regard he carries for women—he's entirely dichotomized. He'll kill a man in a heartbeat, but he won't touch a woman. And the most tragic moment in *The Cold Six Thousand* is when he's coerced into killing a woman.

Interviewer: Yes, I guess to mention Pete Bondurant, he has a very small role in *White Jazz* that leads to a kind of cross-series continuation. You do map out your fictional universe very, very carefully. We've talked about outlines. Is there anything you would see as the most unusual fictionalization of a real event or a real character that you've done?

Ellroy: Well you haven't read the book yet, and I would guess that it would be published in Great Britain in the fall of '09. But the novel that I'm writing now, the sequel to *The Cold Six Thousand* . . .

Interviewer: *Blood's a Rover.*

Ellroy: *Blood's a Rover,* yeah. Takes place largely, the big middle section which I should finish this afternoon, takes place in the Dominican Republic and Haiti. And for years I had planned to, and you know this is very interesting, it's preposterous but . . . I planned on setting it in Nicaragua, somewhere in Central America. The Mob—Ward Littell has set up the Mob to plant foreign casinos in friendly right-wing dictator-run tropical locales.

And Nicaragua, they had a lot shit going on there and the Somozas[2] and all that stuff. I started looking at it—didn't give a shit. Didn't give a shit. The place looked like a shithole. It had no romance to it. Too many of the people were still alive, too many. The United States' foreign policy was too ingrained over decades, too hard to render concisely. And then I went back annotating *American Tabloid* and *The Cold Six Thousand*, as I was preparing the notes and outline for *Blood's a Rover*, when I realized I'd left myself an out when near the end of the book, and parenthetically near the end of his life, Ward Littell is telling our Mob unholy trio Carlos Marcello, Santo Trafficante, and Sam Giancana, "We can plant in Central America *or* the Caribbean," and I've never looked at a map. I'm just encyclopedically ignorant in some ways. I'm not being disingenuous here. But I thought that the Dominican Republic was in Central America, next to Guatemala. I didn't know, and I looked at a fucking atlas, an atlas that I had on my desk. You know every once in a while you get the urge to look at a map. The Dominican Republic is on the island of Hispanola to the east of Haiti! Cuba is within speedboat range. Haiti. Black people. Black militants in the book. Voodoo. Dead dictators. And no discernable Nixon administration policy. Not much of anything goin' on after the '65 Civil War. I had greater latitude to fictionalize, and thus the tropes, the actual tropes of the two preceding novels *American Tabloid* and *The Cold Six Thousand* are very well established, harbingers of the Kennedy hit '58–'63, and then *The Cold Six Thousand* the big book of the sixties. This book of '68–'72, and it's largely shit that nobody could have come up with because it's Haiti and the Dominican Republic and nothing was goin' on, so you may as well fictionalize it.

Interviewer: I read in interviews how you chose that path to bypass Watergate, and what you see as a fictional no-go area. Whilst we're on the subject of research, you're known as a kind of father to all things related to the Black Dahlia. You've mentioned that John Gregory Dunne's *True Confessions* was something of an inspiration on you. I was wondering if other works like *The Blue Gardenia* and Theodora Keogh's *The Other Girl*, did they provide any template or inspiration?
Ellroy: What was the second one you called?

Interviewer: *The Other Girl* by Theodora Keogh. She was related to Roosevelt.
Ellroy: *The Other Girl*? I don't know that book at all.

Interviewer: Right, okay. I haven't read it myself. I looked it up on a Black Dahlia website of some sort. But I was just wondering whether . . .
Ellroy: When was it published?

Interviewer: 1962.
Ellroy: And it was about the Black Dahlia?

Interviewer: It was a fictionalized take on the case with name changes. A rather sensationalized pulp . . .[3]
Ellroy: I have no idea . . . You are the first person, Steve, to mention this book to me!

Interviewer: Right, okay.
Ellroy: *The Other Girl.*

Interviewer: Okay, right. But my question was, was there any other sources outside of *True Confessions* or Jack Webb's *The Badge* which formed, aside from your mother's murder obviously, which formed a kind of basis of inspiration for *The Black Dahlia*?
Ellroy: No, but it's very interesting. There's a very slight homage to John Gregory Dunne who died recently, may he rest in peace, in *Blood's a Rover*, which is if you look back at the book it begins with "NOW," on a page all by itself in the first-person very long prologue of Tom Spellacy. Then you go to "THEN," third person and "NOW" the conclusion and the epilogue. And I've done that in *Blood's a Rover*. I wonder if anybody would comment on it. *True Confessions*, and I know nothing of Irishness or Catholicism at all, and he transposed, he, Dunne, transposed 1940s Boston, in reality Hartford, Connecticut, where he was from, to 1940s L.A. And it's a very fanciful portrayal of L.A. then. White L.A. could not have been that ethnically Irish. And it's a wonderful, wonderful raucous witty profane book. And it made a big influence on me. And the positive upshot of it, although it wasn't a direct stylistic influence on *The Black Dahlia*, was that the success of the book deterred me from writing *The Black Dahlia* for many years because I didn't understand publishing and didn't understand well that's Mr. Dunne's book, that's not mine. And he only adhered to the facts of the case in so far as it's a dead young woman chopped in half, dumped on a vacant lot. Beyond that, it's entirely extrapolated and not steeped in the real history of the forties. So I decided to write an entirely different book, and I realized LAPD

would never let me see the file. Wouldn't see it if I could—there's six thousand pages in six filing cabinets. And so I went out—I was kid writer living in New York, caddying, living in New York City suburbs—and I went out: I got three hundred dollars in quarters, put them in three triple reinforced pillowcases. Went into downtown New York City library, the one at Forty-Second Street and Fifth Avenue, and got on interlibrary loan the L.A. newspapers from that time. Fed quarters to it and made photocopies. Reprinted white on black and extrapolated off the actual facts of the case with fictional characters. That's how I built that book.

Interviewer: Would the fact that your book was more based on research than Gregory Dunne's be reflected in how much more Bucky Bleichert cares from the beginning about women than perhaps Spellacy because one thing about *True Confessions* is its black humor.

Ellroy: Black humor and misogynistic humor, and it's something that's very, very important. I'm just—I'm fuckin' sixty years old, and I'm just so stupefyingly horny and crazed for women. It's rather shocking and wonderful. I look great, and I'll never age, but I'm not out of fuckin' adolescence yet. And I carry it strong, and Bucky carried it strong, and that's the first time I consciously addressed it. I think that the actual black humor and all that misogyny is appallingly stale in *The Cold Six Thousand*. It's just all the talk about cunts and pussies and shit like that. I mean, my books and my books in their regard to women are almost chaste! And there's more sex in this novel, *Blood's a Rover*, than in any other because it's largely based on the last two women who broke my heart and kicked my ass, and I use their actual first names, Joan and Kathy,[4] in this book. Yeah, the black humor when it actually works, race shit, crazy hilarious Catholic Mick shit in *True Confessions* is great. But the undercurrent of women hatred is unsettling and ugly—and just ugly. And then you get to that, that level where you realize that the author, God bless him he's dead and he can't respond, thought this is the truth, thus it's moral. I don't believe that. I just don't believe, you wanna dwell on the squalid for four hundred pages, make an editorial comment about its squalor, or assert greater control of your facts.

Interviewer: Yes, well as I said you have become a kind of Black Dahlia father figure. You originally endorsed Larry Harnisch's theory that Walter Bayley was the killer. Then you . . .

Ellroy: Tenuously, tenuously, Steve. You'll note at the end of that documentary, have you seen the documentary?

Interviewer: Yes, *Feast of Death*.

Ellroy: Yeah, and I think it's out of control. I think there's far too much of Harnisch and that whole dinner, but I say that in the end we're never gonna know. Steve Hodel's theory is somewhat better because at least his father was a suspect in the case, but it's full of a lot of specious reasoning. And it's unprovable. Also it turns out that a lot of those women killings that he attributes to his father were actually solved.

Interviewer: Really?

Ellroy: Yeah. I wish I hadn't endorsed it in print. I led with my heart.

Interviewer: Okay, because one controversial aspect of the book was when Steve Hodel hypothesized that his father's friend and associate Fred Sexton is a plausible suspect for your mother's murder, Geneva Hilliker Ellroy.

Ellroy: Bullshit, bullshit, just bullshit, and I told Steve that. Just bullshit.

Interviewer: Right. He's not the first person to do that in print. Was Janice Knowlton the first when she wrote *Daddy Was the Black Dahlia Killer*.[5]

Ellroy: Did she name Fred Sexton?

Interviewer: No, she named her own father.

Ellroy: Yeah, she named her own father. Yeah, and just preposterous that she watched her father chop up Elizabeth Short, dump the two halves of the body off a pier and then get in and coral them in saltwater, drive them to Veterans of Foreign Wars in Culver City and then drop them. Nahh! Nahh! She's dead now.

Interviewer: Yes, I heard she committed suicide.

Ellroy: Yeah.

Interviewer: So there are tensions perhaps when people approach you about the Black Dahlia or rope in figures with your mother. As I've made out, I'm very interested in the visual aspect of your work, and you mentioned you were very unhappy with the film *Dark Blue* with what it did to your story, "The Plague Season."

Ellroy: I wasn't unhappy. I wasn't unhappy. I have a secondary income and a secondary life writing films. And I've been divorced a couple of times, so I need to earn money. And I can't write up a full board novel or memoir twenty-four/seven, so I get film jobs. And without condescending to the film business, and I would never bite the hand that feeds me, I will tell you that compared to writing novels, writing screenplays is very easy and for very quick turnaround on your buck. So you have to know going into the film business writing movies, any novelist, it is highly unlikely that any screenplay that you write or work on will ever be made into a movie. And if they do, they'll fuck it up past redemption. And so I don't . . . the same thing with *Street Kings*. I don't wanna rag it for retribution, but there were four other writers in it and a total of twenty-two drafts on it, and there was something similar on "The Plague Season," which became *Dark Blue*.

Interviewer: Yes, with a lot of postwar American writers, and perhaps Raymond Chandler would be a perfect example of this, it becomes rather a love-hate relationship with Hollywood. Would you describe your relationship with Hollywood as love-hate or is that overly simplistic?

Ellroy: No, it's fond because I enjoy earning the money and some part of me is removed from the final outcome.

Interviewer: You mention that part of you is removed from the final work. After *White Jazz* you said you'd never write another L.A. crime novel, but you have turned to L.A. in films or short stories. Is it because you find there's more distance between a film than a novel with your name on it?

Ellroy: It's because I don't expect the movies to see final form unless they were published, and I think in my screenplays publishing rights are ambiguously phrased. So I live back in Los Angeles now, I kept getting divorced so I kept moving back south. So I'm here now, and for the longest time I ran away from L.A. And now I live here. Yeah I've lived here for two years. I just can't let it go.

Interviewer: Where can you go after historical fiction? Could you summarize in so many words where you're heading as a writer?

Ellroy: Deeper into historical fiction.

Interviewer: You have a relationship with the LAPD right now which is very amicable shall we say. You've won the Jack Webb award. But your portrayal of the LAPD in the L.A. Quartet is unflinching. Do you feel there's a contradiction there?

Ellroy: Well that's another good question. There has always been rogue elements within the LAPD, but the LAPD was on a course of reform from the time William Parker took over the Department in August of 1950 up until the present, and I hope that point is made implicitly that this is the perspective of rogue cops. And I admire the LAPD greatly: they're not perfect, but they have been unduly castigated in the media. And cops love me because they think I'm honest and I tell the truth of their lives.

Interviewer: Yes, from your novels say post–Lloyd Hopkins you gave up on the maverick outsider within to show that all 1950s cops had to embrace certain aspects of racism, certain aspects of misogyny. But would you say that current, or moderately current LAPD scandals like Rodney King or O.J. Simpson are more beyond the pale compared to the good work the LAPD does in the majority?

Ellroy: Well a couple of things. First of all, I wouldn't call O.J. Simpson a scandal, it's just, it's not even a botched murder case—it's a bad acquittal. And the second thing, Rampart[6] wasn't much of a scandal when truly dissected. Same thing with Rodney King if you see the entire three-minute tape. The fifty-six hammer blows that put Rodney on the ground, and the contact slash don't look good, but moment to moment the entire three minute tape leads me to say, and I realize this is revolutionary, I don't think they did anything wrong. There's a moment when one of the policeman, and it might have been interestingly enough a man named Powell,[7] kicked Rodney King in the head, which was the only out-of-line and out of policy thing that they did. Yeah he attacked Stacy Koon. The other people in the car were led to safety. He kept attacking: he took a taser, he kept getting up, getting up, getting up. He's six foot five, two hundred and fifty pounds, and on angeldust, and you don't engage people like that in one-on-one fights. And I think it was an aesthetic call that people made: they could either see this in the context of white racism and police corruption or overall police misconduct, or they could see it in a more localized context, which in this case, I think, is also a more broader context—that these are the exigent factors of police work, ad hoc, day to day. And you can't let angeldust-addled shitbergs drive around at one hundred and ten miles an hour on the freeway, where they will kill people: interdict and suppress them. It doesn't look good, the footage a million people have seen, many millions of people have seen. In a larger context, it reveals itself to be something entirely different, and so pointing to these things, and Rampart's a crock of shit, and accepting them as historical fact is very dangerous and specious. And so what I'm morally obligated to do with interviewers is try to give them a different view of these speciously alleged facts.

Interviewer: Yes, accepting things as historical fact is dangerous. You've mentioned many times your dislike of the word *closure* or the term *closure*. In your novels there is a kind of contradiction between solving the case, finding the murderer, but not finding the internal psychological emotional closure. Do you think that your novels are heading towards an emotional solving?

Ellroy: I think they're becoming more deeply emotional, and I think this is a very open-hearted book that I'm writing now. What I wanna give you is the sense that the ramifications of the bad deeds continue after the first book, after the last page has ended. And that the men and women involved in these webs of intrigue will continue to pay the moral and psychological cost of having engaged the horror.

Interviewer: In *Clandestine* you mention "the Wonder." Does the horror come out of the Wonder paradoxically?

Ellroy: It's part of it. I still feel a young person's awe over life and all its vicissitudes, and I still feel the Wonder very strongly at this stage of my life—and I've been writing books for almost thirty years.

Notes

1. This interview took place during the primaries of the 2008 presidential election.

2. The Somoza dynasty was a hereditary dictatorship that effectively governed Nicaragua from 1937 to 1979. They were finally overthrown by the Sandinista National Liberation Front.

3. I've since read the book and gave a copy to Ellroy. Theodora Keogh (1919–2008), was the granddaughter of Theodore Roosevelt, socialite, costume designer and author of nine dark and distinctive novels published between 1950 and 1962, before she completely disappeared from the literary scene. *The Other Girl* was her last published novel and gives a fictional account of events leading up to the murder of Elizabeth Short.

4. Kathy actually became Karen Sifakis in *Blood's a Rover*.

5. Knowlton also wrote to Ellroy claiming her father may have murdered his mother, Geneva Hilliker Ellroy.

6. The Rampart scandal was a case of alleged widespread corruption in the Community Resources against Street Hoodlums anti-gang unit of the LAPD Rampart Division in the late 1990s. Ellroy's screenplay "Rampart", a fictionalized version of events, was in postproduction at the time this manuscript was being prepared.

7. Sergeant Stacey Koon and Officer Laurence Powell and two other LAPD officers were acquitted of assault with a deadly weapon, but Koon and Powell were later found guilty of violating Rodney King's civil rights and were both sentenced to thirty months in prison.

Coda for Crime Fiction

Steven Powell/2008

This interview was conducted on August 15, 2008. Previously unpublished.

Interviewer: Your early novels featured many references to music such as Anton Bruckner,[1] rock 'n' roll, black bebop jazz. Why the link between music and crime in your novels?

Ellroy: There's not so many references to rock 'n' roll, they're here and there. *Brown's Requiem* mirrors my flat-out obsession with classical music and Bruckner, the Romantic composers, a line that started with Beethoven and Bruckner—the enormousness, the idea of spiritual transcendence. The idea of seeking God, transmogrification, the bigness of it, the complexity of it has always floored me. And I've got a big poster of Bruckner. It's an early photograph of Bruckner who died in 1896, on my living room wall, and there's Beethoven shit all over this place. And thus that, and then the later book, *White Jazz*, which is in the fractured, disjointed style of a very bad, racist white cop whose life is breaking down, who inexplicably gets hooked on black bebop jazz. I'm not a fan of bebop, but I understand it as the means to express confusion and disorientation. And music is a very pure form of expression, and it's been important to me to include it.

Interviewer: That's interesting because I was thinking the link between classical music and German classical composers and some of your earlier villains, if that's not too crude a term, Doc Harris, Dr. John Havilland almost model themselves on Nietzschean Superman. Is there perhaps a link there between the music and how these villains model themselves?

Ellroy: Yeah, I don't associate classical music with odious philosophy. The greatest musician of all time, Beethoven, was German and his music is entirely about God and liberty and equality. We've all seen a lot of movies and television shows where the genius or the villain—the Anthony Burgess, Kubrick piece *Clockwork Orange* where the hoodlums dig Beethoven. I wasn't trying for that at all.

Interviewer: Well, we talked a little about John Gregory Dunne last time and his novel *True Confessions* and its influence on *The Black Dahlia*, and you also mentioned it was influencing your latest novel in the Underworld U.S.A. trilogy.

Ellroy: Well it's referenced in the Underworld U.S.A. trilogy in that there are first-person prologues preceded by "NOW" in the present on a single page, and the flashback bulk of the book which is in the third person—"THEN." And I do that in this novel. That's as far as it goes. There's raucous . . . and you've read the novel right?

Interviewer: *True Confessions.* Yes.

Ellroy: There's raucous, profane humor to it. You know it's full of racist shit and crude humor that I dug wildly, and in that sense, that book of Dunne's, and it's the only book of his I've read cover to cover (I started reading *Dutch Shea Junior* and didn't dig it), influenced me. But I know nothing about the Catholic Church or Irishness at all.

Interviewer: Right. Well, it is interesting how your influence seems to have changed over the years. *Brown's Requiem* is very much influenced by Raymond Chandler, now you seem to have an aversion to Raymond Chandler.

Ellroy: I think he was lightweight compared to Dashiell Hammett. And I think that the language is overripe, the philosophy is gasbag. He came out of L.A., and he wrote in the first person. And it's the L.A. of my early childhood and the L.A. before my birth, which is intensely romantic to me. And I sure as shit loved the books while I read them, but Hammett and Cain and Ross Macdonald have held in better in my mind. And I had to reread a little Hammett, because I wrote the Everyman Library introduction to one of their volumes, and was amazed at how my sensibility of the goon and the political fixer and the bagman and the hatchet man strike-breaker came out of that.

Interviewer: Yes. Is it fair to say that reading these books changed you not only as a writer but perhaps as a person? I think I read in an interview, it might have been in a documentary, you said that Joseph Wambaugh actually made you more conservative as a person.

Ellroy: I'm a natural Tory. And I had a long conversation last night with a woman I just met and I'm deeply, beautifully in love with. She said, "Just how right-wing are you?" because she doesn't share a lot of my religious and political social beliefs, and we had that discussion and it was just nothing but gracious. And I'm an authoritarian, and I'm just not a leftist. And I may have a little bit of a Marxist social sense and distrust of authority, but in the end, I'd rather err on its side than on the side of chaos. And Wambaugh's books are VERY, VERY MEASURED in their approach to this because you have authoritarian men whose lives are personally disordered. And so the cops in the early novels are always trying to impart order on the world at large because their individual lives lack it and because they're very, very passionate in their deepest hearts, and I'm that way. And cops are the best bunch of people I've ever met.

Interviewer: You have met people on the other end of the spectrum though. I mean that must be a strange experience. You met Gary Graham.[2]
Ellroy: Yeah I met Gary Graham, and I think he's guilty, and I was appalled. And I had a very good policeman friend of mine in the room with me at Death Row, Texas. I mean, I was appalled. Why mince words? I hate criminals and gangbangers and dope dealers, and I feel no social obligation to portray their lives sympathetically. None.

Interviewer: Yes, so hypothetically if you could meet Pete Bondurant, how would you feel about that?
Ellroy: I can't. So I've never given it any thought. I create, and they represent conflict in me, these guys. But in the end, I judge them harshly, and as with most of my big male characters, they either are somewhat redeemed by love, or fully redeemed by love, or die looking for love. And that's why I love 'em. That's why I consider myself a moral writer.

Interviewer: Yes, well speaking of moral judgments, you've made your feelings quite clear about President Clinton, and also your book *American Tabloid* led to widespread revisionism of the J.F.K. administration and that historical period. How important to you is it that people will make historical conclusions from reading your novels?
Ellroy: All I want them to do is get to the point where they say maybe. Maybe. And the inestimable debt of *American Tabloid* and the Underworld U.S.A. trilogy and *Blood's a Rover*—it's influenced by *Libra*. And I really need to write Mr. DeLillo a letter about this and credit him for attribution personally one more time. And so it's *Libra* more than anything else that made me think—"Holy shit! How come I didn't get to Lee Harvey Oswald,

the ultimate American loner loser malcontent fucker before this?" Well, because DeLillo did. And when I saw that I could write a physically larger, physically broader book that would track all the harbingers of the assassination from five years earlier, I mean DeLillo just lobbed me that one. Okay, you can't use Oswald. You can't use Oswald. And I'll be the first to admit that my Jack Ruby is not as indelible as Mr. DeLillo's because I never went inside Ruby's viewpoint and frankly I'm just not as bright as Mr. DeLillo. I'm a more vulgar, urgent, communicative, emotional guy than he is. So I got that one lobbed at me. And as for the morality of portraying the world that way, I think the answer is I trust the morality, my personal morality, and the moral journeys of my characters, and so I don't give a shit. And if it didn't happen that way—crazy, crazy right-wing Cuban exiles, renegade CIA guys, Mob—it sure as shit should have because it's such a fucking good book.

Interviewer: So, you're not trying to create a theory like the Jim Garrison theory or the Jim Marrs theory, the Oliver Stone theory . . .

Ellroy: I'm not telling you that it's true. No, I'm not. And I think I have to be credited with a certain amount of restraint there. I am not telling you it's true.

Interviewer: We were talking earlier about your crime writer references. Would you say that Don DeLillo is the first author who is not necessarily a crime author who is an influence on your work?

Ellroy: If you look back at the odd bunch of books that influenced me . . . Hammett, and I like *Red Harvest* better than *The Maltese Falcon*. The three novels, *Serenade, Postman Always Rings Twice, Double Indemnity*, Cain. His best novel, *Mildred Pierce*, and his greatest character, the Woman of Stone, the eponymous character. Two early novels by George V. Higgins about the Boston Underworld, white ethnic shit that I know nothing about, Italians and Irish, *Friends of Eddie Coyle* and *The Diggers Game*. It's a conversational style and it's a milieu I couldn't have imagined, may he rest in peace, Mr. Higgins. Meyer Levin's novel *Compulsion* about Leopold and Loeb, which exists on many levels—for one thing it's a book about psychoanalysis. It was published in '56 at the height of the craze. It's a period novel. It's about Jewish-American, upper crust Jewish-American life in Chicago in 1924, and it's Leopold and Loeb and the turbulent psychology of the two killers. It's a great book. I don't know many people who've read it . . .

Interviewer: I've read it, and I read your introduction. It's a fascinating book.

Ellroy: Did you dig it? Did you enjoy the book?

Interviewer: Yes, definitely, Strauss and Steiner[3] are fascinating characters.

Ellroy: Let me ask you this because it suddenly came to me: is Great Britain still a reading culture?

Interviewer: Oh, that's an interesting question. I think it is, but I think there's a lot of easy ways out these days. Tabloid easy reads. Celebrities or quasi-celebrities publishing autobiographies at twenty-five. Just terrible, terrible books really.

Ellroy: It's the best, there's some of the best book audiences I've ever run into. I love British book tours. For one thing, it's a foreign country and everybody speaks English. And it's not so much that my people came from there, it's just that in places like Manchester you'll see a working-class guy with his last fifteen pounds, who'll go buy your book in hardcover. And you see a little bit of that in France, but it's almost always followed by some kind of weirdass, fucked up ambivalent reaction to America which you don't get in Great Britain.

Interviewer: I'm married to an American, and she does get some occasional snide comment about her country, but yes I don't think it's as widespread as perhaps on the continent. But speaking of *Compulsion*, there's that interesting thing about Strauss and Steiner—they have this fascination for ornithology, of course they're poisoning birds, which I believe pops up in *L.A. Confidential*. I can't remember the name of the killer now . . . Loren Atherton.

Ellroy: Loren Atherton. Yeah I don't think . . . does he poison birds?

Interviewer: No, but he stitches bird feathers onto his child victim.

Ellroy: Okay, yeah you're right. You're right. You're right. Yeah, Wee Willie Wennerholm, he kills the kid yeah. Fuck.

Interviewer: Did you get that from *Compulsion*?

Ellroy: Best answer, I don't know. I just don't know. I don't know. I dig animals. I also dig a good steak. I love animals. I wouldn't go shoot one, but I'll sure as shit eat the piece of steak you put on my plate.

Interviewer: [Laughs] Wonderful! Alright, you've investigated cases like Stephanie Gorman, fascinating case. Is going over cases like that like investigating ghosts? I mean metaphorically speaking, going over these long dead cases?

Ellroy: The best answer to that is—it's over. It's over. I can't read homicide files. I gotta stop, murdered, murdered women. A couple of things parenthetically and, yeah, you're the first person I've told about this. *Playboy*, you know American *Playboy*, in the Christmas issue, which goes out to many millions of people published—it'll come out in the States here November 10—there's a ten-thousand-word excerpt from *Blood's a Rover*. And I had planned before I write the next novel to do a second book like a memoir. A companion piece to *My Dark Places*, and it was just simply gonna be called "The Big Hurt" subtitled "My Pursuit of Women." I decided not, because there's so much about a couple women in my life in *Blood's a Rover*, and I just don't wanna go there book-length, so instead I'm doing a three- or four-part serialization of the memoir in *Playboy*. And I'm not calling it "The Big Hurt," I'm calling it *The Hilliker Curse* with the same subtitle. And so the idea of a dead woman has been replaced with the idea of women, which is so richly what this novel is about. And without blowing the plot for ya, the first thing that everybody who's read the book most specifically comments on is the women. And so the whole, "I will avenge her," "My mother was killed" thing, I just feel like it's gone away.

Interviewer: How do you make decisions as to what books go forward and which ones don't? You started a book called "The Confessions of Bugsy Siegel." You mentioned you once had an idea of a book about the Wisconsin State Police. Is there something that really tells you, "No, I have to write *Blood's a Rover* now and not that book"?

Ellroy: When you know you know, and "Bugsy Siegel" followed my third novel, which became *Blood on the Moon*, which was a mess I had to rewrite. It was full of shit. I was just a kid running amok. Thirty-four years old, which is not a kid, but I mean I was running amok in New York City, and I was just holed up one winter and wrote half of this thing. And you know I got the brainstorm for the serialization of *The Hilliker Curse* while I was in New York City walking to dinner with the editor whose name is Amy Lloyd and Chris Napolitano, and I got the idea then, and it was impulsive and it's correct. So, as far as the Wisconsin State Police book goes, yeah, somewhere down the line probably.

Notes

1. Anton Bruckner (1824–1896) Austrian Romantic composer. In the conclusion to *Brown's Requiem* the villain-ous Haywood Cathcart compares himself to Bruckner.

2. Shaka Sankofa (born Gary Lee Graham 1963–2000). In 1981 Graham was sentenced to death by a Texas court for the murder of Bobby Grant Lambert. Graham was executed by lethal injection in 2000. Despite his comments here, Ellroy argued that Graham should not be executed on the grounds of reasonable doubt in his article for *G.Q.* "Grave Doubt".

3. Leopold and Loeb become Strauss and Steiner in the novel.

James Ellroy: The Art of Fiction

Nathaniel Rich/2008

This interview is an excerpt of a longer interview that first appeared as the following: "James Ellroy: The Art of Fiction no. 201," *Paris Review* (Fall 2009), no. 190. Reprinted by permission by Nathaniel Rich.

Interviewer: You were away from Los Angeles for twenty-five years. Why'd you come back?

Ellroy: One reason: *Cherchez la femme*. I chased women to suburban New York, suburban Connecticut, Kansas City, Carmel, and San Francisco. But I ran out of places, and I ran out of women, so I ended up back here.

Interviewer: Did you miss the city?

Ellroy: While I was away, the Los Angeles of my past accreted in my mind, developing its own power. Early on in my career I believed that in order to write about L.A., I had to stay out of it entirely. But when I moved back, I realized that L.A. *then* lives in my blood. L.A. *now* does not.

Interviewer: And what about the L.A. of the fifties has a hold on you?

Ellroy: A lot of it is simple biography. I lived here, so I was obsessed with my immediate environment. I am from Los Angeles truly, immutably. It's the first thing you get in any author's note: James Ellroy was born in Los Angeles in 1948. I was hatched in the film-noir epicenter, at the height of the film-noir era. My parents and I lived near Hollywood. My father and mother had a tenuous connection to the film business. They were both uncommonly good-looking, which may be a hallmark of L.A. arrivistes, and they were aware of that generation of migrants who came because they were very poor and L.A. was a beautiful place.

I grew up in a different world, a different America. You didn't have to make a lot of dough to keep a roof over your head. There was a calmness that I recall too. I learned to amuse myself. I liked to read. I liked to look out the window.

It's rare for me to speak about L.A. epigrammatically. I don't view it as a strange place; I don't view it as a hot-pot of multiculturalism or weird sexuality. I have never studied it formally. There are big swathes of L.A. that I don't even know my way around today. I'm not quite sure how you get to Torrance, Hermosa Beach, Long Beach. I don't know L.A. on a valid historical level at all. But I have assimilated it in a deeper way. I had lived here for so long that when it became time to exploit my memory of the distant past, it was easy.

Whatever power my books have derives from the fact that they are utterly steeped in the eras that I describe. L.A. of that period is mine and nobody else's. If you wrote about this period before me, I have taken it away from you.

Interviewer: What did your parents do?

Ellroy: My mother was a registered nurse. She worked a lot. At one point she had a job at a nursing home where movie stars brought their aging parents. She was fluent in German, and when the patients spoke about her in Yiddish, behind her back, she could understand them. She was a big reader of historical novels, and she was always listening to one specific Brahms piano concerto—I remember a blue RCA Victor record.

I have more memories of my dad. He was a dipshit studio gofer, a big handsome guy, a scratch golfer. He worked for a schlock producer named Sam Stiefel.

He was always snoozing on the couch, like Dagwood Bumstead.[1] He was a lazy motherfucker. God bless him. He was always working on some kind of get-rich-quick scheme. This is what my dad was like: I'd say, Hey, Dad, we studied penguins today in school. He'd say, Yeah? I'm a penguin fucker from way back. Dad, I saw a giraffe at the zoo today. Yeah? I'm a giraffe fucker from way back. That's my dad. My dad was a giraffe fucker.

He said to me once, I fucked Rita Hayworth. He said that he once introduced me to Hayworth at the Tail O' the Pup, circa 1950. I would have been two years old at the time, but I don't recall it. He said I spilled grape juice all over her. I never believed that he had worked for Hayworth, but after his death I saw his name in a Hayworth biography. Sure enough, for a period of time, he was her business manager.

Interviewer: What was your childhood like before your mother's death?

Ellroy: I don't remember a single amicable moment between my parents other than this: my mother passing steaks out the kitchen window to my father so that he could put them on a barbecue.

I had my mother's number. I understood that she was maudlin, effusive, and enraged—the degree depending on how much booze she had in her system. I also understood that she had my father's number—that he was lazy and cowardly.

There was always something incongruous about them. Early on, I was aware of the seventeen-year age gap. When I knew her, my mother was a very good-looking redhead in her early forties. My father was a sun-ravaged, hard-smoking, hard-living guy. He looked significantly older at sixty than I do know. Everybody thought he was my granddad. He wore clothes that were thirty years out of style. I remember that he had a gold Omega wristwatch that he loved. We were broke, and then all of a sudden, one day, the watch wasn't there. That broke my heart.

Interviewer: In *My Dark Places* you describe a sense of foreboding not long before your mother's murder. Where did that come from?

Ellroy: Near the end of January 1958, my mother sits me down on the couch. She's half blitzed, and I can tell. She says, Honey, you've never lived in a house before, so we're going to move to a nice little town called El Monte, in the San Gabriel Valley. I sensed that there were some other, more sinister reason we were moving to El Monte, but I still hadn't figured it out. I think she was running away from something, or someone.

We go out there, and it was very upsetting. It was a dirty little stone house with a single bathroom. It was half the size of the apartment that we had in Santa Monica.

Five months later, I come back from a weekend with my father. He put me in a cab at the El Monte bus depot. The cab pulls up to my street, our little stone house is on the left, and there are men in brown uniforms and gray suits standing around. And right then, I knew it: my mother was dead. I knew it in that moment.

Someone said, "There's the kid." A cop got down on my level and said, "Son, your mother's been killed."

I swooned. My field of vision veered off in one direction. But I didn't cry. I started calculating. I began performing almost immediately. I loved being the center of attention. The cops took me to our neighbor's garage, and they took a photograph—often reproduced—of me standing in front of a work-bench. I was goofing, mugging and making faces. The El Monte police chief was dispatched to pick up my dad and me in separate rooms. They gave me a candy bar. When they finally let my dad out, I ran to him and put my arms around him. We went back to his pad on the freeway bus. I recall a stream of cars going by with their lights on in the opposite direction, and I forced myself to cry for just a few minutes. I remember thinking that I should. I was already at a great emotional distance from my mother's death.

When I got back to my dad's crib, I immediately fell asleep. I woke up on Monday morning, June 23, 1958, and I swear to you, the whole world seemed light powder blue, like a '56 Chevy Bel Air.

Interviewer: It sounds like you were in a state of shock.
Ellroy: It technically could have been a state of shock. I had a nervous breakdown much later in life, and I'm still subject to panic attacks: big swells of emotion and anxiety, an aging person's unsuppressable fear of catastrophe and death. All I can tell you is what went through my mind at the time. I couldn't express my thoughts about my mother because my relationship with her was too compromised. I thought, I got what I wanted. My mother is dead. Now what do I do?

I felt death all around me. For a period of some weeks, my dad was very permissive. I began to wonder how much time he had left. I'd stay up late watching TV, waiting for him to come back from sporadic all-night accounting jobs—if indeed he wasn't out fucking every woman who'd let him.

I began to read mystery books: the Hardy Boys, Ken Holt. My father would buy me two of these things a week. I could read the damn books in four or five hours. I started stealing them when I was ten years old.

At the time I had no creative outlet, no indication of genius or a literary gift. I was fearful and occasionally violent, physically outsized, and out of my mind. But I knew right then that I had discovered a secret world.

Interviewer: Why is crime an important subject in American fiction?
Ellroy: We're a nation of immigrant rabble. A great rebellion attended the founding of this republic. We've been getting into trouble for two-hundred-and-thirty-odd years. It's the perfect place to set crime stories, and the themes of the genre—race, systemic corruption, sexual obsession—run rife here. In a well-done crime book you can explore these matters at great depth, say a great deal about society, and titillate the shit out of the reader.

Interviewer: You've said film noir hasn't influenced your writing, but you watched a lot of it in your formative years—and you say you were born and raised in the heart of film-noir culture.

Ellroy: I dig film noir. The great theme of film noir is, You're fucked. There are very few fine films: *Double Indemnity*, *Sunset Boulevard*, and, of course, *Out of the Past*. Robert Mitchum sees Jane Greer in Acapulco, and he *knows*. She sees him, and she *knows*. He's passive, inert, but very resourceful. She's murderous and altogether monstrous. He just wants to forfeit to a woman, to give up his masculinity. She wants to be enveloped in her masculine side. They each want *the other*. When film noir is deeply about that, it can be very powerful. But noir is overexposed now. I'm over it.

Interviewer: How did you do in high school?

Ellroy: I did poorly, and I had an unimaginably dim social sense. I was horrified when the civil rights workers were killed in Mississippi in '64, but I made light of it in school. I knew it was wrong, but I had to be superior to the events themselves. You can see this in my books. There's the reactionary side of me as well as the critique of authority, the critique of racism and oppression. Back then, though, I possessed no social awareness.

Interviewer: Did you graduate?

Ellroy: No. I flunked the eleventh grade and got expelled. I decided I wanted to join the Marine Corps because I wanted to be a shit kicker, which I certainly was not. I did not want to go to Vietnam; I never thought about Vietnam. I had a vague desire to shoot guns. My father's health was deteriorating ever more rapidly—he started having strokes and heart attacks—and he let me enlist in the army.

Interviewer: How long did it last?

Ellroy: If you think I'm skinny now, at a hundred and seventy pounds, picture me at a hundred and forty. I got shipped out to Fort Polk, Louisiana. Flying bugs all over the place. Right away, I went from being a big egotistical bully to a craven scaredy-cat dipshit. My dad had another stroke the first week I was at Polk. I got flown home to L.A., in my uniform, on emergency leave. Two weeks later, he had yet another stroke. I got flown back again, just in time to see him die. His final words to me were, Try to pick up every waitress who serves you.

Interviewer: Is that when you started writing—after your father died?

Ellroy: The first thing I did after he died was snag his last three Social Security checks, forge his signature, and cash them at a liquor store. From '65 to '75, I drank, I used drugs. I fantasized. I swallowed amphetamine inhalers. I masturbated compulsively. I got into fights. I boxed—though I was terrible at it—and I broke into houses. I'd steal girls' panties, I'd jack off, grab cash out of wallets and purses. The method was easy: you call a house and if nobody answers, that means nobody's home. I'd stick my long, skinny arms in a pet access door and flip the latch, or find a window that was loose and raise it open. Everybody has pills and alcohol. I'd pop a Seconal, drink four fingers of Scotch, eat some cheese out of the fridge, steal a ten-dollar bill, then leave a window ajar and skedaddle. I did time in county jail for useless misdemeanors trespassing.

The press thinks that I'm a larger-than-life guy. Yes, that's true. But a lot of the shit written about discusses this part of my life disproportionately.

Interviewer: Aren't you responsible for this? You written a lot about this period, and you frequently talk about it in interviews.

Ellroy: I've told many journalists that I've done time in county jail, that I've broken and entered, that I was a voyeur. But I also told them that I spent much more time reading than I ever did stealing or peeping. They never mention that. It's a lot sexier to write about my mother, her death, my wild youth, and my jail time than it is to say that Ellroy holed up in a library with a bottle of wine and read books.

Interviewer: Still, writing couldn't exactly have been in the forefront of your mind at the time.

Ellroy: But it was. I was always thinking about how I would become a great novelist. I just didn't think that I would write *crime* novels. I thought that I would be a literary writer, whose creative duty is to describe the world as it is. The problem is that I never enjoyed books like that. I only enjoyed crime stories. So more than anything, this fascination with writing was an issue of identity. I had a fantasy of what it meant to be a writer: the sports cars, the clothes, the women.

But I think what appealed to me most about it was that I could assume the identity of what I really loved to do, which was to read. Nobody told me I couldn't write a novel. I didn't live in the world of graduate writing schools. I wasn't part of any scene or creative community. I happened to love crime novels more than anything. So I wrote a crime novel first. I didn't buy the old canard that you had to start by writing short stories, so why the fuck should I want to write one? I only wanted to write novels.

Interviewer: Did you feel that your period of homelessness and delinquency was giving you experiences that you could turn into a novel?

Ellroy: If I did, it was false. The real education I had was from the books I had read and TV shows and movies I saw. When I watched a film or read a book, I was engrossed. I learned in an unmediated way. I didn't know what I was taking in—I wasn't thinking about theme, content, or style—but I took it all in.

Interviewer: You started caddying at golf courses near the end of that period. Did you think you needed the stability of a paying job in order to write?

Ellroy: What happened was that I quit drinking. I knew I couldn't write a novel as long as I drank or used drugs. And I was on fire with a sense of urgency. A buddy took me to an A.A. meeting, and I quit drinking in June of 1975. I continued taking uppers and smoking weed until August 1, 1977. That's when I really got sober. I started writing a year and five months later, in late January of 1979. I was not quite thirty-one.

Interviewer: Did you have an idea for a novel? Or just the general notion that you wanted to write one?

Ellroy: I concocted a story idea. A friend of mine at the country club had taken a job as a process server. He asked me to come work for him. He said it was fun. So I went out as a process server and looked for a couple of witnesses that we never found. It was like being a private eye. I was a big guy in a suit.

I started to plan a novel about a guy who gets involved with a bunch of country-club golf caddies, who does some process serving, who grew up at Beverly and Western, who was a tall, skinny, dark-haired guy with glasses, all of which is me. But he was an ex-cop, which I am not. I invented a nice arsonist—a psychotic, anti-Semitic firebug named Fat Dog Baker. I knew a caddy who was called Fat Dog who slept on golf courses.

That's *Brown's Requiem*. It's wish fulfillment, it's crime, it's autobiography. But it's mostly a work of imagination.

Interviewer: What did you learn from your early novels?

Ellroy: When to use first person versus third person. How to set a scene. Where to put a line break or a new paragraph. How to write an ending. How to develop a tragic sense of the world. Where to put a love scene. When to stress autobiography. When to realize you're actually not that important.

Interviewer: Why did it take so long for you to turn to the Black Dahlia case in your writing? It's your seventh novel, after all.

Ellroy: Because I thought for a long time that the success of John Gregory Dunne's novel about the Black Dahlia, *True Confessions*, would preclude a successful publication. That's a wonderful novel, but it doesn't truly adhere to the facts of the Black Dahlia murder case. Mr. Dunne calls the Black Dahlia "the Virgin Tramp." Elizabeth Short becomes "Lois Fazenda." When I took on the murder for my novel, ten years later, I adhered to the facts of the case more than Mr. Dunne did. His book is phantasmagoria. My book is a much more literal rendering of the truth.

Interviewer: How did that book change your career?

Ellroy: It liberated me. It was a bestseller, I was earning a living as a writer for the first time, and I was exponentially more committed to creative maturity. I'm the most serious guy on earth, but I can bullshit with the best of them, and I play to my audience. There's a concept in boxing that you fight to the level of your competition. You're in with a big guy, you bring the fight. You're in with a bum, you do just enough to win. But if you get lazy, then you put yourself at risk. I've always come to fight, from the very first page.

Interviewer: Some authors say that their characters are flesh and blood. Other authors say that they are puppets that the author moves around on the page.

Ellroy: It's disingenuous when writers say that they have no control over their characters, that they have a life of their own. Here's what happens: you create the characters rigorously, and make clear choices about their behavior. You reach junctures in your stories and are confronted with dramatic options. You choose one or the other.

Interviewer: Are you religious?

Ellroy: I'm a Christian. I'm a proponent of Judaism, and I see Judaism and Christianity as the through-lines of the rule of law in world history. I love the Reformation. I am *of* the Reformation—that moment when you stand alone with God. More than anything else, I am an enormous believer in God, the God who saved my wretched, tormented ass so many times.

I feel that I have a responsibility to portray the spiritual, religious aspect of life. I hate squalor. I'm always astonished when people come up with the nutty idea that my books are nihilistic. I try to show the result of immoral actions: the karmic comeuppance, the horrible self-destructiveness. I explicate the dire consequences of historical and individual misdeeds. What happens to you when you do not know that virtue is its own reward.

Interviewer: How do you begin writing a novel?
Ellroy: I begin by sitting in the dark. I used to sleep on the living-room couch. There was a while when that was the only place I felt safe. My couch is long because I'm tall, and it needs to be high backed, so I can curl into it. I lie there and things come to me, very slowly.

Interviewer: What happens after the sitting-in-the-dark phase?
Ellroy: I take notes: ideas, historical perspective, characters, point of view. Very quickly, much of the narrative coheres. When I have sufficient information—the key action, the love stories, the intrigue, the conclusion—I write out a synopsis in shorthand as fast as I can, for comprehension's sake. With the new novel, *Blood's a Rover*, this took me six days. It's then, after I've got the prospectus, that I write the outline.

The first part of the outline is a descriptive summary of each character. Next I describe the design of the book in some detail. I state my intent at the outset. Then I go through the entire novel, outlining every chapter. The outline of *Blood's a Rover* is nearly four hundred pages long. It took me eight months to write. I write in the present tense, even if the novel isn't written in the present tense. It reads like stage directions in a screenplay. Everything I need to know is right there in front of me. It allows me to keep the whole story in my mind. I use this method for every book.

Interviewer: Your outlines resemble first drafts. Is that how you think of them?
Ellroy: I think of the outline as a diagram, a superstructure. When you see dialogue in one of my outlines, it's because inserting the dialogue is the most complete, expeditious way to describe a given scene.

Interviewer: Do you force yourself to write a certain number of words each day?
Ellroy: I set a goal of outlined pages that I want to get through each day. It's the ratio of text pages to outline pages that's important. That proportion determines everything. Today I went through five pages of the outline. That equals about eight pages of the novel. The outline for *Blood's a Rover*, which is 397 pages, is exponentially more detailed than the 345-page outline for

The Cold Six Thousand. So the ratio of book pages to outline pages varies, depending on the density of the outline.

Interviewer: What happens after you finish writing a book?
Ellroy: I go over it, editing fifty pages a day. I send it to a typist, who enters the changes. Then I proofread it once—make some more additions and subtractions. At that point, there are two sets of corrections. In copyediting, I continue to make small changes. Every opportunity that I have to reach perfection, I take.

Interviewer: What do you do once you have a draft that you're happy with?
Ellroy: I show it to my agent, Nat Sobel, who is a stickler for the logic of the dramatic scenes. He makes certain that each character's motivations and actions are sensible. I'm a perfectionist. I go to great lengths to get it all right. It's the biggest challenge I face when I'm writing. If you're confused about something in one of my books, you've just got to realize, Ellroy's a master, and if I'm not following it, it's my problem. You just have to submit to me.

Interviewer: Did you conceive of all four books in the L.A. Quartet at once?
Ellroy: No, it was only when I decided to write *The Big Nowhere* that it became a quartet. Thus, the last three novels—*The Big Nowhere*, *L.A. Confidential*, and *White Jazz*—were linked more closely with one another than with *The Black Dahlia*.

My intention was to re-create the world that my mother lived and died in, as a homage to her, a conscious address to her, and a sensuous capitulation to her. I wanted to tell big love stories, big crime stories, and big political stories. I wanted to honor Elizabeth Short as the transmogrification of Jean Hilliker Ellroy. Whenever someone asks me what the L.A. Quartet books are about, I say, Bad men in love with strong women.

Interviewer: After the L.A. Quartet, you said you wanted to go in a more "mainstream" direction. I wonder what the word means to you.
Ellroy: I realized that I had taken the police historical novel as far as it could go. I had written a series of masterworks about L.A., so I decided to do the same thing with full-scale America. Hence, the Underworld U.S.A. Trilogy: *American Tabloid*, *The Cold Six Thousand*, *Blood's a Rover*.

Most of all I credit Don DeLillo. Mr. DeLillo's novel *Libra* was published in '88. I was astounded by it. The book detailed the J.F.K. snuff, largely through the eyes of the horribly persistent loser Lee Harvey Oswald. I said to myself,

You can't write this book—DeLillo got there first. He had created the entire metaphysical worldview of the Kennedy assassination. Jack Kennedy was responsible for his own death. His death was no more than the world's most over-glorified business-dispute killing, on a huge geopolitical scale.

I was kicking myself that I didn't come up with this idea first. And then, very slowly, I started to see that I could write a trio of novels, placing J.F.K.'s death in an off-page context, with a giant social history of the United States to follow.

When Knopf was slated to publish *American Tabloid*, I sent Mr. DeLillo a copy in advance to thank him for the influence. I included a thank-you note, telling him that I would attribute his contribution in all my big interviews. I got a very nice note back from Mr. DeLillo. He sent it on March 4, which is my birthday. It was 1995, but he incorrectly dated his note 1955, which seemed appropriate. He praised the book, and that was that.

Interviewer: Why, after *American Tabloid*, did you interrupt the trilogy and turn to a new form—the memoir?
Ellroy: I was forty-five and very happily married. I was living in New Canaan, Connecticut. Life was good. For Christmas one year, my wife got me a photograph taken of me by the *Los Angeles Times* at the time of my mother's death. She had it framed. She said, "Do you remember this?" And all of a sudden—boom. It was like a little knife to my heart. I thought I had locked my mother away after *The Black Dahlia*.

A month later, a reporter for the *Pasadena Star-News* told me he would be seeing my mother's file, as part of a piece he was doing on unsolved San Gabriel Valley homicides. Immediately the opportunist in me said, I have to see my mother's file and write a piece about it. *G.Q.* gave me the assignment.

I visited the unsolved-homicide unit at the L.A. County sheriff's office, and I met Sergeant Bill Stoner. We joked around a little bit and talked about other murder cases. I realized that I was avoiding looking at the file. Finally, he showed it to me. I looked at the pictures first. They weren't terribly shocking, perhaps because I'd lived with the event mentally for so many years.

Then I read the police reports and saw immediately how I would write the book. I knew that it would be my autobiography, my mother's biography, and Bill Stoner's biography. I knew I'd get a significant advance. I knew each of the book's sections would begin with italicized addresses to my mother. I knew that we would try to find the killer. I knew that we wouldn't find the killer. I knew that we were going to get a lot of publicity, and that it wouldn't help the case. The book would be about my journey to reconcile with my mother. And all of this came about just as I had thought it would.

Interviewer: Is your mother as present in your life now as she was when you were writing the memoir?

Ellroy: There is a quotation from Dylan Thomas that I think of often, "After the first death, there is no other." He was writing about the firebombing of London, but for me the first death will always be my mother's. She's with me still, but no amount of effort will allow me to touch her concretely. I have fulfilled my moral debt to her to the best extent that I could. I have granted her a mythic status through my work. The price for that is public exposure. I am a gloryhound, I've always wanted to be famous. She never sought these things. I have a need to refract myself through her, and I owe her a deep spiritual debt.

Interviewer: You've called yourself "the greatest crime novelist who ever lived," and it's difficult to think of another living writer who presents himself as aggressively as you do. How important is it for a writer to have swagger?

Ellroy: You want swagger, look at Norman Mailer. I don't go around beating people up. I'm just James Ellroy, the self-promoting Demon Dog. It comes naturally to me. You call it swagger, I call it *joie de vivre*.

Ultimately, I'm impervious to criticism. The ass kicking I got by a lot of critics for the style of *The Cold Six Thousand* was a real motherfucker, but I stopped reading the reviews. You can't start thinking that critical consensus is a guarantor of quality. This is something I feel very strongly about. I remember that when *L.A. Confidential* went to the Cannes Film Festival, a critic from the *Hollywood Reporter* wrote a negative review. He just didn't think the movie cohered. But by then all the other critics had loved the film, and this guy at the *Hollywood Reporter* had to join the club, so he included *L.A. Confidential* on his list of that year's best films. The irony is that I think much of what he wrote in his original piece was actually dead-on.

Interviewer: Did you think the extreme style of *The Cold Six Thousand* was a success?

Ellroy: Helen Knode, my second ex-wife, is my best friend and the greatest Ellroy scholar on earth. Helen said to me, Big Dog, it's a great book, but it's too difficult. As a reader, you want less style and more emotion.

Interviewer: It seems as if most sentences in that book are four words or fewer. It's been called minimalistic.

Ellroy: Minimalism implies small events, small people, a small story. Man, that's the antithesis of me. Telegraphic means straight sentences—subject, verb, repetitions with slight modifications.

Interviewer: In *Blood's a Rover*, as in many of your novels, several of your main characters undergo extreme shifts of allegiance—from fascistic reactionary, say, to Castroite leftist, and sometimes back again. Why?

Ellroy: I wanted to dramatize the seismic shifts that took place during the sixties and seventies. I wanted to show the positive effects of ideological transformation. So I have two right-wing-toady assassins who can't live with the horror of their misdeeds, chiefly the assassination of Martin Luther King. They are two men who embrace revolution, driven by a hope for redemption and by the women in their lives. It's a more hopeful book than the others in the trilogy. As a character says at one point, "Your options are do everything or do nothing."

Interviewer: Are your books received differently abroad?

Ellroy: I'm a God in Europe—the dominant American writer of our time. And that's no shit. America is the cultural top of the world, and my books are viewed in Europe as realistic critiques of America—at least by those Europeans who worship and loathe America equally and wish *they* were Americans and wonder why *they're* not the height of culture for the entire world. I sell more books in France than in America.

Interviewer: You've talked about your competitive instinct. Who do you feel you're competing against?

Ellroy: No one. I'm only fighting myself. I have a duty to God and to the people who love my books, and that is to get better and better. At this stage of the game, I'm entirely self-referential.

Note

1. Main character in the long running *Blondie* cartoon strip (1930–present).

The Romantic's Code

Steven Powell/2009

This interview was conducted on June 30, 2009. Previously unpublished.

Ellroy: When I was a kid going through the L.A. County jail system, invariably there was a Mexican drag queen called Peaches. Now by and large the county jail back then was safe, but it would take fourteen/sixteen hours to get across, it's a very big facility. And it was all warrant checks with early mainframe computers, and you go through one tank, one cage about the size of this entire apartment to another to another, and there were periods of isolation. You'd get a blood test. You'd get deloused. There'd be a chest x-ray. There'd be questions about your medical history. At one point they said who's a homosexual and they'd get isolated. But there was invariably some little Mexican drag queen named Peaches, I didn't know his real name, he was always named Peaches. And we were in a tank and Peaches was over here next to me, and he kept going like this to my knee (*affects effeminate voice and motions as if patting someone's knee*), "Hi, I'm Peaches." And there's a bunch of white guys watching this. I knew I gotta pop Peaches or people'll think I'm a sissy, and I'd be subjected to some unwanted scrutiny. So Peaches was here, and I'm a big guy, and I just went around and went POP and watched Peaches fall over. And all the guys were looking and went "yeah." But then Peaches gets up, and Peaches has hands like Muhammed Ali, and Peaches kicked my fucking ass. So, he never had a sex change, he couldn't afford it, but he kicked my ass!

Interviewer: That's where you get your strong homosexual characters from perhaps?
Ellroy: Yeah, Peaches! Gene the Short Queen and his boyfriend Donkey Dan. Ask me some questions. I'm gonna lie down like I'm in shrink's office. Can I do that?

(Proceeds to lie on his couch and pretends I'm a psychiatrist)
OOhh scary shit!

Interviewer: You describe your recent work as rewriting history to your own specifications. With the murder of the Two Tony's in *White Jazz*, were you breaking your own rule in that case because that murder was actually committed by Jimmy Frattiano?

Ellroy: The historical record says that Jimmy Frattiano "the Weasel" killed Tony Trombino and Tony Brancato. The way I get around it in *White Jazz* is that there's the rumor that it was "the Weasel." But it was really, and it was attributed to him, but it was really Dave "the Enforcer" Klein. That's what you do, you provide the human infrastructure to large, or if not large, scrutinized form of events. So there was animus between Klein, Trombino, and Frattiano pertaining to Meg Klein Agee, Dave's beloved sister who he is incestuously in love with. And they were messing around with her. And Dave decided they had to go, and it got pinned on the Weasel. That's the specific story pertaining to it. You just have to physically state quite often the action of the story and give the reason for it. So, you will find these inaccuracies throughout the text of my books, and you generally find they're dramatically justified. I find a way to get round it.

Interviewer: You do sometimes avoid the more outrageous historical rumors such as J. Edgar Hoover being a transvestite or the whole Marilyn Monroe murder rumors, the J.F.K. affair. Why do you avoid those historical rumors but other rumors, allegations you might run with?

Ellroy: I had the immediate reaction to all of the Anthony Summers research—"Hoover is an overt fag, transvestite"—preposterous! I feel that way, so does everyone who knew the man. So do true scholars. He was much too discreet. He was much too repressed. He was much too circumspect. Helen Knode, my second ex-wife the novelist, and my very best friend even though were not married anymore, just considered him and Clyde Tolson to be a Victorian gay couple. They never did it. They took vacations together. I doubt he ever had sex with man, woman, or beast. Hence my portrayal of Hoover: effeminate, arch, antique collector, smarter than everyone else. Vicious. As far as Marilyn Monroe goes, I've never liked her. I've never gotten her. I've never seen high tragedy in her. I was never in any way sexually engaged by her. I never dug her. I think she was just a fucked up, usurious, sad, wasteful drunk and dope fiend. By the way Robert Kennedy did not have an affair with her. The Kennedys did not kill her. She was not murdered for any reason. She OD'd. I always considered it a preposterous story and an over-told story. Whatever their flaws, and they were very, very different men, John and Robert Kennedy did not go around murdering movie stars, and you cannot get conspiracy-minded people away from that. Specifically conspiracy-minded Europeans, and I don't think the British are Europeans, who think that America is capable of anything. You can't dissuade them. No, Bobby . . . it wouldn't occur to them to kill Marilyn Monroe. Nobody would've believed her, "I fucked Jack Kennedy." And as far as them being lovers goes, Jack Kennedy wasn't lovers with anyone. They met in '54 at the house of a man named Charlie Feldman—a big Hollywood agent that I caddied for on a few occasions.[1] And they probably had seven or eight assignations between '54 and the time of her death in '62 because Jack would never give a woman more than an hour. He was a two-minute man.

Interviewer: Bad back Jack.
Ellroy: Bad back Jack. Hung like a cashew.

Interviewer: It was Freddy Otash that told you that story right? You met Freddy Otash.
Ellroy: I met Freddy Otash. Freddy Otash is briefly mentioned in *White Jazz* and is in *American Tabloid, The Cold Six Thousand, Blood's a Rover*.

Interviewer: I'm sure you had a very amicable relationship with Freddy Otash, but the way you portray him in *The Cold Six Thousand*—probably the novel he's in the most thus far apart from *Blood's a Rover*—he's deeply grooming James Earl Ray and Sirhan Sirhan. Was that some sort of back-handed compliment to the man?
Ellroy: He was a dipshit. Freddy was a dipshit. God bless him. I was gonna use him in the Pete Bondurant role in *American Tabloid*. I was gonna give him money, and I told him that "I'll pay ya. Part of the deal is that I don't want you contradicting me in anything for attribution. Everyone knows you bugged the Kennedys—Wink, wink, wink—Alright, shut your mouth." I didn't trust him not to betray me on this. Then he died of a heart attack, and I could have used him anyway, but I had already created Pete Bondurant.

Interviewer: Back to individual scenes: *Clandestine* features a monologue by Dudley Smith in which he describes the staged morgue incident pertaining to the Black Dahlia, which later reappears in *The Black Dahlia* in a different format. Why did you go back to this scene?

Ellroy: Well Dudley Smith is in *Clandestine* and is not in *The Black Dahlia*, but he reappears in the final three books of the Quartet. The reason for that is I was somewhat intimidated by John Gregory Dunne's novel *True Confessions*, which is so suffused with Irishness. Now I'm not Irish, and I know nothing about it. I know nothing about Catholicism, and Dudley Smith is very Irish. And I didn't want that presence in *The Black Dahlia*, and then realized I erred on the side of caution in my earlier book and reinserted Dudley Smith in *The Big Nowhere*. It was a good scene, and I simply dramatized rather than just referred to it in *The Black Dahlia*. So I was aware of having written the scene and consciously went back to it.

Interviewer: Would you describe what goes into one of your "jam" sessions?
Ellroy: I have a great deal of knowledge on a forthcoming book. I have research briefs. I have my innate knowledge of the historical period. I have plot ideas. I have character ideas. I have real-life history to derive from; real-life history that I am conversant with; real-life history in the research briefs. I've had a series of dramatic ideas in my head for a long time. I put more and more plot notes together—the police investigations, the romantic stories merged with the historical stories—and I get to the point where I have a great deal of information. So much so that the months of note-taking have strained my abilities of comprehension, and I had better start corralling and containing my information before my fucking brain explodes, and I'm starting to lose the drift! So I'll take a big gulp, get up in the morning and write "jam." Have my notes and my research all of it on the desk beside me. Of course you know I write all of it by hand, and start at the beginning and block it out in shorthand. The shorthand blocked notes for *Blood's a Rover*, my longest outline at 397 pages, is fifteen pages shorter than *The Cold Six Thousand*, and a somewhat less complex, more accessible book. Everything was worked out in the most minute detail. Why do I do that? I wanna write books that are dramatically inviolate, deeply historical, suffused with verisimilitude, teeming with great human stories and the history itself, and I want a seamless interplay of plots. And so you'd better plan all that shit out or it won't fly dramatically. So no one has written the books that I've written. No one has ever written books that started out to be mysteries, then crime novels, then historical crime novels, then plain historical political novels because nobody that I know of has the patience or the stamina to outline like this. And the grand design for the rest of my career, after I finish this memoir that I'm working on, is to write five more novels. And this process will see me through. You don't want

to be an aging writer writing ever more modest books because you're in poor health and you're running out of steam.

Luckily it's English speaking and I'm writing in English. I don't have to do one of those hokey Martin Cruz Smith[2] things where you're in Russia but you're writing the book in English, but the guys are really speaking Russian! Like the Nazis with the British accents!

Interviewer: Well, on the question of dialect, a very simple question, how important is the American dialect to you?

Ellroy: I don't see it as a dialect because I'm American. There's actually an L.A. accent, I have one. It's discernible to people in the west of the country, and people understand that. I listen to people talk. And more than anything else the answer to that is I just make it up. That's the answer with a lot of shit with me is having the superstructure of all the notes and the outline allows me to live improvisationally within the text. And the dialogue comes, and I come at each scene from the standpoint of differentiating the verses.

Interviewer: As in subjective third person.

Ellroy: Right. Absolutely right. Yeah.

Interviewer: Studying your manuscript, the shorthand, block capitals, very little punctuation or paragraph breaks, is there something, aside from the brilliant planning—is there an element of stream of consciousness?

Ellroy: If you look at the sixteen or seventeen—*The Hilliker Curse*—books that I've written. There's a stylistic evolution, and I begin to move towards concision very strongly in *L.A. Confidential*. There's a publishing mode of mine in which the book was too long and an editor at Warner Books wanted it cut. So I developed a telegraphic style that fit the story that I was telling, yet the dialogue was normal humanspeak. When I went on to *White Jazz*, the normal conversational first-person Dave Klein's voice felt flaccid to me, so I did the book in that style. I expanded the style for comprehension's sake and kept it terse for *American Tabloid*. Expanded the style and kept it terse for *My Dark Places*. Drastically reduced the style, some would say—like Helen Knode and myself upon retrospect—that *The Cold Six Thousand* was too abbreviated in its presentation of a very complex text. And then *Blood's a Rover*, which will be out in America in the fall, is my most explicated style in years. I needed to write a more accessible, more emotionally fulsome, reader-friendly, less rigorous book. And I did.

Interviewer: Speaking of *L.A. Confidential* and *White Jazz*, you described the former as "epic noir" and *White Jazz* as "ultimate noir." Would you be able to define those terms?

Ellroy: Someone attached "noir" to me early on, and what you're talking about, and these are my own dust-jacket quotes. I co-opted noir before I'd ever really watched film noir. I mean, I'd seen a half dozen film noirs, *Out of the Past, Double Indemnity, Sunset Boulevard*, and a few more, *Plunder Road, The Killing*. What they are, and Curtis Hanson will tell you this about *L.A. Confidential* the movie, is not film noir or roman noir but historical novels set in the film noir era in L.A. the film noir epicenter. So, noir, the concept of noir has been bastardized. It's commonly misused. What people really mean by the overall designation of noir is hardboiled and there's even the phrase political noir on the dust-jacket of *Blood's a Rover*, and I'm fine to sit with it.

Interviewer: Your work is often described as pessimistic—that's not something I agree with—but would you say, paradoxically, that despite the corruption, there is something positive in your depiction of America?

Ellroy: Yeah, I love America and my books are all about one thing and one thing only, a man needs a woman. This is the Romantic's code, and I'm talking about Romanticism from that guy on [*points to a portrait of Beethoven hanging on his wall*]. The books are utopian. The books are about the seeking of personal transcendence. I'm a Christian: the books are about redemption. They're specifically and devoutly Protestant, and the Protestant idea that there need be no intermediaries between you and God is very, very much in play. These are documents practically of the Reformation. And the notion that the books are pessimistic or squalid is generally a critical reflection of younger rock 'n' roll influenced critics who dig me because I'm dark and who misread the texts completely.

Interviewer: On the subject of Christianity, you describe yourself as very Calvinistic. Would you say that there's redemption for Kemper Boyd and Ward Littell if they're predestined to live their lives that way, as Calvinism is all about predestination?

Ellroy: Yeah well, Calvinism is misused as well, there's nuances to it. There's the Protestant Eucharist as expressed by John Calvin in Geneva, Switzerland, an acolyte of Martin Luther, and there's Calvinists who denote a Protestant personal faith within the parameters, that's driven by stern, stern moral boundaries. And it's the second definition that I use to describe myself. Being a human being, as the Bible will tell you, it's a battle between dark and light of the human appetite. And I'm writing a memoir now about the eternal struggle. You figure this shit out later on, and I'm enjoying figuring it out, enjoying both the fight and the succumbing to it. And the books themselves are in essence about men who come to their humanity learning the lesson of self-sacrifice later in life and not early, and there is invariably a transcendent woman involved.

Interviewer: Is the woman then part of the salvation? Is she the means to it, or is she just present at the time the man has this realization?
Ellroy: The woman presents the man with a moral truth that prevents him from going on the way that he is. And there is a pay-off in the woman in feminine persona and softness and in sexuality and in the possibility of love. The man knows that if he continues on the immoral path he'll squander that.

Interviewer: Pete Bondurant is probably the most striking example of that. Pete Bondurant and Barb.
Ellroy: Right. Yeah.

Interviewer: You wrote the introduction to *Scene of the Crime: Photographs from the LAPD Archive.* How important is the visual imagery or photography in your writing?
Ellroy: I picture things in my mind's eye when I write them. So I can tell you what things look like as I have been in the process of composing. I don't spend a lot of . . . I don't have a lot of pictures that I look at. When this place was decorated, I knew I wanted red walls, dark wood, a long couch, and the decorator presented me with ideas and a photo archive of pictures. And I picked them out. And so I love an old documentary which shows me L.A. and America the way it was then, but it's sufficient, more than anything else, now more than ever. Largely because I'm solitary at this stage of my life, and happily so, and then I'm writing this memoir. I do what I do when I was a kid, or a younger man. I brood every night, usually have early dinners. I think about women. I talk to women on the telephone. And if I have an opportunity to go out with people, I'd rather lie here because some woman might call. And I think about shit. And I'm obsessed with Beethoven. I'm just obsessed with Beethoven. The music itself, the man's transcendent courage.

Interviewer: So would the knowledge of composers seep into characters? In *Brown's Requiem*, the bad guy whose name I can't remember off the top of my head . . .
Ellroy: Hayward Cathcart.

Interviewer: Cathcart, yeah. He says to Brown at the end of the novel shortly before he dies . . .

Ellroy: "I have been Anton Bruckner." I'm not going that far Steven! I have been Beethoven? What I love is the worse it got, the greater he got. In his famous quote when he started to go deaf, "I will take fate by the throat." It's just almost unfathomable courage. And the older he got, and he was dead at fifty-six, the more unfathomable and great and uncategorizable his music. So this is largely what Christianity asks of a writer in a secular world. Will you ascend to Christ's example? What Beethoven asks of you, will you ascend to my example? Who do you want to be? Do you want to be Beethoven or do you want to be Hunter S. Thompson? I mean, really, do you want to go out and abuse women and use drugs and squander your potential because it's cool. It's one of the reasons that I devoutly dislike rock 'n' roll and the mindset of rock 'n' roll, and the fact that there's sixty-five- and seventy-year-old rock 'n' rollers out there in a state of perpetual reaction and perpetual rebelliousness. And I see it a lot in Britain. These aged ass rock 'n' rollers. Holy shit! And you're sentencing yourself to a life of the puerile. And I would rather, and I'm not in any way saying that I'm Jesus Christ or Beethoven, I would rather always ascend because I have that knowledge that's the way it's supposed to be.

Interviewer: In his book *Like Hot Knives to the Brain*, Peter Wolfe links the bulk of your fiction to actual events in your life.

Ellroy: There were a lot of things that were wrong in that book. Physically wrong.

Interviewer: So would you say that his main hypothesis that all fiction is directly related to autobiography is right or wrong?

Ellroy: It is emotionally, but the point he misses, and the point you can hit on, is the proportion and even how truthful nonfiction distorts. I'm having a dialogue. It started on Facebook with a woman I haven't seen in person yet. And she's a writer who lives in L.A. And she's a little frightened of me because of a recent Playboy channel publicity stunt that I did pertaining to my memoir *The Hilliker Curse*, miming masturbation outside Hancock Park. And it unnerved her a little bit. She quoted it was "Nervy, pervy, dirty old man." I'm not old! But here is proportion. I broke into houses fifteen, eighteen, twenty, twenty-two times between Christmas time '66 and the summer of '69, circumspectly, very, very cautiously, great concern to cover my tracks. Shamefully, I knew it was wrong. And in-between each one of those little episodes I'd read twenty or thirty books. So the amount of time spent housebreaking was proportionally tiny. Yet it's given amazing sway in my biography. You can't tell someone . . . There's a marked language gap between America and Europe that doesn't quite exist in America and Britain. We speak the same language and are the same people much more than Americans and Europeans. Burglary is not robbery. County jail is not prison. I couldn't have survived in prison. We're talking about three, five, six, seven months aggregate, small amounts in the L.A. County jail system when there was no racial violence. It was just one big bullshit session. You kept your bunk tidy and hosed down cellblocks and did some crummy job. Big fucking deal. It's not the big house with the torture and rape and gang warfare. And I haven't lied. I haven't been disingenuous. But I've been misrepresented. The facts have been distorted. And I was never a bad-ass. I'm a complete bad-ass compared to this generation of young men out there today. They all wanna be artists, and they all don't know if they're gay or straight. And young women are completely flummoxed by them. It's another story entirely. So autobiography to me is growing up in L.A. when I did. The extrapolative power of my mother and her death. The romantic configuration that attends it. The way that I will rectify previous autobiographical writings in the book I'm writing, *The Hilliker Curse*. And the fact that autobiography, if you're honest and compassionate, changes as a writer changes. My mother and I, as I say in *The Hilliker Curse*, were a love story. We were never a friendship story. So my relationship to autobiography is changing as I address the corollary of the central story of my mother and her death. And address it not as an encapsulated or unencapsulated murder story with no formal solution, BUT as an address of the question that her life and death begs, which is why this overweening/overwhelming desire for women. And what is the male's romantic urge? And I'm sixty-one years old, and I'm crazed that way. And I may be coming out of it, and the means to it may be this dialogue I'm having with a married woman, a happily married woman with children, who informed me last night, "Ellroy, no sex! Don't even think about it. It ain't on the table." So before you got here today, I sent her a note back through my assistant to email to her, "Alright! I guess that means I really do have to be your friend." Because I don't wanna be a piece of shit. So autobiography in these books of mine, it's the starting off point. But then there's the journey within the journey within the journey—L.A.'s criminal and social history. America's. The big political books, *Blood's a Rover*, which is in every way a novel of belief. And what created the seismic shift in *Blood's a Rover*—Women. What's it about more than anything else—Women.

Put a character within a context of action and their philosophy, their heart, their soul is up for grabs. Then the larger forces at play explicate their character because their physical shifts of loyalty will define who they actually are. When I look at literary fiction—I'll glance at books because I'm at BookExpo America—I'm amazed at how bad it is because these people don't have to tell a complex and dense story with big shit at stake. And so it's not storytelling by implication at all. It's just arid descriptions or over-rushed descriptions of small moments, and they tell you everything that a person is in the moment. And some people find that very artful. And I don't. I wanna big story about events that were bigger than anything I might interact within. And so those are the stories that I create. I don't wanna be a mid-level or lower-level CIA goon getting embroiled in the Kennedy hit. I don't wanna murder Civil Rights leaders with the Klan. I don't wanna go on scalping raids with Cuban exiles to Varadero Beach, Cuba, but I like the idea dramatically and I wanna write about it. And I don't give a shit about some fuckhead who has an epiphany in a phone booth while walking to the store to buy a newspaper, *à la* Raymond Carver. Small lives mean nothing to me. I hate irony. I dislike satire. I hate nihilism and squalor and smallness.

And I haven't been to a movie in a year and a half. I think I'm gonna see *Public Enemies*, even though I don't think it will be convincing. I mean, Johnny Depp's a pansy and he's not John Dillinger! But Michael Mann made it. It's three hours long; it's a three-hour gangster movie. You know a lot of Tommy gun shit.

Interviewer: On a tangent, I think Michael Mann's been off-form recently so hopefully this will be a return to form.
Ellroy: Yeah.

Interviewer: You're well known as a publicist's dream client. You have stupendously busy publicity tours, and you're a wildly entertaining figure. Would you say there's a difference between James Ellroy, the "Demon Dog of Crime Fiction" and just James Ellroy?
Ellroy: I like to perform, and I'm very grateful for what I have. And the older I get the better I get at performance, and the more grateful I become. And I've had some raw years of plight that I describe in *The Hilliker Curse*. And I'm coming out of it with a new novel and this memoir, and it's been a gas. It's just been a gas. And I've enjoyed being solitary lately. I spend a lot of time alone here, and then all of a sudden you let the animal off his leash,

ripe to perform. Oh shit, come on what a blast. And I actually like Great Britain as the best place for book tours. British readers are the best in the world. They have a sense of America as strange and foreign, yet they read the language. And have no great animus for America, whereas the French are utterly tweaked and fucked up by America and resentful of America, and resentful of their own slavish adulation. So I love to perform, and I'm coming to perform in Great Britain this fall.

Interviewer: I'll look forward to that. In your article "The Great Right Place" you describe yourself as a Tory Mystic. Does being a conservative in the liberal world of Hollywood and publishing paradoxically make you more of a radical?

Ellroy: I don't subscribe to a lot of the liberal social text. And you see here, you have to realize that you're in Los Angeles, and you'll see in New York a profound idiot liberalism that has been in play for years. You go to Middle America, the South, the upper Mid-West you'll see a profound idiot conservatism. And the best way to describe these views of mine is that I'm not a liberal. And it is so mandated and so unexpected and so bewildering in media circles to find someone who isn't, who doesn't have the same cultural antecedents. For example, I have no affinity for rock 'n' roll, so it has nothing to do with my development as an artist. Again for example, I have friends, contemporaries who were big in the punk rock movement. And it's just silly, puerile noise to me. I asked a magazine editor, a friend of mine, a woman who's fifty-six, "What was punk rock about?" and she said it was a reaction to Reagan. And I said history has been very, very kind to Ronald Reagan. Very kind to this man who I think even the most reluctant liberal historian would concede as being one of the greatest American leaders of the past two hundred years. He was a massive presence. He took down the Soviet Union and did amazing things, and he was flawed in other ways as well. You know, *OR* a bunch of spiky-chinned, purple-haired kids jumping up and down. Come on! Just come on! It's just the reluctance with which people would step back from the precipice of their own belief that shocks and appalls me. And you can't get people to, on either the right or the left. You can't tell a liberal, well, "read Edmund Morris's book, *Dutch: a Memoir of Ronald Reagan*, and to one degree or another," you'll notice I qualified that, "you'll dig Ronald Reagan." You can't tell right-wingers, "read any one of the great biographies of Franklin Roosevelt, step back a bit, you will dig Franklin Roosevelt." You can't.

Interviewer: So did you choose "Tory" because it seems more nuanced? It's not a particularly American term "Tory," it's distinctly British.

Ellroy: Yeah, you're right, I did it for just that reason. Because right-wing is loaded. I remember I had a date with a woman. It was a go-nowhere love affair. Recently, I've had major obsessions and go-nowhere love affairs. Dissecting them. Major self-destructive obsession or go-nowhere love affairs.

Interviewer: In the sense of what might have happened, you dissect them, what went wrong?

Ellroy: In the obsessive ones or the go-nowheres?

Interviewer: Are you dissecting the sense of what went wrong or what might have been?

Ellroy: Yeah, it's the Rod Stewart song: "If I listen long enough to you, I'd find a way to believe it's all true." Yeah, I bought that line of shit. You know what my ex-wife Helen Knode says, "No, Big Dog, you sold it to yourself! You wanted to get laid and you sold it to yourself." So there was a woman: a forty-five-year-old woman, a writer, twice-published novelist, lived out in the San Fernando Valley. I said, "What street do you live on?" She said ___. I said, "I go to Church out there." Immediately! This is a woman who's an atheist: Jewish mother, Gentile father. She looks me over. She's looking at an abortion clinic bomber, gay basher, who lynches black people with the Klan, who goes to Church—just immediately! And there's a lot of that. And I told her, "I don't bomb abortion clinics, beat up gays, or lynch black people," and then I said, "I'd like to, but I resist the urge!" And she laughed.

Interviewer: In the acknowledgements to his book *Hollywood Station*, Joseph Wambaugh thanks you for persuading him to return to his L.A. roots. What would you want your, not to say you're particularly old, legacy and inspiration to be for writers today and in the future?

Ellroy: My gift to them? The gift of meticulous and assiduous planning. The idea of moral fiction and Romanticism.

Notes

1. Is Ellroy teasing me here? Charles K. Feldman died in 1968, and Ellroy did not start caddying until the late 1970s.

2. American novelist. Author of the Arkady Renko series.

James Ellroy Previews *Blood's a Rover*

Art Taylor/2009

From *Art and Literature: The Literary Blog of* Metro Magazine *(Raleigh, NC)*, 20 September 2009. Reprinted by permission of Art Taylor.

On Tuesday, September 22, Alfred A. Knopf will publish James Ellroy's *Blood's a Rover*, the third and final installment of the Underworld U.S.A. novels that began with *American Tabloid* and *The Cold Six Thousand*. The new book is not only a fine finish to that trilogy but also strikes me as both Ellroy's most ambitious novel (drawing on seven different perspectives) and the most accessible entry into the trilogy. As with its predecessors, *Blood's a Rover* continues to explore how private lives can impact very public and highly political events, spanning in this case from the aftermath of the King and Kennedy assassinations to the eve of the Watergate break-ins. But this new book is also, at its heart, a love story, with each of the three leading men—Wayne Tedrow Jr., employed by Howard Hughes; Dwight Holly, reporting to J. Edgar Hoover; and Don Crutchfield, a window peeper turned obsessive investigator—falling under the spell of women, including a radical liberal activist, Joan Rosen Klein, who may stand as the most complex female character in all the author's books.

Interviewer: *Blood's a Rover* marks a magnificent end to the Underworld U.S.A. trilogy, a crowning achievement for sure. Had you seen these books as a trilogy from the very beginning?
Ellroy: I knew the second novel would be my big novel of the 1960s. The history was easy to foresee: the civil rights movement, the ultimate assassination of Robert Kennedy and Martin Luther King, more Cuban exile shit, more mob shit, Howard Hughes buying up Las Vegas, general civil rights unrest, the Klan, and my two survivors from *American Tabloid*, Ward Littell and Pete Bondurant, getting further into the shit. It took longer to put

Blood's a Rover together, because going from '68 to '72, you're going to have the summer of the political conventions and the '68 election and all that hoo-ha, but my mob guys had to get to a cool locale, and it took me a while to come up with the Dominican Republic and Haiti. It's full of voodoo, which is cool shit and certainly intensifies all the black militant shit in L.A.

Interviewer: It's been interesting to try to chart the line between documented/accepted history and your revisioning of that history in all of these books. How do you approach that research?

Ellroy: One of the questions I never answer is what's real and what's not. The established history is there to be culled, to be analyzed, and then I extrapolate off of it fictionally with both real-life and fictional characters. For example, Don Crutchfield in *Blood's a Rover* is a real-life private eye here in L.A. He has a website, and he's a very successful Hollywood private eye, largely involved in the Michael Jackson pedophile cases. [Note: This interview took place before the death of Jackson.] I realized I could utilize Crutchfield differently. But he and I will never say what's real and what's not. Did he really go to the D.R. and kill all those people, kill a lot of Castroite Cubans? Well, maybe, maybe not.

Interviewer: *Blood's a Rover* looks at the wages of right-wing political action and explores liberal activism in new ways—with characters examining their own ideologies and changing as a result. Is any of this related to recent history in America, or is it solely embedded in the history of that era, or do various characters' choices and actions stem from your own reflections on politics?

Ellroy: This has nothing to with the world today or the world over the past several years—either the current man in the White House or his predecessor. I conceived of this book before any of that shit started to happen. What I wanted to write was a book that's about the necessity of belief and about the exigent factors of political conversation and spiritual conversion. I wanted to create a diverse panoply of characters who thought a great deal about what things meant. Wayne Tedrow was utterly exhausted morally from his racist journey in *The Cold Six Thousand*, and he certainly did not start out as a racist. And he keeps blundering around, killing black people, and then he falls in love with a black woman. This represents a seismic shift in my dramatic thinking. Dwight Holly becomes radicalized, and so does Don Crutchfield. It was the time, and I didn't realize it until a lot of personal events intersected within my life: the dissolution of my marriage, my turbulent love affair with a left-wing woman named Joan, and my turbulent love affair with a married woman named Kathy who had a daughter who wasn't mine, the basis of Karen in the book.

Interviewer: Each of the characters here seem to be looking for women—Dwight Holly is looking for love and family with Karen and finds a passionate connection with Joan; Wayne Tedrow is trying to find something with Mary Beth Hazzard; and Crutch is literally looking *at* women and pursuing the women central to the case *and*, poignantly, searching for his own vanished mother. In other interviews, you've said you were putting aside talking about your own mother, but Crutch seems to be echoing some of that longing and obsession, and your new series for *Playboy* is all about your "pursuit of women." Women have often played important roles in your fiction, but it feels like the goals are different here, the stakes a little higher somehow, yeah?

Ellroy: Yes, it is. I'm writing a memoir that will come out in book form next year. The first two parts have been serialized in *Playboy*—in the April and June issues—and then the rest will appear in September and November. Women have been the big obsession of my life. It's the biggest story of my life. It's *bigger* than the story of my life. My mother and her murder, so I'm writing this memoir which is called *The Hilliker Curse*.

Interviewer: Tough to get away from that story?

Ellroy: Yeah, it is tough to get away from it. So why run?

Interviewer: Each of your novels has been consistently more ambitious than the one before—an admirable raising of the stakes as an author—and in this book it strikes me that you're delving into different social and political viewpoints more completely than you have in previous books: Marsh Bowen's journals, Karen Sifakis's journals, Joan's letters and then her own section at the end. Was delving into those viewpoints part of a self-conscious "upping the stakes"? Or what, in your opinion, makes *Blood's a Rover* stand out as different from and better than your previous books?

Ellroy: The emotional resonance of this book. It's not quite as complex as the last two novels. It's a more open-hearted book. There's the pathos of Don Crutchfield who's the voice of American ingenuity. I transposed my past, being a window peeper with a dead mother, to his past. I made Crutchfield younger than he is in real life. I didn't go around killing communists or fomenting revolution in the D.R. But I did a lot of the early perverted shit that Crutchfield does in the book. And it's wrenching, his love for Joan, it's wrenching. And they have very few moments together toward the end of the book. Dwight Holly's relationship with Karen Sifakis is wrenching. It's pre-established in the text that the relationship has been going on for a period of years when the book opens. There's children in this book, there's a lost child in this book, there's families. It is utterly different from any other book I've ever written. There's a closeted gay black cop—very, very bright and very, very guarded and seethingly angry.

Interviewer: And that black cop, Marsh, and Dwight Holly develop a re-spect, a relationship.
Ellroy: Yeah, a Klan boy and a bright black kid from L.A. These people—they may be specious. Karen calls herself on her speciousness all the time. They may be hypocritical. Karen is the most introspective character in the book and calls herself on that all the time. But they pay for their lives in blood. And they change and they care about the world and they want to change the world. And their thinking and their actions shift radically. And then everybody's does. And then it just all goes away at the end. It disperses, leaving the kid alone. If the last hundred pages of that book don't break your heart, then you don't have one.

Interviewer: Critics of your other books have accused you of being racist, sexist, homophobic. Do you pay any attention to that criticism?
Ellroy: I don't pay attention to it. I'm empathetic with people. This book does not represent an exponential shift in my thinking. It's about people from 1968 to 1972 and about the lessons I learned from Joan. All I really want is to get her one up in San Francisco. I still have her address. I just want to put it in her hands with all my love and an expression of my thanks. And then maybe see her at a book gig and just wave to her across the room.

I had a series of relationships with women that burned my life down, and I wrote a different kind of book. And then I wrote a book about women. And then I'm gonna write a new kind of book next that I'm not gonna talk about.

Star of the Noir: An Audience with *L.A. Confidential* Author James Ellroy

Alix Sharkey/2009

From the *Daily Telegraph* (November 9, 2009). © Telegraph Media Group Limited 2009. Reprinted by permission.

Somewhere between the low-rent end of Hollywood and the mansions of Hancock Park stands an Art Deco tower with a temperamental elevator. On the third floor, at the far end of a carpeted hallway, an apartment's blood red walls are hung with vintage photos of L.A. crime scenes. Cops with fedoras and overcoats. Sprawling corpses. Dark stains on the sidewalk.

Beethoven and Bruckner glower across the living room at a black and white photo of two boxers mid-punch. It's 3 pm but the blinds are down and the table lamps have that forties nightclub glow, romantic and sickly. Black leather sofas barricade the slab-like coffee table.

No television, computer, magazines, cushions, family photos, plants, or flowers. The feminine absent, the present banished save for the rows of shiny new books on the shelves. A dozen titles, multiple copies, all by the same writer. His name is James Ellroy, and this womblike lair is his home. He lopes out of the kitchen and thrusts a mug of black coffee at me, spilling a few drops as he rushes to open the front door.

A tall, rangy, athletic sixty-one-year-old, Ellroy has the professional writer's hump in his upper back. White polo shirt, grey shorts, and trainers.

We settle onto the sofas as he stretches out his long knotty legs, stacks his feet on the table, raises his mug and says: "Shoot."

Best known for his 1990 bestseller *L.A. Confidential*, Ellroy's latest, *Blood's a Rover*, is his thirteenth novel and the last in his Underworld U.S.A. trilogy.

A claustrophobic, labyrinthine tour of the United States in turmoil between 1968 and 1972, it links and contrasts four central characters with the hippy counterculture and black militancy, the Mob and the CIA, J. Edgar Hoover and Howard Hughes, the assassinations of M.L.K. and R.F.K., Vegas casinos, L.A. detectives, and Haitian voodoo, dictators and bank robbers, junkies and spooks, hit men and hookers. And yet it ends on a poignant, almost wistful note. That surprised me, I say.

"It's about a lost boy," he shrugs. "Don Crutchfield, who is also a real person, a real Hollywood private eye. He's older than me in real life, so I had to make him younger in the book."

The book's voice is clipped and edgy, cool and sardonic, spitting out hipster jive, racial epithets, and blithe profanity, gurgling with violence, lust, and paranoia. It's also a voice from a distant era, one you don't hear now. Does he feel those momentous events of the late sixties still weigh on the American psyche?

"No, they've gone," he says, waving them away. "It's more than forty years since Dr. King and Bobby were killed. People have got the general idea; it was a free-floating conspiracy of some kind; we'll probably never know the full truth. Meanwhile, we got our love lives, a bum economy, a war in Iraq, and a lot of other s--- to deal with. So people don't dwell. It's kind of understandable."

Then why write about that era?

"I love living history. I mean, look around this place. It's why I'm looking forward to going to Great Britain next month. To being in a place that's older and possesses a greater civility.

"I've always found Great Britain so very civil. Even your soccer hooligans, none of whom can fight by the way. I was in a soccer riot in Birmingham and they were swinging away, but they were all too drunk to hit anybody."

Your own sense of history allows for some fascinating artistic liberties, I suggest, in particular the febrile portraits of J. Edgar Hoover and Howard Hughes.

"Hoover was nuts," Ellroy says. "He never had sex with man, woman, nor beast. He was a celibate homosexual who loved power. Imagine staying in power at the FBI for forty-seven years, amid a bunch of ambitious lawyers and accountants holding guns and badges. Of course you'd want to create an atmosphere of fear and paranoia.

"Hughes was a freak. A racist. Addicted to blood transfusions. Tertiary syphilis. Addicted to every narcotic on God's green earth, intravenously. You can't make up characters like that. You can only embellish, with details.

Hughes once went to a cinema screening at the Goldwyn Theatre and sat in a seat that he learnt had recently been occupied by a black actor. He was so freaked out he left, booked into a suite in the Beverly Hills Hotel and was never the same again.

"That's true, it's a matter of record. But I have him stretching condoms over door handles that black people might have touched. Made up. You know why? Funny s---."

So does he believe, having written an 840-page novel about conspiracy, assassination, and covert operations, that the principal agencies in his book—the FBI, the CIA and the Mob—are any less influential today?

"Well, we're forty-odd years into an era of supposed public accountability, so you would think there was less subterfuge, but I couldn't really tell you," Ellroy admits.

"What I do know is we've just concluded the most duplicitous American presidency in living memory. And the new guy is coming to grips with the facts: America has to rule the world, or someone worse than us will. A capitalist economy has to prevail, because massive social programs tend not to work. Still, I don't think it's that much of a shock to him. Obama is much more of a Tory than most people realized."

He takes a slurp from his mug. He'll drink another before we're done, on top of the three or four he's already had today. Having quit drinking in 1977, caffeine is practically his only vice these days.

He gets up around 5.30 am, has black coffee and oatmeal, and sits down to write at his desk, in an office whose walls are covered with memorabilia about himself: book and film posters; photos from signings; and awards.

He writes with a fountain pen on white ruled paper. He edits the draft with red ink before an assistant types it up—he has never learnt to type, let alone use a computer—then goes over it again in red ink.

When he's not doing that he drinks more coffee, stretches out on his sofa and lets his mind run, following his characters into confrontations, racial quagmires, and ethical quandaries. I read him back a quote where he once said: "I am a thinking machine." Is that what he was talking about?

"Yeah. I like to think, I like to brood. I like to lie around and let my mind run. I go for a drive so I can think. I lie awake in bed and just follow my imagination," Ellroy says.

Does it ever become self-destructive, letting the mind run into paranoia, betrayal, and violence? He stares at me in a distracted kind of way.

"I'll tell you how I got to this point," Ellroy finally says. "The preceding book in this trilogy, *The Cold Six Thousand*, was too stylistically rigid. I knew it was flawed. My ex-wife, Helen Knode, who's also a novelist, said: 'Get back to your heart.'"

"Well, Helen and I broke up and later I met a woman in San Francisco. She was Jewish, I'm Gentile. She was Marxist, I'm a Tory. She was atheist, I'm religious. She was bisexual, I'm straight. It was a very passionate, wild, all-encompassing thing. And it didn't work out. It was a deeply romantic relationship, where a man and woman were united by both physical passion and trauma.

"It ended badly. I moved to L.A., she stayed in San Francisco. It was an affair that burned my life down. But I learnt a lot and when it ended, I thought: 'You can turn this to s---, or you can write a book.'"

So he pondered the clash of philosophies and emotional turmoil he'd just lived, and started to construct his new novel's enigmatic female lead—"a titanic revolutionary figure, who happens to be Jewish"—called Joan Rosen Klein. He spent eight months making notes, writing and rewriting, thinking, reading and researching, until he'd written four hundred pages.

That was the outline. Then he sent a friend to the Dominican Republic, to do some more research and take some photos. Going there himself, he says, would have been a waste of time: "If you're a novelist all you need to do is look at a picture and you've got it." Finally, he gathered his materials and sat down to write. Eleven months later he had an epic novel.

While the revolutionary Joan is based on his bisexual ex-lover, another principal character, the would-be private eye and obsessive peeping Tom, a "dips--- twenty-three-year-old virgin" called Don Crutchfield, incorporates elements of his younger self. He, of course, becomes infatuated with the older, wiser, and less predictable Joan.

Yet even the most absurdly caricatured version of Ellroy pales alongside the facts, detailed in his 1996 memoir, *My Dark Places.* An astonishing book, it follows Ellroy's attempt, aged forty-six, to investigate his mother's unsolved murder, which happened when he was ten.

She had gone out drinking and ended up strangled and dumped on waste ground in El Monte, about twenty miles east of Los Angeles. With the help of a retired L.A. homicide detective named Bill Stoner, Ellroy waded through evidence, interviewed elderly suspects and witnesses, and slowly learnt to mourn the loss of a woman he'd never really known or understood.

They ultimately failed to identify the "swarthy man" seen with Jean Ellroy that night. But along the way, the author exposed his own tawdry past—addiction to drugs and booze, shoplifting, homelessness, voyeurism, petty crime, white supremacism, incarceration, and marathon masturbation sessions—with a remorseless scrutiny.

This almost total lack of shame would border on the pathological if not for a corresponding absence of self-pity and his brilliance at shaping the brutal facts of his life into a compelling redemptive narrative. Still, it's both humbling and intimidating to sit across from a man who, after exposing himself so fully, must have nothing to hide.

Ask him about his mother, for example, and he will tell about how she instilled in him "self-sufficiency by negative example," by repeatedly telling him never to trust people. How she gave him "the gift of obsession," that helped him to focus once he finally cleaned up and started writing. And how he felt relief at her death, because it meant he could finally go live with his father, as he'd long wanted.

Ask about his father, on the other hand, and he'll tell you that after his death from a stroke, he stole the old man's last three social security checks, forged his signature, cashed them at the liquor store and spent a week bombed on booze and drugs.

Ask about his early life, and he'll talk about getting expelled from high school at sixteen, how he became a voyeur, spying on women through bedroom windows. How he drank and used drugs for an entire decade. How he was constantly getting into street fights and bar brawls.

It doesn't take much prodding to get a great anecdote. Like the one about the scar on his hip, which he got back in 1964. He'd gone into a Safeway just around the corner from here and stolen a bottle of Thunderbird wine. The cashiers saw him, gave chase, and tackled him onto the pavement. The bottle in his waistband shattered.

"It hurt like a mother------. The store guys just laughed at me and left me there, rolling around. It got infected and full of pus. So I stole some antibacterial spray and cleaned it up."

Perhaps the most curious aspect of his current life is that he has moved back to the scene of his former dissolution: within a few minutes' walk of his apartment are houses he once burgled, places where he scored drugs, corners where he slept on the sidewalk. He went to school just a few blocks from his current residence.

I read another quote back to him, from 1995, when he was living in Kansas City with ex-wife Knode, and he told an interviewer that he'd never live in L.A. again. What changed his mind? He ponders the question, nods his head, then says: "A woman I'd known all of ten seconds."

I laugh. He says: "That's cool, right?"

The thing is, he's only half-joking. He freely admits to being obsessive about women. Towards the end of the interview he turns and starts talking to the attractive female photographer, sitting patiently at the other end of his sofa. He locks onto her. There's nothing sleazy about it, in fact, he's almost puppyish in his attentiveness. He listens carefully, then asks polite but incisive questions about her opinions, her life, and her children.

"All of my best friends are women," he eventually says. "With women I can make friends, with guys I'm competitive." It doesn't take a psychology degree to draw a direct line back to his childhood, and the loss of an absent, alcoholic, drug-abusing mother whose taste for "cheap men"—as he says in *My Dark Places*—probably got her killed.

When he "lies around brooding," does he actually feel his characters' emotions? Only they don't read like the emotions of imaginary people.

"They live in me," he says. "I'm not crazy. I write big outlines. I'm a solitary guy, but I have a girlfriend, so I have a very strong human connection. And I put it out at the end of the day. I don't go around with race hate language in my head. I don't live this world, I just write about it."

There's something about this reply, so fractured that it startles me. Not that I think Ellroy has racist slander swilling around in his mind. But it's hard to believe the line between his fiction and his inner life is as sharp as he says. I think that's even a prime reason for his success.

Ellroy has willed himself to become what every writer dreams of being; a disciplined, hard-grafting, thinking machine with an original voice, cranking out big books with big themes that make big sales. Financially secure, internationally acclaimed, lauded by critics, loved by his fans.

But he has also willed himself into a life many writers dread: the isolated figure sliding into late middle age with a couple of divorces behind him, living alone with his thoughts in monastic luxury, intensely self-absorbed, outside interests down to a minimum, managing an obsessive personality, plundering the past for material, constantly cannibalizing his own life, even as he crawls from the wreckage of another broken romance.

And constantly looking for female approbation, if not absolution.

With the interview over, he follows the photographer into his bedroom to do the portrait. Afterwards, she mentions how neat the room is and he talks about his need for order. "Have you ever met another guy with such a tidy bedroom who wasn't gay?" She hasn't.

"You wanna see my closet?" Ellroy says, slowly opening the door to reveal a row of pristine clothing. Not more than a dozen pieces, laundered and pressed, hanging in perfect color-coded order. All of it high-end Ralph Lauren.

The photographer, already laughing, squeals with delight. Ellroy is visibly aroused, eyes wide at learning she approves. They swiftly agree to do another shoot, for the style supplement of an American paper.

His face is open, like . . . what was the phrase describing the main character in his new novel? This tough guy of American crime fiction looks for all the world like a lost boy.

James Ellroy and David Peace in Conversation

David Peace/2010

From the *Guardian* (London), 9 January 2010. Reprinted by permission.

Interviewer: Pete Bondurant appears as a minor character in *White Jazz* and then becomes one of the principal characters in *American Tabloid* and *The Cold Six Thousand*—is that where the spark for the whole Underworld U.S.A. trilogy came from? With you wanting to run with this character, to see where Pete took you?

Ellroy: There was an overlap that began with my reading of Don DeLillo's novel *Libra*. I saw that it was so superbly done that I couldn't write another book specifically about the assassination of John F. Kennedy. But that's when I began to see that the harbingers of the assassination started to percolate in '58. And I saw that I could do a book where the assassination could be a concluding event, but appear off-stage. And then turn it into a trilogy. So I was originally going to use the real-life private eye Fred Otash, who's been a supporting character in three or four other books, but I was going to pay him because I didn't trust him.

Interviewer: Is he dead now?

Ellroy: Yes, he's dead now. So I could've used him for free. But I had already created Big Pete, so I decided to use him.

Interviewer: Did you write *American Tabloid* knowing it would be the first book of a trilogy?

Ellroy: As I began the finishing of *Tabloid*, I saw that it was a trilogy, and I saw that the second book would be the big book about the '60s.

Interviewer: Had you also envisaged the third book?

Ellroy: Not in any kind of detail, no. Because the politics and the social upheaval of America during the '60s are so obvious—you've got the anti-war protests, the civil rights movement, the racism of the South, Howard Hughes buying up Las Vegas—I had a lot of it right at the gate. But when you go into 1972, as this book [*Blood's a Rover*] does, it's less charted territory.

Interviewer: At what point did you decide on the various timeframes for each novel?

Ellroy: I had decided to end the first two books with the assassinations (of J.F.K. in 1963, and Martin Luther King and Robert Kennedy in 1968), and then the death of Hoover in '72 unfolded as the logical conclusion to the trilogy.

Interviewer: These are huge stories, huge histories. What are your research methods?

Ellroy: They are threadbare. I hire researchers who compile factsheets and chronologies for me, so that I won't write myself into error. And then I extrapolate, fictionally. Which is what you do; you just extrapolate . . .

Interviewer: Well, I use the library a lot more; I spend a year in the library. And then the fiction comes. So I admire your ability to do this without a net . . .

Ellroy: I like to lie in the dark, Mr. Peace. I just lie in the dark and I . . . think. And history has been kind to me. I am a good thinker. I am a single-minded man. I spend so much time . . . do you have a family?

Interviewer: Yes, I do.

Ellroy: I don't have a family. I've never had a family. It's the strangest thing. I am sixty-one years old. I'm very healthy. I am more obsessed with women than I've ever been. And I've finally met the woman. I've finally met her. But I'm the guy with no place to go on Christmas and Easter that ends up getting, you know, some pitiful invitation, shit like this. So I spend a lot of time alone, thinking. And I avoid the culture. I don't go to movies. I don't read newspapers. Here's what I mean: I'm not a rich man. I pay alimony. I pay taxes. But I don't have to support a family. So I have this assistant. So I don't have to go to the fucking store. I don't have a computer. She does my email.

Interviewer: That must be very useful.

Ellroy: Yeah, I live a very, very simple interior life that allows this stuff to build in me and come to me slowly over time. And the voices come to me. And the situations come to me. So I don't think about very many things. And those few things I think about, I think about intensely. So I am able to take small bits of information and infuse them with verisimility.

And so I sent the researcher for *Blood's a Rover* to the Dominican Republic. Haiti's too hazardous to go to. She came back with slides for me. She had three hours of slides. After one hour I said, "Kid, that's enough! Jesus Christ, I can see it! I've got the maps. I've got everything I need." And part of this is viewpoint. It's that you got this dipshit kid, Crutchfield, out of the States for the first time, looking at this impoverished third-world country, blithely watching kids dive into sewer-infested waters for crawdaddy.

Interviewer: This character, Don Crutchfield, he's an actual person . . .

Ellroy: He's still alive, yeah.

Interviewer: At some point, then, were you lying in the dark, thinking this real man, this Don Crutchfield, could work as a character within this fiction?

Ellroy: Here's what happened—I had a nervous breakdown. I was on a book tour. My marriage went to shit. I fell in love with a woman in San Francisco. A left-wing woman named Joan. Red Goddess Joan. It went bad. Big time. Fucking bad. I got the fuck out of L.A. Then I met a married, pregnant woman . . .

Interviewer: Bloody hell.

Ellroy: Yeah. Ha! We had a thing. You know?

Interviewer: Right. And Don Crutchfield?

Ellroy: Well, I'd already paid Crutchfield to be in the book. And my ex-wife Helen Knode, crime writer herself, was saying, "Get back to a more explicated style. Show your heart!" And I wanted to write a book about ideology, about bad men cracking up, and I wanted to honor Joan, and I wanted to honor the real woman Kathy, who is Karen in the book, and I saw that this kid Crutchfield, who in reality is thirteen years older than me—I'm sixty-one and he's seventy-four and so I made him twenty-three when I was twenty—this dipshit kid is the voice of American history. He is malleable. He is politically naive. He's never been laid. He spends four years tracking one woman to have twenty minutes with her, and then spends the rest of his life looking for her. It's fucking heartbreaking. The last hundred pages of this book are heartbreaking.

Interviewer: And very different from *The Cold Six Thousand*. Reading that book, I wondered how you could go beyond that; it almost seemed a dead stop.

Ellroy: I think it's flawed. I think I needed to go back to an easier read. And especially since these people [in *Blood's a Rover*] were ideologically inclined. These people think about things. And you've got such a diversity of character and motive. So I could not use that hyper-concise style one more time.

Interviewer: You alternate narratives from chapter to chapter. When you are writing the book, do you go from chapter to chapter; chapter one, two, three? Or do you follow one narrator all the way through and then go back?

Ellroy: No, I have a four-hundred-page outline of the book: chapter one, two, three; viewpoint, viewpoint, viewpoint; Holly, Crutchfield, Tedrow. Holly, Crutchfield, Tedrow.

Interviewer: So even the outline is broken down into the separate chapters?

Ellroy: I start out where I have the research notes. I have pages of notes on character, historical events. Soon things start coming together. And then I do a shorthand version of the entire story, and then I flush it out into a big outline. And the outline is just, Chapter one: Pete Bondurant / Beverley Hills Hotel / Watching Howard Hughes shoot dope / Following leads / Following information / Boom, boom, boom.

Interviewer: You are writing about a period you lived through, 1968–72. How much memory is involved in the writing?

Ellroy: I have a very dim social sense. I recall the time. I recall the specific events. But I didn't give a rat's fucking ass. I was self-absorbed. All I wanted to do was drink, use drugs, perv around after women, unsuccessfully. And read. I didn't give a shit. I was never left-wing. I was never a war protestor. I would just steal and hole up in libraries and sleep in parks and act like an asshole, in a minor way. But I read and nurtured notions of being a great writer. And I sensed history bombing around beside me. I knew I was living through tumultuous history. And I had a sense, even then, of the human infrastructure of big public events: the guy with the attaché case holding the gun, the Bondurants, the Ward Littells, the Crutchfields. And they came back to me consciously when I was plotting *American Tabloid*.

Interviewer: Some of the characters in *Blood's a Rover* are making a political journey, from right to left, and I think that also separates this book from the others . . .

Ellroy: It is a political journey. It's also a racial journey. It's the symbiosis and synthesis of the left and the right meeting each other and their contrasting, conflicting, and cohering agendas. The most moving part of the book for me is when Joan says to Dwight, "What do you want?" And he says, "I want to fall and I want you to catch me." That's always what I've wanted; I want to fall and I want someone to catch me. And the surprise of this book is that Dwight Holly and Joan Klein are lovers in blood and to the death. And you think she'll betray him, you think she's using him. No, she's a woman deeply in love.

Interviewer: *Blood's a Rover* has an element of personal redemption but the trilogy overall is still, I think, an indictment of a country and its political system. It doesn't make me want to vote. Do you personally feel this cynicism and distrust towards the political system, towards politicians?

Ellroy: No. I trust our system of governance. But I am not a liberal and people find that shocking. Just utterly shocking. And I wanted to honor in this book the lessons learnt from a woman whose beliefs were inimical to mine and to talk in the abstract about the necessity of conversion and of revolution. But I have not moved left. I have just described the journeys of people who have done so.

Interviewer: Knowing what comes later in the '70s and '80s, with Reagan and Iran-Contra, will you go on—another book, another trilogy?

Ellroy: I actually greatly admire Ronald Reagan. History has been very kind to him. And I think history will continue to be kind to him. And so this is it. This marks the chronological conclusion of my life's work as a historical novelist.

Interviewer: Being presumptuous, looking in from the outside, I would have thought that Reagan was the logical conclusion, the perfect character, for your writing, the marriage of Hollywood and Washington.

Ellroy: I always assume people are more left-wing than me.

Interviewer: I think it's a fair assumption.

Ellroy: Well, I am quite often right. And I tell people who are right-wing, you cannot read the James MacGregor Burns or the Joseph P. Lash biographies of Franklin D. Roosevelt and not dig him. And I tell people who are left-wing, you cannot read Edmund Morris's *Dutch: A Memoir of Ronald Reagan* and not come away admiring Ronald Reagan. You will dig him. He was a titanic human being. And even his sternest biographer, Lou Cannon, said, I never knew him to lie. And so I think during Iran-Contra, he had already begun to go senile. So then you're just in a territory I don't want to enter.

Interviewer: In England, we get quite hysterical about the difference between fact and fiction, particularly writing about "real events" and recent history in novels. So I'm going to ask you a question I get asked a lot: why do you write history as a novel, and not as nonfiction?

Ellroy: Because I want to change things. If I don't like something and the way it plays out, I don't want to be beholden to the facts. And I want to tell the private stories. If you look back at what I call the private nightmare of public policy, then these fictions of mine are actually valid. I can just imagine the web of bad people, dubious people, that even clean politicians know.

Interviewer: Is there a difference for you when you are writing about someone who actually lived and a character you've imagined?

Ellroy: I get a kick out of writing someone like Sal Mineo because he kills his boyfriend. He keeps falling in the shit . . .

Interviewer: But what about someone like Bayard Rustin? This man is a legendary Civil Rights activist and pacifist . . .

Ellroy: Well, I had a biography on him, and I read a subversive person's summary list on him. It's a document insert in *The Cold Six Thousand*. I didn't copy it over verbatim but that's pretty much his real story.

Interviewer: But don't you feel a responsibility to that person who lived?

Ellroy: I want to be fairly true to the real-life people, yeah. I want to be true to their lives. And then I want to have fun with it and fuck with them.

Interviewer: You've written a second memoir . . .

Ellroy: Yeah, *The Hilliker Curse*. It's about women and me.

Interviewer: You wrote the first memoir, *My Dark Places*, between *American Tabloid* and *The Cold Six Thousand*. Was that difficult for you, going from a novel to a memoir and then back to a novel?

Ellroy: It was easy for me. *G.Q.* magazine gave me a big commission to go look at my mother's murder file, and I saw that I could turn it into a book that would be her biography, my autobiography, the chance for me to investigate her death, and I jumped at it. I knew I could always come back to the novel.

Interviewer: And what was the motivation to write a second memoir?
Ellroy: I saw that my mother and I were not a murder story, we were a love story. And I was just thinking, what is the single biggest fixation in my life, and it's women. And it always has been. And this was after Joan. And just as I was meeting Kathy. And now I've met the ultimate woman, so I've got to expand the text.

Interviewer: But is it an uncomfortable experience writing such a memoir, or is it cathartic? Can you shine that light on yourself?
Ellroy: Yes, I can. And you know what it is, Mr. Peace? I'm just an exhibitionist.

Interviewer: John Dos Passos . . .
Ellroy: Never read him.

Interviewer: Well, in 1932, John Dos Passos wrote that the novelist should aspire to be "the architect of history." And I think that is what you have achieved in your best work. Would you be happy with that description, the architect of history?
Ellroy: I'd be happy with that.

Interviewer: Do you feel blessed or cursed to have lived through the times, the histories you have lived through?
Ellroy: Blessed. Yeah, blessed.

Index

www.ingramcontent.com/pod-product-compliance
Lightning Source LLC
Chambersburg PA
CBHW020654030726
47498CB00002B/504